African Americans and the Criminal Justice System

CURRENT ISSUES IN CRIMINAL JUSTICE
VOLUME 13
GARLAND REFERENCE LIBRARY OF SOCIAL SCIENCE
VOLUME 1019

CURRENT ISSUES IN CRIMINAL JUSTICE
FRANK P. WILLIAMS III AND MARILYN D. MCSHANE,
General Editors

AFRICAN AMERICANS AND THE CRIMINAL JUSTICE SYSTEM

MARVIN D. FREE, JR.

GARLAND PUBLISHING, INC.
NEW YORK AND LONDON
1996

Library of Congress Cataloging-in-Publication Data

Free, Marvin D.
    African Americans and the criminal justice system / by Marvin D. Free,
Jr.
        p.   cm. — (Garland reference library of social science ; v. 1019.
Current issues in criminal justice ; v. 13)
    Includes bibliographical references and index.
    ISBN 0-8153-1982-7 (alk. paper)
    1. Criminal justice, Administration of—United States.   2. Discrimination
in criminal justice administration—United States.   3. Afro-American criminals.   4. Afro-Americans.   I. Title.   II. Series: Garland reference library of
social science ; v. 1019.   III. Series: Garland reference library of social science. Current issues in criminal justice ; v. 13.
HV9950.F74   1996
364'.089'96073—dc20   95-23142
                                                                            CIP

Printed on acid-free, 250-year-life paper
Manufactured in the United States of America

In memory of my parents, Marvin D. Free, Sr., (1917-1990) and Julia Margaret Free (1917-1995).

CONTENTS

TABLES

SERIES EDITORS' FOREWORD

It is easy for people to be sidetracked or blindsided by the controversial cases involving race and the criminal justice system. The O.J. Simpsons, the Rodney Kings, and the Eulia Loves all create an image that does not mirror day-to-day, criminal justice experiences. After each sensational event, we find ourselves redirecting attention to the research, to the data, to the trend. Although thousands of research studies have incorporated race as a variable and many articles have examined the effects of race on virtually all aspects of the criminal justice system, we still lack comprehensive statements that allow us to clarify racial issues for our students, the general public, or even for ourselves. Marvin Free undertakes such a task in this work.

As with all the volumes in this series, readers may expect this to be a readable, well-researched work. Professor Marvin Free has written, as far as possible, in a jargon-free style and the result is a volume of information that is easily accessible to the novice. At the same time, however, those readers familiar with the subject matter will find new concepts and ideas, excellent summaries of research findings, and a comprehensive view of a major issue in criminal justice today.

One of the strengths of this work is that it includes historical perspectives as well as insight into the research questions that drive our inquiries. Although this book represents a guide to the issues of race and the criminal justice system, there are also many points of departure along the way where readers may want to explore various points for someone else's reaction, or simply expand the depth of coverage through their own additional reading. This, we believe, is the mark of scholarship, the creation of curiosity and the desire to know more. Professor Free's work serves this purpose admirably.

Marilyn D. McShane
Frank P. Williams III

PREFACE

Anyone with an interest in criminology and criminal justice is immediately struck by the overrepresentation of minorities, particularly African Americans, in official crime statistics. Having taught criminology to undergraduate students, I have grappled with the problem of satisfactorily explaining the intricate relationship between race and criminal justice in a limited amount of time. This book represents an attempt to address this issue in an objective, comprehensible, and informative manner.

The selection of African Americans (rather than minorities in general) is defensible on three grounds. First, it is a logical choice in that African Americans constitute the largest racial minority in the United States, and most of the studies of minorities focus on this group. Second, by concentrating on a single group, the analysis can be more specific. Finally, the overrepresentation of African Americans in the criminal justice system is personally interesting to me as I lived for a number of years in a region of the United States where black-white relationships have traditionally been strained.

The reader will notice that this book is written so that minimal knowledge of the subject matter is required. It is hoped that this will increase readership and encourage further research on this topic. For the novice I have included an introductory chapter (Chapter 1) and a brief analysis of the black experience in America (Chapter 2). The first chapter provides a succinct overview of African Americans as perpetrators of crime, victims of crime, and agents of social control. Contained in the second chapter is an historical account of the black experience in America during the antebellum and postbellum periods. There is also a discussion of current relations between African Americans and whites.

The remaining chapters are written for both novices and more advanced readers. Chapter 3 contains an examination of theoretical explanations of African American crime. This chapter analyzes selected sociological, social psychological, psychological, and biological theories of race and crime. Minority views on crime are also presented.

Chapter 4 looks at African American encounters with the police and judicial system. Some of the topics covered are police discretion in arrest decisions, police use of force against African Americans, African American involvement in the juvenile justice system, and African American involvement in the criminal justice system. Supplementing these topics is an analysis of racial disparities in sentencing.

Incarcerated African Americans are investigated in Chapter 5. Explanations of racial disparity in prison and an examination of prison life are reviewed in this chapter. Black solidarity in prison and black participation in prison programs and work assignments are also examined. The chapter concludes with a discussion of incarcerated African American women.

Because it is all too easy to forget that most African Americans are law-abiding citizens, Chapter 6 examines African Americans as agents of social control. This chapter focuses on African Americans who serve as police officers, correctional officers, judges, and jurors.

Chapter 7 investigates the future of race and criminal justice. An assessment of demographic trends and the war on drugs is used to project future participation by African Americans in those crimes most likely to be detected by the police. Moreover, the chapter evaluates the state of the current research on race and criminal justice and offers suggestions for increasing African American participation in criminology and the administration of the criminal justice system.

The book concludes with an epilogue which addresses the issue of racial disparity in criminal-justice processing. In addition to preventive measures, suggestions for reducing black crime also focus on needed changes within the criminal justice system.

No book is possible without assistance from others. Although it is impossible to acknowledge everyone who contributed in some way to this book, three sources of assistance must be noted. First, I am grateful to the University of Wisconsin Centers for awarding me a sabbatical which made the book a reality. It is certain that I would not have attempted this task had it not been for the release time afforded me by my sabbatical. Moreover, I am indebted to the faculty secretary, Charlene Schmidt, whose proficient word-processing skills made frequent revisions of the manuscript feasible. Lastly, I must recognize the assistance provided by Frank Williams and Marilyn McShane, editors of the Current Issues in Criminal Justice series. The book was substantially strengthened by their thoughtful suggestions.

AFRICAN AMERICANS AND THE CRIMINAL JUSTICE SYSTEM

CHAPTER 1
RACE AND CRIMINAL JUSTICE

The United States Bureau of the Census (1992, p. 17) estimates that approximately 30 million African Americans live in America. Comprising 12.1 percent of the country's population, African Americans are the largest racial/ethnic minority. The second largest racial/ethnic group is Hispanics, who constitute 9 percent of the U.S. population. Within this heterogeneous group, Mexican-Americans, at 5.4 percent of the U.S. population, make up the largest single category.

A majority (52.8 percent) of African Americans still live in the South, although 18.7 percent live in the Northeast and a similar percentage (19.1 percent) reside in the Midwest. The smallest concentration of African Americans is found in the West, where they comprise slightly less than 10 percent of the total African American population (U.S. Bureau of the Census, 1992, p. 21).

African Americans today are heavily concentrated in urban areas. In 1980, 80 percent of African Americans lived in urban areas (Pinkney, 1987, p. 46).[1] Moreover, African Americans frequently live in large urban centers, thereby increasing their visibility among law enforcement officers. In 1990, for example, African Americans constituted a majority of the inhabitants in 14 of the cities in the U.S. with at least 100,000 people. They also made up a significant percentage of the population in such large cities as Chicago (39.1 percent), Philadelphia (39.9 percent), and New York City (28.7 percent) (U.S. Bureau of the Census, 1992, pp. 35-37).

Also important is the composition of African Americans by age. Census data (1992, p. 18) reveal that 26.5 percent of the African American population is 15 to 29 years old, and another 26.9 percent is under the age of 15. Because the likelihood of arrest is greatest among younger people, the youthfulness of the African American population makes it a particularly fertile area for study in criminology and criminal justice.

AFRICAN AMERICANS AND CRIME

Measures of Race and Crime

Official statistics, self-reports, and victim surveys represent three sources of data commonly used by researchers to ascertain the relationship between race and crime. Each contains methodological biases making any evaluation of minority crime a precarious undertaking. In particular, official measures of crime, as exemplified by the Uniform Crime Reports (UCR), are frequently criticized on a number of grounds. First, although a majority of the police jurisdictions report their activities to the Federal Bureau of Investigation for inclusion in the UCR, there are still some jurisdictions that do not disclose their activities. Crime data for 1992, for instance, were reported by law enforcement agencies that represented 97 percent of the population in Metropolitan Statistical Areas (MSAs), 90 percent of the population in cities outside the MSAs, and 86 percent of the rural population (Federal Bureau of Investigation, 1993, p. 1). Another problem stems from the fact that definitions of crime used by the FBI do not always coincide with those definitions of crime used by the various states, resulting in inconsistent reporting of felonies (Savitz, 1982).

Additional methodological problems include (1) inaccuracies resulting from the manner in which the offenses are to be recorded, (2) the use of inappropriate measures for determining rates of crime (e.g., basing the rate of forcible rape on the total U.S. population, rather than on the female population only), and (3) combining completed and attempted offenses for four of the Index Crimes (Vetter & Silverman, 1986, pp. 44-46). The recording of offenses is especially problematic. The two-step procedure involves classifying the criminal event and then scoring the most serious offense. Since only the most serious crime occurring in a criminal event is typically recorded, some information known to the police is immediately lost. Further, whether the most serious offense is a property crime or a violent crime will affect the way it is to be scored. If the offense is a crime against property, one offense is recorded for each criminal event. However, if the offense is a crime against the person, then the number of offenses is determined by the number of victims (thus, if one woman is raped by five men, there is only one rape, but if four people are seriously injured in the same fight, there are four aggravated assaults).

McNeely and Pope (1980) suggest that the use of official statistics can distort the actual involvement of African Americans in crime because laws and law enforcement patterns differentially impact African Americans. This selection bias is difficult to pinpoint as it can occur as a result of "changes in penal laws, administrative leadership, citizens' reporting patterns, or the deployment of law enforcement agency personnel; or there may be overt discrimination in the enforcement and application of criminal sanctions" (Pope, 1979, pp. 352-353).

To address some of the criticisms of the UCR, changes are presently underway. An expansion of crime categories, a revision of the definitions of many crimes, the inclusion of statistics from federal law enforcement agencies, the separate reporting of data on hate crimes, and more detailed data on individual criminal events are currently being implemented (Siegel, 1992). The redesigned UCR Program, known as the National Incident-Based Reporting System or NIBRS, will result in data being collected on 22 offenses. For each offense, data on the incident, victim, property, offender, and arrestee will be included when known to the police. As of 1993, six states (Alabama, Colorado, Idaho, Iowa, North Carolina, and South Carolina) supply data in the NIBRS format. Fifteen additional states have submitted test tapes or disks with this information and 19 other state UCR Programs are developing these procedures (Federal Bureau of Investigation, 1993, p. 3). Although these enhancements will reduce the number of criticisms leveled at UCR data, their reliance on crimes known to the police severely restricts their utility as an accurate gauge of actual illegal behavior. Moreover, the potential problem of selection bias raises additional questions about the use of official statistics in ascertaining African American involvement in crime.

While selection bias can be eliminated through the use of self-reported data, this measure is not without its critics. Some of the more frequently mentioned limitations include: (1) potential problems associated with respondent recall and honesty, (2) crime categories may not be comparable to those employed in official statistics, (3) an overemphasis on trivial offenses (although this is less of a problem today than in the past), (4) sample limitations (e.g., overreliance on high school populations, small number of African Americans, etc.), and (5) heavily dependent on perceptions of past activity that may vary across racial lines (McNeely & Pope, 1980; Pope, 1979). Because self-report studies have only recently used national samples, it is also frequently difficult to generalize the results obtained in these studies to other populations. Further hindering the usefulness of these data is the fact that few self-report studies have focused on adult populations.

National victim surveys first appeared as a measurement of crime in the mid-1960s (Pope, 1979). The most widely used victimization survey, the National Crime Victimization Survey (NCVS), was first conducted by the U.S. Census Bureau in 1972 (Inciardi, 1990). This measure suffers as well from problems of recall and honesty. Additional limitations include: (1) the activities reported by the respondents may be difficult to recast into legal categories of crime, (2) neither white-collar crimes nor crimes to businesses are measured, (3) offender descriptions are limited in that only crimes in which the respondent has had personal contact with the perpetrator permit a description of the offender, and (4) criminal accounts may be distorted because they depend entirely on the perception of the victim to determine what actually occurred (Pope, 1979). The third limitation represents a significant obstacle to ascertaining the racial identity of the offender as only about 15 percent of the respondents come into contact with their victimizers (Chilton, 1993).

These limitations notwithstanding, what do we "know" about the relationship between race and crime? Pope (1979) concludes that official data reveal, and victim surveys concur, that African Americans are overrepresented in crime. However, self-report studies generally fail to detect large black/white differentials in criminal activity. Because the crux of the debate over race and crime centers on official data, let us now turn to a discussion of arrests.

Arrests of African Americans

Overrepresentation of African Americans in arrest statistics is not a new phenomenon. From January through June of 1924, African Americans comprised 24.4 percent of those arrested in Philadelphia, despite being less than 8 percent of Philadelphia's population (Berry & Blassingame, 1992). Arrest data from 1990 paint a similar picture: 28.9 percent of all arrests in the United States involved African Americans (Flanagan & Maguire, 1992, p. 444).

Table 1.1 discloses the 10 most and least common crimes based on arrests for whites and African Americans in 1990. By analyzing crime

Table 1.1
Most and Least Common Crimes Based on Arrests for
Whites and African Americans in the United States in 1990

----

10 Most Common Arrests

Whites	African Americans
1. Driving under the influence (1,227,221)	1. **Larceny-theft** (374,968)
2. **Larceny-theft** (827,860)	2. Drug abuse violations (349,965)
3. Drunkenness (566,075)	3. Other assaults (269,560)
4. Other assaults (510,552)	4. Disorderly conduct (186,671)
5. Drug abuse violations (503,315)	5. **Aggravated assault** (143,540)
6. Liquor laws (478,873)	6. Drunkenness (130,226)
7. Disorderly conduct (379,324)	7. Driving under the influence (118,729)
8. **Burglary** (230,310)	8. **Burglary** (101,855)
9. **Aggravated assault** (223,952)	9. Fraud (90,708)
10. Vandalism (191,269)	10. **Robbery** (83,165)

10 Least Common Arrests

Whites	African Americans
1. Gambling (7,251)	1. **Arson** (3,410)
2. Suspicion (7,462)	2. Embezzlement (3,816)
3. Embezzlement (7,900)	3. Gambling (7,294)
4. **Murder/nonnegligent manslaughter** (7,942)	4. **Murder/nonnegligent manslaughter** (9,952)
5. **Arson** (11,154)	5. Suspicion (10,125)
6. **Forcible rape** (16,973)	6. Curfew & loitering (11,379)
7. Vagrancy (17,617)	7. Vagrancy (12,644)
8. Offenses against family and children (42,469)	8. **Forcible rape** (13,309)
9. Forgery & counterfeiting (47,330)	9. Sex offenses (except forcible rape & prostitution) (16,271)
10. Curfew & loitering (50,721)	10. Offenses against family and children (19,602)

NOTE: Crimes in boldface type are index crimes. The numbers appearing in parentheses refer to number of arrests.

Source: Table compiled from data in Table 4.9 of Flanagan, T.J., & Maguire, K. (Eds.). (1992). *Sourcebook of Criminal Justice Statistics 1991* (U.S. Department of Justice, Bureau of Justice Statistics). Washington, DC: U.S. Government Printing Office.

in this way, we can see that the *pattern* of offending is similar for whites and African Americans. Eight of the 10 most common offenses resulting in arrest for whites are also found on the list of 10 most common offenses resulting in arrest for African Americans. Moreover, 9 of the 10 least common offenses resulting in arrest are shared by whites and African Americans. This view of arrest data reveals an aspect of official data that tends to be overlooked when racial comparisons are restricted to index crime categories.[2]

Because African Americans represent only 12.1 percent of the population of the United States but account for 28.9 percent of those arrested, they are proportionately more likely than whites to be arrested. The racial disparity in arrests is especially evident in large urban areas. Blumstein and Graddy (1981/1982) estimate that African Americans living in cities in excess of 250,000 people have a 51 percent chance of being arrested during their lifetime (the lifetime rate of arrest for whites is 14 percent). Does this differential reflect bias within the criminal justice system or greater criminality on the part of African Americans? Although the answer varies in the extant research, Petersilia (1983, p. 46) contends that, based on her sample of male prisoners from three states, there was "no strong evidence of consistent racial differences in the probability of being arrested for any of the crimes we studied." Support for her conclusion tends to come primarily from a lack of significant racial differences in probability of arrest for specific crimes among frequent offenders. However, if racial discrimination is present, would it not be more evident among the least frequent offender categories since this is the point at which the police may be able to exercise some discretion? Using the least frequent offender categories for the 10 crimes analyzed, we find that African Americans are significantly ($p < .05$) more likely than whites to be arrested for burglary, auto theft, theft (other than auto), and property crimes (excluding drugs). In none of the crime categories were whites significantly more likely than African Americans to be arrested. Moreover, Petersilia (1983) does note that recent data from California suggest that African Americans are more likely than whites to be arrested without sufficient evidence to support criminal charges.

The Uniform Crime Reports tend to mislead the public about the costs to society of black crime. Because some of the more costly crimes, such as white-collar crimes that are disproportionately committed by whites, are not included in the index crimes that are emphasized in these reports, the average citizen is often left with the impression that African Americans are primarily responsible for losses due to crime. Yet, Berry and Blassingame (1992), citing a 1974 study in *U.S. News and World Report*, conclude that less than 10 percent of the cost of crime can be attributed to predominantly black crime.

RACIAL DISPARITIES IN SENTENCING

Numerous instances of racial disparity in sentencing can be cited (e.g., Martino, 1989; South, 1993; "Virginia Blacks Get Tougher Sentences," 1983; Zalman, Ostrom, Guilliams, & Peaslee, 1979). An analysis of sentencing in Michigan in 1977, for example, found that after controlling for relevant offense and offender characteristics, nonwhites were significantly ($p = .01$) more likely than whites to be incarcerated for 6 of the 10 offenses studied. Additionally, after controls were introduced, nonwhites were significantly more likely than whites to receive longer sentences (Zalman, Ostrom, Guilliams, & Peaslee, 1979). Petersilia's (1983) analysis of 1980 data from California disclosed that after being convicted of a felony, African Americans were more likely than whites to be sentenced to prison. Moreover, after being convicted of a misdemeanor, African Americans were more likely to be sentenced to a county jail, whereas whites were more likely to receive probation. These differences remained even after controlling for prior record, conditional status (on probation or parole), and other relevant factors.

Studies of southern states also indicate racial disparities in sentencing. A 1983 study of robbery in Virginia revealed that African American recidivists (i.e., repeat offenders) were more likely than white recidivists to receive longer sentences ("Virginia Blacks Get Tougher Sentences," 1983). A recent analysis of court cases in Georgia found that African American men convicted of burglary were more likely than their white counterparts to be sent to prison. The same held true for convictions of violent crimes and drug selling (Martino, 1989). An extensive examination of almost 8 thousand felony convictions in the seven largest counties of Texas in 1991 disclosed that in most cases where sentencing differences existed, minorities (African Americans and Hispanics) had the highest rates of imprisonment. African Americans with no prior felony convictions were more likely than whites to be sentenced to a state penitentiary for convictions of homicide, sexual assault, drug possession, other drug offenses (e.g., forging a prescription, manufacturing a controlled substance, etc.), and indecency with a child (including incest). If on probation and convicted of assault, African Americans were over twice as likely as whites to be sentenced to a state prison (South, 1993).

Historically, African Americans have been much more likely than whites to be sentenced to death. In the United States there were 3,909 executions between 1930 and 1985. Over half of those executed were African American (Flowers, 1990, p. 157). The racial discrepancy is particularly pronounced in cases of rape and murder, where the race of the victim is important. As Flowers (1990, p. 169) has noted, "Black rapists have been far more likely to be put to death when their victims were white females rather than black females, whereas the death penalty has been imposed on white rapists exclusively when their victims were also white." Nevertheless, there is some evidence that the amount of discrimination against African Americans has decreased since the death penalty was reinstated in 1976. Between 1977 and 1985 fifty persons were executed in the United States. Of the persons executed during this time, only 34 percent were African American (Flowers, 1990, p. 170).

In cases involving murder, evidence suggests that killing a white person is more likely to lead to execution than killing a black person. Two studies cited in Flowers (1990, p. 158) are especially illustrative of this point. One study examined murders from 1977 to 1984 in states with death penalties. The study found that (1) people who murder whites were more likely than those who murder African Americans to be prosecuted and (2) murderers of whites were 11 times more likely than murderers of African Americans to be executed. The unequal justice indicated in the preceding study is further evident in cases of interracial murder. In Texas between 1977 and 1984 thirteen African Americans were executed for murdering whites, but no whites were executed for murdering African Americans.

Still, African Americans as a percentage of those sentenced to death has steadily declined since 1973 when 65 percent of convicted offenders sentenced to death were black ("Less Racial Disparity," 1983). African Americans remain overrepresented in statistics regarding capital punishment, nevertheless. Forty percent of the prisoners under sentence of death on December 31, 1990, were African American (Flanagan & Maguire, 1992, p. 705). This percentage translates into 943 African Americans awaiting execution at the end of 1990 (Flanagan & Maguire, 1992, p. 708). Although the number of African Americans actually executed in a given year is rather low (since 1980 the largest number of African Americans executed has been 12 in 1987), over a five-year period ending in 1990, 41.9 percent of all persons executed were African American (Flanagan & Maguire, 1992, p. 713).

AFRICAN AMERICANS IN JUVENILE FACILITIES, JAILS, AND PRISONS

African American Juveniles

A national program to deinstitutionalize status offenders (i.e., those who have violated laws that apply only to minors) and divert juveniles involved in minor offenses from the juvenile justice system can be traced back to 1974. The main impact of decarceration occurred between 1977 and 1979. Concomitantly, a number of states changed their juvenile codes in order to confine for longer periods of time their more serious juvenile offenders. The overall result was a decline in the number of confined juveniles between 1977 and 1979 and a 15 percent increase in the number of confined juveniles between 1979 and 1982 (Krisberg, Schwartz, Fishman, Eisikovits, Guttman, & Joe, 1987). The authors largely attribute this increase to the longer periods of confinement imposed on violent and chronic offenders rather than an increase in admissions.

These changes impacted black and white juvenile offenders differently. Seventy-five percent of the decline in confined juveniles between 1977 and 1979 was due to a decrease in incarcerated white youths. Between 1979 and 1982, when there was an increase in the total number of incarcerated youths, minority incarceration accounted for 93 percent of the increase (Krisberg, Schwartz, Fishman, Eisikovits, Guttman, & Joe, 1987).

The disproportionate representation of African American youth continues today. In 1987, 41.4 percent of the juveniles in long-term state youth correctional facilities (i.e., those facilities that are used to hold juveniles who have already been adjudicated delinquent) were African American (U.S. Department of Justice, 1990, p. 81).[3] Although unable to control for a number of factors that might have influenced the outcome, Tollett and Close (1991) report that African American juveniles (in particular, males) were overrepresented at every stage of the juvenile justice system in Florida. Among their more interesting findings were the following: (1) the arrest rate for African American youth in 1989 was two-and-a-half times that of the white youth rate, (2) from 1982 to 1990 delinquency referrals increased by only 36 percent for whites but increased by 113 percent for African Americans, and (3) African American juveniles in 1989 were eight-and-a-half times more likely than white juveniles to be incarcerated in adult prisons in Florida. Perhaps the most remarkable finding concerned felony drug cases in that state. From 1982 through 1989 the number of felony drug cases doubled (from 299 to 606) for white male juveniles while the number of felony drug cases for black male juveniles increased 68 times (from 54 to 3,675). The overrepresentation of African American youth in juvenile correctional facilities for drug offenses is not confined to Florida, either. A single-day survey of juvenile drug offenders in Georgia during the spring of 1990 disclosed that all 110 of the juvenile drug offenders being held in Georgia's juvenile correctional facilities were African American ("Single-Day Study Finds," 1990).

African Americans in Jail and Prison

Information on jail populations is sparse and fragmented. The extant data suggest, however, that African Americans are disproportionately represented in jail populations. Two government publications by the U.S. Department of Justice (1988, p. 47; 1990, p. 80) indicate that African Americans made up 40 and 42 percent of the jail population in 1984 and 1987, respectively. A more conservative estimate is provided by Backstrand, Gibbons, and Jones (1992). Examining six jails in Oregon and Washington State, they found that 32 percent of the newly booked individuals charged with felonies were African American. Although lower than the percentages reported earlier, this figure is considerably higher than the composition of African Americans in the general population of these areas.

The United States has historically had a disproportionate number of African Americans in its prisons (Mann, 1993). For example, in 1923, when only 9.3 percent of the total adult population was African American, 31.3 percent of the total prison population was African American (Berry & Blassingame, 1992). In 1939 the prison rate for

African Americans was almost 3.2 times greater than the white rate (Myrdal, 1987). The median state incarceration rate in 1973 was 43.5 per 100,000 whites, while the rate was 367.5 per 100,000 African Americans. Moreover, the states with the greatest discrepancies between black and white incarceration rates were not always in the South. Some non-southern states with large disparities were Iowa (633), Oregon (628), Nebraska (561), Washington (522), Minnesota (543), Arizona (510), and Wisconsin (456) (Christianson, 1980). The U.S. Department of Justice (1988, p. 47) estimates the chances that an adult man will have been incarcerated in either a juvenile or adult correctional facility by the age of 64 is 18 percent for African Americans and 3 percent for whites.

When we look at the most serious offense that state prison inmates are charged with, some interesting findings emerge. Table 1.2 depicts a breakdown of state prison inmates for 1986 and 1991 by race (white/African American) and most serious offense. This table suggests that, contrary to many news-making stories of crime, African Americans were less likely to be charged with violent and property crimes in 1991 than 1986. There was, however, a dramatic increase in the percentage of African American inmates charged with drug offenses (from 7 to 25 percent). Put another way, from 1986 to 1991 the number of African American inmates serving sentences for drugs increased 447 percent (compared to a 115 percent increase for whites during the same time).

Table 1.2
State Prison Inmates for 1986 and 1991 by Race and Offense

| | Percent of inmates | | | |
| | White | | African American | |
Most Serious Offense	1986	1991	1986	1991
Violent	50%	49%	59%	47%
Property	36%	30%	29%	22%
Drug	8%	12%	7%	25%
Public-Order	6%	8%	4%	5%
Number	177,181	248,705	202,872	321,217

Source: U.S. Department of Justice. (1993). *Survey of State Prison Inmates, 1991*. Washington, DC: Bureau of Justice Statistics, Figure 4.

An area of special concern in criminal justice involves the uncertain future of African American men. As Mauer (1990, p. 9) has noted, there were more 20-29-year-old African American men under the jurisdiction of the criminal justice system in 1989 (609,690) than *all* African American males enrolled in institutions of higher learning in 1986 (436,000).[4] The extent of the problem is indicated in Table 1.3. A comparison of African American and white criminal justice control rates (expressed as a percentage of each race, ages 20 to 29 years, that is either on probation or parole or incarcerated in a jail or prison) reveals an African American male control rate that is almost four times greater than the control rate for white males (23.0 percent control rate for African American males versus 6.2 percent for white males).

Although African American and white women are less likely than their male counterparts to be under the jurisdiction of the criminal justice system, African American women in their twenties are 2.7 times more likely than white women in their twenties to be incarcerated or on probation or parole (see Table 1.3). Examined in a different light, however, one finds that an estimated 50 percent of all incarcerated women are African American, a figure comparable to that for African American men. The most common offenses that imprisoned black women are charged with are drug-related crimes, murder, robbery, and larceny. African American women are also disproportionately likely to be sentenced to death. Between 1930 and 1967, 37.7 percent of the women executed in the United States were African American (Flowers, 1990, pp. 171-172).

In a review of the literature French (1983) observed that African American women are disproportionately found at all levels of the criminal justice system. More specifically, he noted that in Minnesota, where African Americans constitute less than 1 percent of the population, 17.7 percent of the female inmates are African American. In other states with larger African American populations, the percentage is even higher. For instance, in Alabama, a state in which approximately one-fourth of the population is African American (U.S. Bureau of the Census, 1992, p. 24), 75 percent of the female inmates in state correctional facilities are African American. And the disparity is not unique to state prisons: 54 percent of the female inmates serving time in federal prisons are African American.

Table 1.3

1989 Criminal Justice Control Rates for 20-29-Year-Olds

	State Prisons	Jails	Federal Prisons	Probation	Parole	Total	Criminal Justice Control Rate
Males							
White	138,111	94,616	15,203	697,567	109,011	1,054,508	6.2%
African American	138,706	66,188	7,358	305,306	92,132	609,690	23.0%
Females							
White	6,320	7,099	944	141,174	8,712	164,249	1.0%
African American	6,072	6,095	665	58,597	6,988	78,417	2.7%

Source: Mauer, M. (1990). *Young Black Men and the Criminal Justice System: A Growing National Problem*. Washington, DC: The Sentencing Project, Table 1.

AFRICAN AMERICANS AS
VICTIMS OF CRIME

Data from the 1991 National Crime Victimization Survey (NCVS) provide information on the disparity between white and African American victimization. Once again we tend to find that black rates exceed white rates. Tables 1.4 and 1.5 reveal the extent of the disparity between whites and African Americans. As indicated in Table 1.4, overall African Americans are more likely than whites to be victims of personal crimes and violent crimes. They are as likely as whites to be victimized by theft. If we further divide the data into victimization by race and gender (see Table 1.5), we find that black males are more likely than white males to be victims of all three types of crime. And although the rate differentials between the two races are not as great for females, black females are more likely than their white counterparts to report being victims of personal crimes and violent crimes. White females, however, are somewhat more likely to be victims of theft.

When we analyze the victimization rates for violent crimes for persons 12 years and over, we discover that for all age categories African Americans are more likely than whites to have experienced violent crimes (U.S. Department of Justice, 1992b, p. 28). In contrast, for crimes of theft the rate for African Americans exceeds the white rate for only two age groups: 25-34 and 65 and over (U.S. Department of Justice, 1992b, p. 28).

But what about the overall personal crime and violent crime rate differentials depicted in Tables 1.4 and 1.5? Aren't the differences largely attributed to social class differences between African Americans and whites? An examination of victimization rates for crimes of violence and theft for persons age 12 and over by annual family income reveals some interesting results. For both crimes of violence and theft, whites in the two lowest annual family income categories (under $7,500 and $7,500-$9,999) are more likely than African Americans to be victimized, whereas African Americans with annual family incomes between $10,000 and $24,999 are considerably more likely than

Table 1.4
Victimization Rates for Personal Crimes, Violent Crimes, and Theft by Race

	Rate per 1,000 persons age 12 & over	
	White	African American
All personal crimes	90.9	105.6
Violent crimes	29.6	44.4
Theft	61.4	61.1

Source: U.S. Department of Justice. (1992b). *Criminal Victimization in the United States, 1991*. Washington, DC: U.S. Government Printing Office, Table 6.

Table 1.5
Victimization Rates for Personal Crimes, Violent Crimes, and Theft by Race and Gender

	Rate per 1,000 persons age 12 & over			
	Male		Female	
	White	African American	White	African American
All personal crimes	102.0	130.8	80.5	84.2
Violent crimes	37.7	60.9	22.0	30.5
Theft	64.3	69.9	58.6	53.7

Source: U.S. Department of Justice. (1992b). *Criminal Victimization in the United States, 1991*. Washington, DC: U.S. Government Printing Office, Table 7.

comparable whites to be victims of violence and theft (U.S. Department of Justice, 1992b, pp. 34-35).

A tenable partial explanation for the higher rate of victimization among African Americans with incomes between $10,000 and $24,999 is that racial discrimination and prejudice have precluded the large-scale movement of African Americans with modest incomes from high-risk inner city neighborhoods. Some support for this proposition can be found in the data on victimization by place of residence. Both male and female African Americans living in the central city are more likely than their white counterparts to be victims of violent crimes, while African American males are more likely than white males to be victims of personal crimes. The greater vulnerability of African Americans to crime disappears, however, in nonmetropolitan areas. In fact, male and female African Americans living in nonmetropolitan regions are actually *less* likely than white males and females to experience personal crimes and theft (U.S. Department of Justice, 1992b, pp. 40-41).

That social class cannot fully account for higher rates of black victimization is also evident from Table 1.6 which depicts victimization rates for crimes of violence and theft according to years of college. Whether African Americans have 1-3 years of college or 4 or more years of college, they are more likely than comparable whites to be victims of violence and theft.

Of all races, African Americans are the highest at-risk population for homicide and have been since 1914 when the first statistics based on the race of victims were kept (Rose, 1987). The seriousness of this is revealed in a recent quote from Dr. Robert Froehlke at the Center for Disease Control: "In some areas of the country, it is now more likely for a black male between 15 and 25 to die from homicide than it was for a U.S. soldier to die in Vietnam on his tour of duty" ("'Disturbing Increase' Reported," 1990, p. 1). Although between 1970 and 1983 black homicide rates decreased by 21.7 percent (Wood, 1990), 42 percent of the deaths of 15-to-24-year-old African American males in 1987 was attributed to homicide ("'Disturbing Increase' Reported," 1990). Wood (1990), in a discussion of black homicide, notes that the age of the victims and offenders is becoming younger.

Table 1.6
Victimization Rates for Crimes of Violence and Theft
by Race and Years of College

Years of College	Rate per 1,000 persons age 12 & over			
	Crimes of Violence		Crimes of Theft	
	White	African American	White	African American
1-3 years	34.8	39.0	79.8	113.0
4 or more years	17.8	19.1	69.0	71.6

Source: U.S. Department of Justice. (1992b). *Criminal Victimization in the United States, 1991*. Washington, DC: U.S. Government Printing Office, Table 17.

Further, there has been an increase in the rate of firearm homicide and drug-related homicide.

Turning to other forms of victimization, we find that between 1973 and 1990 the rate of robbery victimization for African Americans remained virtually the same (12.9 victimizations per 1,000 African Americans age 12 or older in 1973 versus 13.0 in 1990), while the white rate dropped from 6.0 in 1973 to 4.5 in 1990 (U.S. Department of Justice, 1992a, p. 35). Thus, the discrepancy between black and white rates actually grew between these years.

Rape represents a contrasting case. Between 1973 and 1990 the rate of rape victimizations per 1,000 African American females age 12 or older has declined from 2.6 to 1.0. The 1990 figure for African American females is identical to that for white females (U.S. Department of Justice, 1992a, p. 23). Since rape tends to be *intra*racial (i.e., whites rape whites, African Americans rape African Americans), these numbers suggest that African American men are no more prone to rape women than white men are.

Property crime victimization statistics provide mixed results. Between 1973 and 1990 African American victimization rates decreased sharply for burglary (from 132.5 incidents per 1,000 black households to 85.4 incidents), increased for motor vehicle theft (from 24.5 incidents per 1,000 black households to 36.4 incidents), and declined slightly for household larceny (from 103.7 incidents per 1,000 black households to 101.1 incidents). However, African American victimization rates for all three categories remain higher than those for whites (U.S. Department of Justice, 1992a, pp. 106, 112, & 118).

Victimization of the elderly is another area of concern. (It should be recalled that for crimes of theft the rate for African Americans exceeds the rate for whites in only two age categories, one of which is 65 years and over.) A national survey reported that 70 percent of elderly African Americans were fearful of becoming victims of crime. The figure for elderly whites was 49 percent. However, a more recent survey conducted in an inner city in the South found that 94 percent of the respondents believed that they were either "likely" or "very likely" to be victimized in the future. Moreover, 7 percent of the sample had been criminally victimized at least once since reaching the age of 60 (Wiltz, 1982). The percentage would undoubtedly be higher if the study had not oversampled women, since elderly women are less likely to be victimized because they are more likely than elderly men to be confined to their homes.

And finally, victimization by the police must also be included. African Americans have historically been singled out by the police for excessive force. During the 1920s half of all African Americans killed by whites were killed by the police (Berry & Blassingame, 1992). Between 1963 and 1968 the police killed 1,826 people, about 50 percent of whom were African American (Mitford, 1974, p. 77). The Rodney King incident in Los Angeles is a vivid reminder that police brutality continues to exist today.

AFRICAN AMERICAN UNDERREPRESENTATION IN THE ADMINISTRATION OF THE CRIMINAL JUSTICE SYSTEM

The lack of African American representation in decision-making positions in the criminal justice system is apparent when examining the racial composition of the police and the judicial system. Particularly interesting is the extent of African American representation on American police forces. Depending on the data that is cited, one can show underrepresentation or proportionate representation in municipal police departments. The U.S. Department of Justice (1990, p. 58) provides statistics on 59 police departments in cities having a population of at least 250,000. Of all part-time and full-time sworn personnel in the state police agencies in 1987, only 6.5 percent were African American. (You may recall that African Americans constitute slightly over 12 percent of the United States population.) Using this figure, then, one can argue that African Americans are *under*represented. However, the same report also states that an average of 14 percent of the full-time sworn police officers in these cities were African American. If this number is used, then one can argue that the number of African Americans employed as municipal police is *proportionate* to their numbers in the general population. Regardless of the position that one takes, it appears that African American representation in large urban police departments is less than the proportion of African Americans found in those urban areas (Mann, 1993).

The judicial system reveals even greater racial disparities. In 1983 only 2.7 percent of all lawyers and judges were African American. This figure was virtually unchanged (2.8 percent) in 1991 (U.S. Bureau of the Census, 1992, p. 392). Moreover, minorities have traditionally been underrepresented on juries in federal and state courts (Fukurai, Butler, & Krooth, 1993). This disparity recently received notoriety when in the first trial of four white Los Angeles police officers indicted for the beating of Rodney King, an African American, the officers were found not guilty on 10 of 11 counts. The jury contained no African Americans.

What accounts for the underrepresentation of African Americans and other minorities on juries? Fukurai, Butler, and Krooth (1993) attribute four factors to African American underrepresentation on juries. First, the personnel responsible for the jury selection process, such as jury clerks and jury commissioners, have frequently limited African American participation on juries. Second, the use of *voir dire* by attorneys has minimized the inclusion of African Americans on juries. Third, "human capital" factors (e.g., race, social class, education, and occupation) have contributed to jury underrepresentation by certain segments of society. For example, because whites from higher social classes are more likely to be registered to vote and therefore be selected for jury service and because whites with better-paying jobs are better able to take time off from work to serve on juries, they are more likely to be found on juries. And fourth, psychological factors contribute to the underrepresentation of African Americans. Exemplary of this factor would be the dismissal of African Americans due to the perception of blacks as being "inherently criminal" and having "impaired intelligence." The perception that African Americans may be anti-police or sympathetic to minority offenders further contributes to their underrepresentation on juries.

The *voir dire* examination poses special problems for minorities. Before potential jurors are actually seated on a jury, an examination of them is conducted by the prosecuting and defense attorneys or by the judge. Each side is granted a certain number of peremptory challenges which permit dismissals of potential jurors without any cause or by stating a cause that is not racial exclusion. After both sides have used their allotted number of peremptory challenges, potential jurors can still be dismissed for cause. If during the *voir dire* examination the prosecution or defense believes that a potential juror may be biased, and if the judge concurs, the potential juror will be excused for cause. However, as Newman and Anderson (1989, p. 346) note:

> In practice, neither peremptory nor for-cause jury exclusions are really designed to obtain an impartial jury. Both sides use both forms of challenges in an attempt to build a partial jury, *favorable* to the side

of the case that the attorney represents, either state
or defense. A historic concern of jury selection has
been the systematic exclusion of blacks and other
minorities from jury duty (italics in original).

Researchers have found that prosecutors are more likely than
defense attorneys to dismiss minorities during the peremptory challenge
stage of jury selection. Moreover, prosecutors in criminal cases
frequently look for certain characteristics in potential jurors that would
make them better identify with the government rather than the
defendant. In practice, this often means favoring whites who are
middle aged and middle class (Fukurai, Butler, & Krooth, 1993).

For many years the Supreme Court accepted one's race as a valid
reason for dismissal. In *Swain v. Alabama* (1965) the U.S. Supreme
Court upheld the practice of racial exclusion on juries during the
peremptory challenge phase of *voir dire*. This case was recently
overturned in *Batson v. Kentucky* (1986) when the Supreme Court "held
that prosecutors may not exclude blacks from juries because the
prosecutor believes they *may* favor a defendant of their own race"
(Newman & Anderson, 1989, pp. 346-347, italics in original). The
effect of the latter case on actual jury selection may be minimal,
nonetheless, if nonracial reasons are proffered for the exclusion of
African Americans and other minorities on juries.

CONCLUSION

The extent of African American involvement in crime is unknown
as a result of methodological problems associated with each of the three
measures of criminal activity. Nevertheless, compared to their
numbers in the general population, African Americans are
overrepresented in arrest statistics. Arrest data further reveal a similar
pattern of offending for blacks and whites.

Racial disparities in sentencing are not restricted to southern states.
Overall, African Americans are more likely than whites to be sentenced
to prison in felony cases and to receive the death sentence in capital

cases. The race of the victim in capital offenses is of considerable importance, as the death penalty is more common if the victim is white than if the victim is another African American.

Both African American men and women in their twenties are more likely than their white counterparts to be on probation or parole or to be in jail or prison. Particularly disturbing is the fact that 23 percent of all African American men in their twenties are in some way under the control of the criminal justice system.

African Americans are also more likely than whites to be victims of personal and violent crimes. In fact, African Americans represent the highest at-risk population of all races for homicide. Data further suggest that African Americans are more likely than whites to be victimized by the police.

Despite their overrepresentation as defendants and victims, African Americans remain underrepresented in the administration of the criminal justice system. In many large urban police agencies, the number of African Americans serving as officers is not proportionate to their representation in those urban areas. Moreover, African Americans are underrepresented in the legal profession, as lawyers and judges, and on juries.

NOTES

1. African Americans, as a group, are actually more urbanized than the general population of the United States. For the population as a whole, 73 percent lived in urban areas in 1980 (Pinkney, 1987, p. 46).

2. Mann (1993, p. 39) looked at African American involvement in crime using both methods. When comparisons were made between groups, the 1986 Uniform Crime Reports indicated a high level of African American involvement in crime: African Americans comprised 46.5 percent of all persons arrested for violent crimes and 30.2 percent of all persons arrested for property crimes. But when one calculates the percentage of all black arrests per crime category, a different picture emerges. Here we find that only 7.7 percent of all African American arrests were for violent crimes and an additional 18.4 percent of all African American arrests were for property crimes. Or, stated another way, 73.9 percent of all African American arrests were for the less serious crimes.

3. This disparity becomes apparent when examining census data disaggregated by race and age. In 1990, for example, African Americans comprised only 15.1 percent of all youths ages 10 to 19 years (U.S. Bureau of the Census, 1992, p. 18).

4. The figure of 609,690 includes those in state prisons, federal prisons, and jails, as well as those on probation and parole.

CHAPTER 2
THE BLACK EXPERIENCE
IN AMERICA

African American mistrust of the criminal justice system has been well documented. Studies in cities such as Pittsburgh (Scaglion & Condon, 1980) and Miami (Wilbanks, 1987, p. 1) tend to show that African Americans are much more critical of the criminal justice system than are whites. More recently, a 1993 national telephone poll of 1,003 adults revealed that whites see equal justice for minorities as a problem by a 4-3 margin whereas among African Americans equal justice for minorities is seen as a problem by a 12-1 ratio (Goldberg, 1993).

It appears that these black-white differentials in perception of criminal injustice are race related rather than class related. Hagan and Albonetti (1982) analyzed data from a national survey of adult Americans and found that African Americans were substantially more likely than whites to perceive criminal injustice. When the researchers analyzed the possibility that socioeconomic status rather than race might actually be the reason for the black-white differential, they discovered that race was a better predictor of perception of criminal injustice than socioeconomic status. In fact, the largest racial difference in perception of criminal injustice occurred among the professional managerial class and not among the working class and unemployed categories. Hagan and Albonetti (1982, p. 352) explain this anomaly in the following way:

> One possibility is that black members of the PMC [professional managerial class] who perceive income discrimination may be sensitive to the perception of injustice elsewhere as well. Another possibility is that a consciousness of race among blacks in the PMC, and their more recent movement into this class, is associated with a consciousness of prior class position that continues to influence significantly their

perceptions of the surrounding world. Finally, it
may be that whites who manage to stay out of the
surplus population [unemployed class] also are able
to avoid criminal injustice, while working class
blacks and black members of the PMC may continue,
directly or indirectly, to experience criminal injustice,
perhaps partly as a consequence of the apparent
contradiction in their race and class positions.

How did African Americans come to have different views of the
criminal justice system? To understand this one must have some
knowledge of the history of black-white relations in the United States.
Although a comprehensive review of African American history is
beyond the scope of this chapter, some appreciation of minority views
on criminal justice can be gained by a rudimentary exposure to the
topic of race relations.

THE EARLY BLACK EXPERIENCE

While historians are unsure when the first black person actually
arrived in North America, in 1619 blacks entered what is now the
United States (Flowers, 1990). It is unclear whether the first blacks in
America were slaves or indentured servants.   However, many
historians contend that these blacks were indentured servants and not
slaves since English law had no precedent concerning slaves (Flowers,
1990). Regardless of their initial status, by the 1650s some of the
colonies had legally begun to differentiate the status of white and black
servants. By the early eighteenth century, the broad legal framework
of slavery in the South had been established (Turner, Singleton, &
Musick, 1984).

Slavery has existed in almost every preindustrial society.
Nonetheless, the specific form that it acquires varies by society.
Legally a slave can be viewed as chattel (or a "thing" that has no
personal rights) or as a legal person who is a lifetime servant having
various obligations to others. If defined as a legal person, the slave
retains some rights that cannot be deprived by the master. Under
chattel slavery, the master has complete property rights. Virginia's

slave code, which became a model for other southern states, embraced the ideology of chattel slavery (Klein, 1967).

The inferior position of the slave was codified into slave codes that constantly reminded the slave of his/her lowly status. For example, slave marriages were not legally sanctioned anywhere in the South. Thus slave families could be legally dissolved at the discretion of the master. The lone exception was Louisiana which forbade the selling of children under 10 years of age from their mothers. Moreover, because blacks were not permitted to testify against whites in court, laws designed to protect the lives of slaves were difficult to enforce (Genovese, 1974).

In 1821 legislation changed the murder of a slave from a misdemeanor to a felony. This law differentiated three causes of death: murder, killing in the heat of passion, and killing by undue correction, which is an euphemism for excessive whipping of a slave (Genovese, 1974). Despite this change in status, it remained difficult to protect slaves from harsh punishment and murder since slaves could not testify against whites. To protect slaves the legal system of South Carolina permitted as circumstantial evidence the physical condition of the slave's body or corpse. The law provided the master with a virtual immunity from conviction, however, as a master's oath of innocence had to be honored (Genovese, 1974).

Rape as a criminal category during the antebellum period did not exist for black women. This crime applied exclusively to white women. If a black man sexually attacked a black woman his master could punish him, but no legal apparatus was in place to charge the offender with a crime (Genovese, 1974).

Lynching as a means of controlling the slaves was largely unnecessary in the antebellum South. Probably fewer than 10 percent of the persons lynched in the South between 1840 and 1860 were black (Genovese, 1974, p. 32).

> . . . for the blacks the danger of lynching remained minimal until after emancipation. The direct power of the masters over their slaves and in society as a whole, where they had little need for extralegal measures against blacks, provided the slaves with extensive protection against mob violence (Genovese, 1974, p. 32).

The treatment of blacks in the North prior to the Civil War was also characterized by inequality between the races. In some northern states blacks were separated from whites in the militia or excluded altogether. Northern states such as Massachusetts and Ohio provided separate schools for whites and blacks, while other states excluded blacks from schools entirely (Franklin, 1968). Although the legal codes of northern states accorded blacks more rights than southern states, "few people questioned beliefs about the inferiority of blacks or the necessity for excluding them from full economic, educational, and political participation" (Turner, Singleton, & Musick, 1984, p. 147).

THE BLACK EXPERIENCE: POSTBELLUM PERIOD

After the Thirteenth Amendment abolishing slavery was ratified in 1866, the rights of the former slaves were restricted by legislation passed by southern states. These "black codes" placed a number of restrictions on African Americans. The former slaves were not allowed to vote, sit on juries, testify against whites in court, and bear arms. Additionally, African Americans were excluded from certain occupations and if found to be vagrants, could be consigned to forced labor (Turner, Singleton, & Musick, 1984).

The Fourteenth and Fifteenth amendments were designed to counteract the black codes of the South. The Fourteenth Amendment (1868) extended citizenship to the former slaves; the Fifteenth Amendment (1870) gave the former male slaves the right to vote (Turner, Singleton, & Musick, 1984).

Christianson (1981, p. 373) contends that "The state prison as we know it arose in part as a replacement for slavery, in order to control newly freed blacks." Indeed, over 95 percent of the state prison population in the South shortly after the Civil War was composed of African Americans. In stark contrast to the antebellum era when errant slaves were infrequently incarcerated, by 1878 1,122 of the 1,239 inmates in Georgia's prisons were African American (Adamson, 1983, p. 565). Myers and Massey (1991) attribute the increase in black male incarceration rates in Georgia from 1868 through 1936 to a strong demand for black convict labor and increased profitability of convict labor under the convict lease system. They found no evidence that the size of the black male population that is most likely to be incarcerated (20-29-year-olds) is related to incarceration rates of black males.

African American and white prisoners were typically segregated. According to Rabinowitz (1976), the size of the facility was a primary determinant of whether separation of the races was feasible. Small jails were probably integrated because of the lack of separate facilities for African American and white inmates. Toward the latter part of the nineteenth century larger jails were constructed in cities such as Atlanta and Nashville to accommodate the demands of racial segregation of inmates.

A primarily African American convict lease system evolved in the South after the Civil War. This gave the financially frail state governments additional revenue for their state coffers, while facilitating the separation of African American and white convicts. Predominantly black chain gangs were also established (Rabinowitz, 1976).

As private companies began leasing state convicts, the state governments surrendered their responsibility for overseeing discipline at the prison camps. Moreover, the states had no control over the work or living conditions of the leased prisoners. High mortality rates prevailed at the lease camps. Living conditions were worse at these lease camps than on the typical plantation under slavery (Adamson, 1983).

White violence against African Americans was relatively common in the South in the postbellum period. Although undoubtedly many murders went undetected, in Texas from 1865 to 1868, there were 499 African Americans killed by whites (versus 15 whites killed by African Americans). For all forms of violence (including homicide), whites committed 1,524 acts of violence against African Americans in comparison to 42 acts of violence against whites by African Americans. There were also 183 incidents of whites victimizing African American women, 15 of which resulted in murder. Nor did African American children escape the wrath of racial hostilities. Black children were victims of whippings, floggings, beatings, assaults, castration, and murder (Crouch, 1984).

Caddo Parish in Louisiana was particularly violent. Between 1865 and 1876 whites murdered 295 African Americans in contrast to 12 incidents of African Americans murdering whites. A further analysis discloses that white involvement was widespread. Vandal (1991) estimates that 30 percent of the white population in Caddo between 18 and 45 years of age was involved in killing African Americans. An examination of the occupations of the perpetrators reveals that many came from the higher social strata.[1] The vast majority of motives were political in nature. As Vandal (1991, pp. 379-380) notes "Evidence clearly shows that whites did not kill blacks at random, but developed a selective and deliberate policy aimed at eliminating black leadership and intimidating the black population."

In general, race relations between African Americans and whites in the South between 1865 and 1890 were characterized by inequality.

> Integration was rarely permitted. When it did occur, it was only at the initiation of whites and was confined as a rule to the least desirable facilities-- cheap bars, inferior restaurants, second-class and smoking cars on trains. Whites were there because they chose to be; blacks were there because they had no choice (Rabinowitz, 1976, p. 350).

THE BLACK EXPERIENCE: THE JIM CROW ERA

Originally Jim Crow referred to a dance tune, but by the last decade of the nineteenth century it referred to segregation of the races in the South. Jim Crow legislation of the South was legitimated by U.S. Supreme Court decisions such as *Plessy v. Ferguson* (1896) and *Williams v. Mississippi* (1898). In the former case the Supreme Court ruled that state laws allowing for "separate but equal" accommodations for African Americans were constitutional. The *Williams v. Mississippi* decision declared that states could use poll taxes, literacy tests, and residential requirements to determine eligibility to vote despite the fact that these devices were designed to diminish the strength of the black vote (Schaefer, 1984).

Lynching later became another way of subduing African Americans in the South. Between 1882 and 1930 in the Deep South, 1,844 African Americans were lynched (Beck & Tolnay, 1990). The largest number of black lynchings occurred during the 1890s when 1,111 African Americans were killed (Flowers, 1990). Beck and Tolnay (1990) propose a relationship between the market for cotton (the dominant crop in the agricultural regions of the Deep South) and black lynchings in the South. They report an inverse relationship between the "constant dollar" price of cotton and black lynchings in the Deep South between 1882 and 1930. The presence of such a relationship suggests that economic conditions, and not the actual amount of black crime, was an important determinant of the number of black lynchings. Additional support for this view can be found in their finding of a positive relationship between inflationary shifts in the price of cotton and black lynchings. Although their relationships were considerably stronger during the late 1800s than in later decades, controlling for a proxy measure of the annual level of black crime had no effect on the previously mentioned relationships. In other words, the amount of African American crime appeared to be unrelated to the number of black lynchings in this region. Although caution should always be exercised in generalizing from a single study, the results "are consistent with the view stressing the victimization of blacks in southern society" (Beck & Tolnay, 1990, p. 537).

THE BLACK EXPERIENCE DURING THE TWENTIETH CENTURY

Between 1914 and 1920 an estimated 400,000 to one million African Americans migrated to northern states in search of factory jobs (Pinkney, 1987, p. 26). The reception that they received was similar to what they knew in the South. As they settled in urban areas they were forced to live in segregated neighborhoods. Moreover, violence was not a stranger to African Americans living in border and northern cities. In 1917 in East Saint Louis, Illinois, 125 African Americans were burned by whites. The summer of 1919 was especially violent.

> The summer of 1919 was called the Red Summer because of the racial violence which took place. From June to September some 25 race riots erupted in American cities, and 14 blacks were publicly burned alive. The most serious outbreak occurred in Chicago, where 38 persons were killed, 23 of them blacks (Pinkney, 1987, p. 27).

Disregard for the value of black lives was expressed in other ways as well. The use of African American men as human guinea pigs in research designed to examine the effects of untreated syphilis on humans illustrates the lowly status of African Americans during much of the twentieth century.[2] Known as the Tuskegee Syphilis Study and headed by the United States Public Health Service (PHS), this experiment ran from 1932 to 1972 making it "the longest nontherapeutic experiment on human beings in medical history" (Thomas & Quinn, 1991, p. 1501).

Originally containing 399 African American men with syphilis and 201 without the disease, the sample was composed of individuals living in Macon County, Alabama, an area where widespread poverty existed among African Americans and many had no access to health care. (An earlier phase of the study had disclosed that this county exhibited high rates of syphilis infection, ranging from 35 percent to 40 percent depending on the age group.) Further fueling interest in this area was speculation in the scientific community that the natural history of this disease differentially affected African Americans and whites. Subjects were not informed of the specific disease that they had nor were they told how they had contracted it. Instead, the vernacular of the black rural South was used and syphilis was referred to as "bad blood," a catchall term used to describe various maladies. Incentives such as free food, transportation, and physical examinations were offered to encourage participation. Moreover, burial stipends were used to receive permission to perform autopsies on the dead (Thomas & Quinn, 1991).

Although some of the men in the experimental group received treatment for syphilis, the dosage was less than that recommended by the PHS. In addition, strong measures were taken to ensure that the experimental group subjects did *not* receive proper treatment. During World War II, for instance, the PHS was able to get about 50 of their experimental subjects exempted from the requirement of receiving treatment prior to military induction. In 1943 when penicillin was first used to treat some patients with syphilis, it was denied to the men in this study. By 1951 treatment of syphilis with penicillin was common, but once again the experimental subjects were refused such treatment. The study was finally terminated in 1972 as a result of a disclosure by an investigator with the PHS in San Francisco that led to unfavorable publicity of the little-known project (Thomas & Quinn, 1991).

African Americans have not been the only minority group to be assigned an inferior status by their government, however. While beyond the scope of this book to elucidate fully, some examples will suffice. The land claims of whites who had "discovered" land occupied by American Indians were upheld by the U.S. Supreme Court in *Johnson v. McIntosh* in 1823. An 1854 California Supreme Court decision upheld a ruling which prohibited Chinese from testifying in court. More recently, in 1944 the U.S. Supreme Court upheld the practice of relocating Japanese living in certain areas of the country without recourse to due process under the grounds of national security (Letman & Scott, 1981).

According to the research of Professor Lilly at Northern Kentucky University, African Americans were disproportionately executed in military courts-martial in Europe during World War II. Recent evidence uncovered by Lilly reveals that black soldiers were almost four times more likely to be executed than white soldiers despite being fewer than 10 percent of the American troops. For rape, the disparity was even greater: 87 percent of the American soldiers executed for the rape of civilians during World War II were African American (Clines, 1993).

There have been some changes in the status of African Americans since World War II, though the changes have been gradual and sporadic. Executive Order 9981 issued by President Truman in 1948 began the process of desegregating the military. In the 1954 Supreme Court case *Brown v. Topeka Board of Education*, the "separate but equal" ruling established in *Plessy v. Ferguson* (1896) was struck down. The Twenty-fourth Amendment, ratified in 1964, removed the poll tax barrier to black voting (Schaefer, 1984).

AFRICAN AMERICANS TODAY

Economic Well-Being of African Americans
Government statistics suggest that African Americans will continue to face many obstacles to upward mobility in the future. Data from the U.S. Bureau of the Census (1992, p. 47) disclose a dramatic rise in the percentage of black family households headed by a female. In 1970 black female-headed households accounted for 28 percent of all African American households; in 1991, black female-headed households

comprised 46 percent of all African American households. (The corresponding figures for white female-headed households in 1970 and 1991 were 9 and 13 percent, respectively.) Because female-headed households are more likely than other households to be impoverished, this trend is especially alarming.

Annual family income is relatively unchanged over the past two decades. Using constant 1990 dollars, the U.S. Bureau of the Census (1992, p. 449) reports that in 1970 the median annual family income for African Americans stood at $21,151. By 1990 this figure improved slightly to $21,423. However, during this same period of time the median annual white family income increased from $34,481 to $36,915. Thus, black income failed to keep pace with white income. Moreover, the changes in black family income were unequally distributed, with increases reported in the lowest (under $10,000) and highest ($75,000 and over) categories.

The unemployment rate is another gauge of the economic well-being of African Americans. Using this measure African Americans are only slightly better off today than in 1980. The African American unemployment rate for civilians 16 years and over was 14.3 percent in 1980 and 12.4 percent in 1991. The 1991 black rate was slightly over twice the 1991 rate for whites (U.S. Bureau of the Census, 1992, p. 39). Perhaps of greater concern is the unemployment of African American youth, the group most frequently found in arrest statistics. Here we find continued high rates of unemployment: in 1991 the unemployment rate for 16-to-19-year-olds was 36.3 percent (down from 38.5 percent in 1980, but up from 31.1 percent in 1990). For 20-to-24-year-olds the 1991 unemployment rate was 21.6 percent (U.S. Bureau of the Census, 1992, p. 399). And these numbers do not reflect those who are *under*employed (e.g., those who need full-time work but are employed part-time) and those who have given up on finding suitable employment.

What accounts for the large numbers of young African Americans who are without work? Schaefer (1984) cites four factors that will not be changing anytime soon which contribute to the high rate of unemployment. First, young African Americans have faced increased competition for jobs from immigrants and illegal aliens who are frequently willing to work for low wages. Second, the influx of large numbers of women into the labor force has further increased job competition. Third, young African Americans are more likely to experience high rates of unemployment because many live in the central cities that are economically depressed. And finally, Schaefer points out that it has become more profitable for young African Americans to engage in illegal activities than to work at whatever low-paying jobs exist. Although not on this list, one could add prejudice and discrimination as additional contributing factors.

Educational attainment is another measure of the potential for economic advancement. Figures for the 1991 civilian, noninstitutionalized population 25 years of age and over reveal that African Americans persist in lagging behind whites. Data from 1991 show that although approximately the same percentage of African Americans (17.8 percent) as whites (18.8 percent) have 1-3 years of college, whites are much more likely than African Americans to have a bachelor's degree or higher (22.4 percent for whites versus 12.1 percent for African Americans). In addition, 4.1 percent of the African American population 25 years of age and over, compared to 1.9 percent of the white population, has fewer than 5 years of elementary school (U.S. Bureau of the Census, 1992, p. 386).

Relations between African Americans and Whites

A recent poll of approximately 1,600 people released by the Anti-Defamation League of B'nai B'rith disclosed that Americans between the ages of 18 and 30 are more prejudiced toward African Americans than Americans between the ages of 30 and 49. This finding reminds us that African Americans have yet to be fully accepted by members of the dominant group. Further, the gains made in the recent past may be deteriorating. The poll also found that a significant number of white Americans continue to perceive African Americans in stereotypic ways. For example, 38 percent of the white respondents believe that African Americans are more violence prone than other races ("Poll," 1993).

This view of the potentially violent behavior of African Americans probably accounts in part for the excessive force by the police in their dealings with African Americans. Illustrative of these police-African American encounters is a 1993 case from Milwaukee. On September 27, 1993, a Milwaukee police officer stopped a car driven by a 30-year-old African American man. As the man stepped out of his car, the police officer shot and killed him when the police officer thought he saw the man raising a gun. The "gun" turned out to be a cassette tape. At the ensuing inquest the jury ruled that the police officer shot the man in self-defense ("Police Car," 1993).

The Rodney King incident in Los Angeles in 1991 provides another example of police use of excessive force. King, a black motorist, was beaten by members of the Los Angeles Police Department. During an 81-second period King was clubbed and kicked 56 times by white police officers. The incident, which was videotaped by a spectator, also showed a 50,000 volt stungun being fired into King. After the second trial in which Stacey Koon, who directed the beating, and Laurence Powell, who delivered 43 of the baton blows, were being tried in a federal civil rights court, the two officers were sentenced to 30 months in prison by a white judge. The maximum sentence the two police officers could have received was 10 years in prison and $250,000 in fines. In imposing this mild sentence, U.S. District Judge John Davies contended that King was a "threat" to the officers and placed much of the blame for the beating on King (Pope & Ross, 1992; Stewart, 1993; Stewart & Fields, 1993; "Twelve Blind Jurors," 1992).

African Americans are also the targets of white supremacist organizations, such as the Aryan Nations and the White Aryan Resistance. The Skinheads, a group that originated in England in the 1970s as a protest against poverty and unemployment and first appeared in the United States in the early 1980s, are seen as such a threat that the Department of Justice's Civil Rights Division has a special task force to deal with the problem (Clarke, 1991). Nevertheless, while the activities of organized hate groups, such as the Aryan Nations, the White Aryan Resistance, the Skinheads, and the Ku Klux Klan, provide the most visible evidence of racial violence, most racially motivated violence against African Americans results from the actions of individuals and unorganized groups (Levin & McDevitt, 1993).

Regardless of the source, African Americans are frequently victims of hate crimes.[3] 1991 marked the first year in which official hate crime data was collected by the Department of Justice for the FBI. Despite limited reporting of hate crime information by law enforcement agencies (only 2,771 of over 16,000 law enforcement agencies provided data), 4,755 hate-related offenses were recorded. Moreover, 35.5 percent of the hate crime victims were African American (Byers & Venturelli, 1994, pp. 10-11).

The primary federal agency responsible for investigating cases of racial and ethnic violence is the FBI. Two criminal investigative programs exist at the FBI: the Domestic Counterterrorism Program and the Civil Rights Program. The Domestic Counterterrorism Program focuses on organized groups (such as the Skinheads, Aryan Nations, White Patriots Party, etc.) that employ illegal force or violence to further their political or social agenda. In contrast, the Civil Rights Program concentrates on individuals or small unorganized groups that engage in hate violence. Successful prosecution of these groups is highly dependent on assistance by state and local law enforcement agencies (Clarke, 1991).

That the FBI is charged with investigating cases of racial and ethnic violence is ironic since this same agency in the 1960s infiltrated civil rights groups for the purpose of discrediting them (Schaefer, 1984). Moreover, a recent story appearing in the *ABA Journal* reveals that a growing number of politicians, lawyers, and researchers believe that the FBI has been engaging in selective investigation and prosecution of black elected officials (Curriden, 1992). Although it is virtually impossible to "prove" the existence of a conspiracy against black elected officials, there is mounting evidence of such collusion.[4] Hirsch Friedman, a white Atlanta lawyer who was once an informant for the FBI, stated in an affidavit that the FBI had an *unofficial* policy of singling out for investigation without probable cause African American officials in major metropolitan areas. Friedman further states in his affidavit that the justification for this policy was "that black officials were intellectually and socially incapable of governing major governmental organizations and institutions" (Curriden, 1992, p. 56).

CONCLUSION

Prejudice and discrimination have accompanied blacks since their arrival in the U.S. in 1619. Legal protection accorded whites was absent during much of the time that African Americans have been in America. Throughout the antebellum period slave codes rigidly defined the position of the slave in southern society. After emancipation southern states replaced the slave codes with black codes designed to restrict participation of African Americans in society. Lynchings of African Americans became more frequent in the South, having previously affected a greater proportion of lower-class whites. The convict lease system in the South, composed primarily of African

American inmates, provided needed revenue for financially strapped state governments trying to rebuild after the Civil War. It further enabled southern penal systems to segregate prisoners according to race. Although people in the North were generally more tolerant of African Americans, they, too, saw African Americans as inferior and systematically denied them full participation in society.

Prejudice and discrimination continued into the twentieth century. Violence in northern cities was especially acute in the first quarter of the century. As we approach the twenty-first century, we see that African Americans have made some gains although the gains are illusory in many ways. From 1970 to 1990 black family income increased somewhat but failed to keep pace with white family income. Further, black wealth is unevenly distributed: the poorest and wealthiest categories have shown increases recently. Moreover, substantial increases in the number of female-headed households hold little promise for meaningful improvements in this area. Unemployment rates for African Americans remain higher than that for whites. And African Americans are reminded of their inferior status by the continued presence of white supremacist organizations that thrive today.

NOTES

1. A similar finding is reported by Corzine, Creech, and Corzine (1983). They detected a negative relationship between percentage of white illiteracy and lynching rates of southern African-Americans between 1889 and 1931. The investigators intepret this outcome as a contradiction of the commonly held assumption that lower-class whites were primarily responsible for black lynchings.

2. A more detailed description of this study can be found in *Bad Blood: The Tuskegee Syphilis Experiment--A Tragedy of Race and Medicine* (1981) by James Jones.

3. A more detailed discussion of hate crimes appears in Chapter 7.

4. Both statistical and anecdotal data have been employed to document the presence of selective enforcement of the law by investigators. For instance, Curriden (1992, p. 55) notes that over 14 percent of the public corruption cases during a recent five-year period targeted African Americans, yet fewer than 2 percent of all elected officials were African American. The situation in the South was even more pronounced: 40 percent of the public corruption cases involved African American officials. Additionally, over half of the members of the Congressional Black Caucus have been singled out for investigation or harassment by federal investigators.

Highly publicized cases, such as the 1990 trial of the Washington, D.C., mayor, Marion Barry, accused of violating drug laws, illustrate the type of anecdotal evidence used to corroborate the selective enforcement view. Although Barry was eventually convicted of only a single misdemeanor, his case is significant in that his defense attorneys were prepared to provide documentation of a hit list maintained by federal investigators that contained Barry's name and other African American public officials.

CHAPTER 3
THEORETICAL EXPLANATIONS OF AFRICAN AMERICAN INVOLVEMENT IN CRIME

There is no one agreed-upon classification for criminological theories as each classification scheme is somewhat arbitrary, emphasizing certain aspects of a theory while excluding others. Despite the lack of consensus, Williams and McShane (1988) list three dichotomous classification schemes that are commonly employed. One dichotomy involves grouping theories into either **classical** or **positive** categories. The former concentrates on the law, the government, and human rights; the latter emphasizes criminal pathology, treatment, and the correction of individual criminality. This typology is based on two prominent schools of thought within criminology: the Classical School, which arose in the eighteenth century, and the Positive School, which developed in the nineteenth century.

The other classification schemes represent more contemporary ways of organizing diverse theories. Some theorists classify criminological theories as either **structural** or **process** theories. Structural theories emphasize the effect of the social structure on human behavior. Some structural theories are called strain theories because they are based on the notion that the social structure creates tension within certain segments of society which can eventually lead to deviant behavior. Process theories, in contrast, attempt to explain how individuals become involved in criminal behavior. Other theorists classify theories according to their views on the existence of shared values. **Consensus** theories assume that common values exist among members of society, while **conflict** theories contend that different groups of people possess different values. Many (though not all) conflict theories focus exclusively on conflict arising from differences related to social class.

Not all authors rely on dichotomies for classifying theories of crime. In particular, authors of criminology textbooks typically use multiple categories for classifying criminological theories. Larry Siegel (1992), for instance, devotes five chapters to a discussion of theory. His categories include choice and deterrence theories, biological and psychological theories, social structure theories, social process theories, and social conflict theories. Freda Adler, Gerhard Mueller, and William Laufer (1991) take a slightly different approach in their grouping of criminological theories. Their five chapters consist of psychological and biological theories, strain and cultural deviance theories, subcultural theories, social control theories, and alternative explanations of crime (labeling, conflict, and radical theories). An even more extensive classification is provided by Stephen Brown, Finn-Aage Esbensen, and Gilbert Geis (1991) who use a seven-category scheme. They divide theories into early theories of crime (including the Classical and Positive Schools), biogenic and psychogenic theories, social structure theories, social process theories, social reaction theories, contemporary neoclassical theories (i.e., deterrence theories), and integrated theories.

Michael Hindelang (1978) suggests a classification system for sociological explanations of the race-crime relationship that centers on the way in which each theory views racial disparities in arrest statistics. At one end of the continuum are theories such as subculture of violence theory, anomie theory, and differential opportunity theory that subscribe to the notion that African Americans actually engage in more crime than whites and are consequently more likely than whites to be arrested. At the other end of the continuum lies labeling theory which promotes the view that the higher arrest rate for African Americans is reflective of differential processing by criminal justice agencies and not greater black involvement in crime.

The theories discussed in this chapter are organized along a modified textbook classification scheme. The chapter commences with a discussion of sociological theories that typically predict a high level of African American criminal behavior and then proceed to an analysis of conflict and labeling theories which typically predict less criminal involvement by African Americans. Psychological and biological theories of crime are examined next. Finally, the chapter concludes with a brief discussion of minority views on crime.

SOCIOLOGICAL THEORIES OF CRIME

Theories Predicting High Levels of African American Criminal Behavior

Strain theories. A number of mainstream sociological theories predict greater involvement in crime by minorities. Strain theories, in general, posit that segments of society experiencing strain due to their position in society are more prone than those not experiencing strain to deviate from society's norms. Three strain theories frequently used to explain crime are anomie theory, reaction-formation theory, and differential opportunity theory. Each intimates that relatively powerless groups, such as African Americans and other minorities, should be more likely to engage in crime than more favorably situated groups.

Merton's (1938) **anomie theory** stresses the need for compatibility between societal goals and the socially-approved means for attaining them. His theory is applicable to the study of minorities because they often are denied access to socially-approved means for reaching their goals. Of the five modes of adaptation enumerated by Merton (conformity, innovation, ritualism, retreatism, and rebellion), innovation is the most common mode used to explain crime. As Flowers (1990) points out, however, the theory contains some shortcomings. For example, although it does help to account for differences in crime rates, it does not explain why one person chooses one mode over another. Furthermore, anomie theory makes a precarious assumption that there is a consensus on what constitutes socially approved goals and means that transcends class, race, and ethnic lines.

Reaction-formation theory (Cohen, 1955) was influenced by Merton's anomie theory and Sutherland's differential association theory (Williams & McShane, 1988). This theory of working-class male delinquency argues that boys from the lower class are typically unable to measure up to the middle-class standards being used to evaluate them. The inability to compete successfully with middle-class boys becomes most noticeable in school, where teachers expect all students to adhere to middle-class standards. As a consequence, lower-class boys suffer status-frustration. Some of these lower-class boys will drop out of school and develop a delinquent subculture whose values are the antithesis of those of the middle class. Because African Americans are disproportionately poor and therefore at a disadvantage in school, reaction-formation (or status-frustration) theory has been used to explain African American male involvement in delinquency and crime.

The theory can be criticized on a number of grounds. Kitsuse and Dietrick (1959) have criticized Cohen's theory on the grounds that he failed to provide *adequate* support for his assertions. However, Martin, Mutchnick, and Austin (1990) contend that the validity of this criticism rests on one's perspective. They surmise that the criticism reflected a disagreement with Cohen's heavy dependence on the ethnographies of earlier researchers to support his theory rather than developing new data sets to test his proposals.

Another criticism of reaction-formation theory is based on Cohen's assumption that delinquency is more prevalent in the lower-class areas of the city than elsewhere. Since this is still an unresolved issue, his emphasis on working-class male gangs may exaggerate the extent of delinquency among male members of the working class.[1]

A third criticism is derived from Cohen's assumption that status-frustration results from working-class boys trying to adhere to middle-class standards. Not all researchers concur with the view that working-class youth strive to acquire middle-class cultural traits (Martin, Mutchnick, & Austin, 1990). For example, Walter Miller (1958), to be discussed later in the chapter, argues that delinquency among lower-class males is the consequence of their loyalty to lower-class cultural values.

Some additional weaknesses of reaction-formation theory are suggested by Flowers (1990). One weakness he mentions is that, while it can explain gang-related delinquency, it cannot adequately account for delinquency involving individuals who are not associated with gangs. Moreover, the theory is unable to explain why some gang members leave the gang while others eventually become adult criminals. He further questions whether Cohen's depiction of lower-class gangs as "nonutilitarian," "malicious," and "negativistic" equally applies to all such gangs. In addition, Matza (1964) contends that some young people participate in delinquency because it can be fun and exciting and not because, as reaction-formation theory asserts, they are committed to a delinquent subculture.

Differential opportunity theory appeared in 1960. Also influenced by both Merton's anomie theory and Sutherland's differential association theory (Williams & McShane, 1988), Cloward and Ohlin

(1960) propose that the type of delinquent subculture to emerge will depend on the opportunities (legitimate and illegitimate) provided by the social structure of the local community. Again, because of its focus on lower-class neighborhoods, differential opportunity theory has been used to explain African American delinquency.

While recognizing greater diversity in delinquent gangs than reaction-formation theory, Cloward and Ohlin's theory also suffers from a number of shortcomings. A critique of differential opportunity theory by Martin, Mutchnick, and Austin (1990) reveals at least six possible weaknesses of the theory. One flaw of the theory is that there is little support for Cloward and Ohlin's assumption that blocked economic aspirations influence attitudes and lead to frustration among lower-class youth. A second weakness is that two of the key concepts, aspirations and opportunity, are not conceptually clear. Another criticism is that their definition of a delinquent subculture is tautological.[2] A fourth criticism stems from the fact that Cloward and Ohlin contend that middle-class delinquency is not the result of a delinquent subculture but offer no empirical data to support their argument. Moreover, although a number of researchers have found support for their argument that gang specialization occurs, the specific types of gangs (criminal, retreatist, and conflict) identified by Cloward and Ohlin have not been corroborated by other researchers. Finally, the implementation of the ideas contained in differential opportunity theory by Presidents Kennedy and Johnson did not result in any meaningful change in the level of delinquency.[3]

Nettler (1974) offers two additional criticisms. First, frustration can manifest itself in many different ways, only one of which produces delinquent behavior. And second, exclusive focus on the opportunity structure may be the result of middle-class scholars attributing *their* values and perceptions to others. Moreover, a recent investigation by Simons and Gray (1989) suggests that the theory may have limited applications as they observed a moderate negative relationship between perceived chance for occupational success and delinquency for lower-class African Americans, but not for lower-class whites or middle-class African Americans.

Theories focusing on learned behavioral differences. Some theories have emphasized the importance of group values and norms in the learning of deviant behavior. Such theories as differential association, social learning, focal concerns, and subculture of violence exemplify this type of theoretical orientation.

Differential association theory was introduced by Edwin Sutherland in the 1939 edition of *Principles of Criminology* (Flowers, 1990). The theory focuses on the process by which people acquire the values and definitions necessary to engage in delinquency and crime. A basic assumption is that all behavior (including illegal behavior) is learned. Moreover, criminal behavior is primarily learned through interaction with intimate personal groups (or what sociologists refer to as primary groups). The extent to which these primary groups value illegal behavior will significantly influence the perceptions and behavior of individuals within the groups. Thus, if one lives in a ghetto where many of the inhabitants define illegal behavior as acceptable, then that person will more likely come to accept those definitions of appropriate behavior as valid than individuals not exposed to such definitions.

Shoemaker (1990) alludes to three criticisms of Sutherland's theory. First, he notes that some critics have argued that the assumption that criminal behavior is learned belies the complexity of motivations for crime and adds little, if any, to our understanding of crime. A second criticism of differential association theory is that it understates the importance of individual factors (e.g., personality variables) that also contribute to delinquency and crime. Perhaps the most serious problem, however, is the issue of measurement of the theory's concepts.

> A major problem of measurement with this theory is its historical and situational focus. Since most criminal offenders are discovered after the fact, so to speak, reconstruction of thoughts and moods at the time the act was committed is exceedingly difficult to develop. When one adds to this difficulty the problem of reconstructing prior events and influences on one's attitudes and behavior, the task becomes almost impossible (Shoemaker, 1990, p. 157).

An additional shortcoming of differential association theory is mentioned by Vold and Bernard (1986). They are critical of the theory in that it cannot explain delinquent and criminal behavior from people who have not been exposed to delinquents and criminals. For example, the lone embezzler who has not been exposed to individuals who favorably define violation of the law cannot be adequately accounted for by Sutherland's theory.

Attempts to reformulate the propositions of differential association theory led to the emergence of **social learning theory** by Robert Burgess and Ronald Akers (1966). Couched in the language of behavioral psychology, the theory argues that learning occurs sometimes as a result of conditioning (direct learning) and sometimes as a result of imitation or modeling (indirect learning). The theory, like differential association theory, asserts the supremacy of social groups in behavior reinforcement. However, unlike differential association theory, social learning theory recognizes the possibility that some behavior may be strengthened by *nonsocial* reinforcers (e.g., the physiological effect of a drug). Stressing the importance of both reinforcement and punishment in the learning of deviant behavior, Akers, Krohn, Lanza-Kaduce, and Radosevich (1978) note that deviant behavior is likely to persist if the behavior is rewarded (positive reinforcement) or if the behavior results in avoidance of punishment (negative reinforcement). Conversely, behavior is less likely to persist if the behavior is either accompanied by aversive stimuli (positive punishment) or loss of a reward (negative punishment). To the extent that an individual finds deviant behavior to be more reinforcing than conforming behavior, the individual is likely to continue engaging in deviant behavior.

At least three criticisms of social learning theory should be noted. First, Reed Adams (1973) contends that, contrary to Akers' theory, nonsocial reinforcers can sometimes be more important than social reinforcers. Gibbons and Krohn (1991) suggest two additional weaknesses of the theory. According to them, one shortcoming of social learning theory is that it tends to be tautological and is therefore unable to be disproved. They see this drawback as the most serious problem of the theory. However, they note another weakness of social learning theory that hinders its practicality: the difficulty involved in operationalizing its concepts. Gibbons and Krohn (1991) indicate that research has yet to establish that social learning theory is more amenable to operationalization, and consequently easier to test empirically, than its precursor, differential association theory.

Walter Miller's (1958) focal concerns theory and Wolfgang and Ferracuti's (1967) subculture of violence theory stress the deviance-enhancing qualities of lower-class culture. **Focal concerns theory** posits that male members of the lower class possess six focal concerns or areas of interest: (1) trouble, (2) toughness, (3) smartness, (4) excitement, (5) fate, and (6) autonomy. Because many lower-class families are headed by women, many lower-class boys do not have adequate male role models in the home and thus turn to the male gang as a way of resolving their problem of sex-role identification. The lower-class gang, by emphasizing these focal concerns, increases the likelihood that its activities will come to the attention of social control agents.

A number of authors have been critical of focal concerns theory. Whitehead and Lab (1990), for instance, have observed that Miller's theory is tautological. That is to say, Miller and his research team of seven social workers observed the behavior of lower-class individuals to identify their focal concerns, and then used the same focal concerns to explain the behavior of lower-class individuals. Brown, Esbensen, and Geis (1991) offer two additional criticisms of the theory. First, they note that it is difficult for persons from the middle class to observe members of the lower class without introducing some class-related bias. (The tendency to use one's own cultural standards as a yardstick to measure the standards of others and the accompanying tendency for this to result in a negative evaluation of the other group is known as ethnocentrism in sociology.) Moreover, they criticize the theory for only addressing the problem of male delinquency, a criticism that is also applicable to many other theories of delinquency.

Other shortcomings of focal concerns theory have been noted by Hagan (1990) and Shoemaker (1990). Hagan (1990) is critical of the theory on two grounds. First, it tends to ignore delinquent acts perpetrated by middle- and upper-class delinquents.[4] And second, focal concerns theory assumes the existence of a distinctive lower-class culture possessing values and attitudes that tend to clash with those of the middle class, yet the heterogeneity of American society casts doubt as to whether a distinctive value system based entirely on social class can exist. Shoemaker (1990), in turn, focuses on the importance that focal concerns theory attaches to the female-headed household. This aspect of the theory is of special significance to the study of African American delinquency as the female-headed household is more common in the black community than the white community (see Chapter 2). Shoemaker's review of the evidence leads him to conclude that there is limited support for Miller's view that delinquency is related to the female-headed household.

Subculture of violence theory is the most widely accepted sociological explanation of criminal homicide. The theory posits that in inner-city ghettos a subculture has arisen that supports the use of physical force as a way of solving problems associated with everyday living. Members of this subculture share some of the values of the larger society. However, they condone the use of violence to solve social conflicts to a much greater extent than the dominant culture. Moreover, failure to act in an aggressive way can result in rejection by the peer group (Wolfgang & Ferracuti, 1967).

Evaluations of this perspective have typically been accompanied by a comparison of official measures of criminal violence for various groups assumed to be differentially exposed to norms and values supportive of violence. Though these investigations appear to be measuring the level of violence, the use of official measures of criminal violence raises the issue of possible bias. Research has documented that such factors as the status of the participants and the preference of the complainant influence the probability that a violent episode will be officially recorded. The use of official homicide rates as a gauge of violence is not infallible either as the availability of medical assistance can determine whether a violent incident is recorded as an assault or a homicide (Luckenbill & Doyle, 1989).

In addition to the use of questionable measures of violence, much research suffers from the problem of multicollinearity, resulting from a substantial portion of the variance in one or more independent variables being explained by other predictors in the model. According to Blalock (1972, p. 457) multicollinearity can affect partial correlations and slope estimates by making them more vulnerable to sampling and measurement errors. That multicollinearity can influence results is corroborated by a recent study by Huff-Corzine, Corzine, and Moore (1991). The researchers compared results obtained using a commonly employed statistical procedure known as ordinary least squares (OLS) to results obtained using normalization ridge regression (NRR), a statistical procedure that they contend is preferable when multicollinearity is present. They note that the findings of their investigation would have been substantially modified if they would have relied entirely on OLS instead of both OLS and NRR.

Further complicating the testing of the subculture of violence thesis is the fact that numerous investigators have used inappropriate units of analysis. Luckenbill and Doyle (1989) argue that, although most researchers have employed *aggregate*-level data to examine this subject, *individual*-level data are actually needed since violence occurs within an interpersonal setting and involves a number of psychological processes which cannot be adequately detected at the aggregate level.

These criticisms of the literature notwithstanding, what support exists for this explanation of black violent crime? A review of the literature by Kennedy and Baron (1993) disclosed little support for the theory. Their review, though, was not restricted to an analysis of an African American subculture of violence and consequently does not specifically address the issue. More pertinent to the discussion is a review of 18 studies by Kposowa and Breault (1993). The studies, all published between 1974 and 1988, investigated the relationship between the proportion of the population that is nonwhite and the homicide rate for various regions, predominantly urban areas. They report mixed support for the theory. While 12 investigations supported the proposed positive correlation between percent nonwhite and the homicide rate, six of the studies failed to uncover such a relationship.

Some researchers have observed that not only do African Americans not have a proclivity for violence as suggested by the subculture of violence thesis, but it is whites, and not African Americans, who are actually more accepting of violence as a way of resolving conflict. For instance, Shoemaker and Williams (1987), using General Social Surveys for seven years, cite evidence supportive of the view that African Americans are less tolerant of violence than whites. Similarly, Christopher Ellison (1991) reports that whites are significantly ($p < .001$) more likely than nonwhites to approve of interpersonal violence in defensive situations.

If the subculture of violence thesis is to be accepted as valid, then there should be varying levels of violence among different groups depending on their exposure to a violent subculture. Yet Kposowa and Breault (1993), after holding constant other factors, found that the average homicide rate for 1979 to 1981 was positively ($p < .05$) related to the proportion of African Americans, Hispanics, and Native Americans in the 3,083 United States counties that they analyzed. These results led the authors to conclude:

> . . . if we interpret the effect of percentage African
> American on homicide as evidence for an African
> American subculture of violence (as some past studies
> have done), arguments could also be raised for
> Hispanic and Native American subcultures of
> violence. Since African Americans, Hispanics and
> Native Americans have disparate cultures, race and
> ethnic-specific subcultures of violence fail to be
> persuasive explanations of homicide (p. 43).

In addition to a general lack of empirical support, Hawkins (1983)
cites other weaknesses of the subculture of violence theory. Hawkins
is especially critical of the failure of the theory to appreciate the
structural, situational, and institutional variables that may contribute to
the use of physical force. For example, the subculture of violence
theory neglects the role of the legal system in black-on-black
homicides.

Social control theory. Travis Hirschi's (1969) social control theory
attempts to explain why people *conform* to society's norms. It begins
with the assumption that people are inherently self-interested and only
the presence of effective social control mechanisms ensures conformity.
According to social control theory, attachment, commitment,
involvement, and belief comprise the elements of the social bond that
tie individuals to conventional society. The weaker the social bond, the
freer one is to deviate.

> Under control theory, the high rate of minority crime
> can be attributed to a weaker attachment to social
> institutions such as school or jobs, economic
> opportunity (as related to their disproportionate
> representation in the lower classes), and family (there
> is some indication that minorities have higher rates of
> broken homes and illegitimacy than whites) (Flowers,
> 1990, p. 69).

However, Boocock (1972) questions the assumption that African
Americans have weaker attachments to school than whites. She notes
that "On attitudes toward school and academic work generally, black-
white differences are negligible or even indicate a higher valuation of

school and achievement by blacks" (p. 43). In addition, a recent review of the research on broken homes suggests that the effect of the broken home on African American delinquency is poorly understood. Of the nine studies examining racial differences, four found no evidence that the broken home-delinquency relationship was differentially affected by race. In contrast, two studies observed that African Americans from broken homes were more likely to use drugs or engage in delinquency than their white counterparts, while three studies reported that drug use and delinquency were more common among whites living in broken homes than among African Americans living in broken homes (Free, 1991).

Despite considerable support for the tenets of social control theory, four possible limitations of Hirschi's theory have been identified. First, even when support for social control theory was found, the social control variables typically explained a very small proportion of the variance in delinquency. Second, the impact of the social bond on delinquency may be age-specific (e.g., the social bond may have a greater deterrent effect on younger adolescents than on older ones). Third, contrary to the theoretical expectation that there will be a one-way relationship between the social bond and delinquency (such that a weak social bond will precede involvement in delinquency), some longitudinal investigations of the theory support the view of a reciprocal effect on the relationship between the social bond and delinquency. In other words, involvement in delinquency can affect the social bond and vice versa. Finally, there is some evidence that the relative importance of these bonds on delinquent behavior may vary according to geographical area and type of culture being studied (Shoemaker, 1990).

Socioeconomic theories. Socioeconomic theories of crime include those that emphasize the importance of social class, economic deprivation, breakdown in the family structure, and racism in the creation of criminal behavior. According to Flowers (1990, p. 72) these theories "are perhaps the most applicable to the crime of minorities compared to general crime theories because these groups tend to be overrepresented in socioeconomic circumstances believed to be most conducive to criminality."

At least four theoretical explanations have proposed a link between racial inequality and violent crime (Messner & Golden, 1992). The first of these is the **social disorganization/anomie explanation.** A previously discussed example of this category is Merton's anomie theory, which draws attention to the strain that is generated whenever there is a discrepancy between societal goals and the culturally-approved means for attaining them.[5] In general, social disorganization/anomie theories focus on the ascriptive quality of racial inequality in the United States. Because American society subscribes to democratic principles and emphasizes *achieved* status, the presence of racial inequality, an *ascribed* status, produces hostile sentiments in African Americans and other minorities. Concomitantly, those norms that function to control hostile sentiments have been weakened due to a lack of social integration. The poor integration and widespread anomie eventually lead to heightened violence.

A second theoretical perspective is referred to by Messner and Golden as the **relative deprivation/frustration aggression explanation**. This explanation postulates that racial minorities will experience a feeling of *relative* deprivation when they compare themselves to the dominant group. As opportunities to redistribute resources are likely to be blocked, racial minorities will become frustrated. This frustration, in turn, ultimately manifests itself in aggressive behavior.

The **relative gratification/reduced aggression explanation** is analogous to the previous one, except that it focuses on white violence. According to this perspective, racial inequality benefits the dominant group. In other words, whites may derive both material and psychological benefits from being relatively advantaged. The advantage whites have over African Americans and other minorities serves to reduce aggressive tendencies in whites through its lessening of frustration. Consequently, whites will have *lower* rates of criminal violence than their disadvantaged counterparts.

And finally, there is the **macrostructural opportunity explanation**. This view hypothesizes that racial inequality leads to racial segregation which thereby reduces the chances of contacts between individuals of different races. Because interracial contact is minimized under racial segregation, racial inequality should be *negatively* related to *inter*racial rates of violent crime and *positively* related to *intra*racial rates of violent crime.

Investigations of the relationship between racial inequality and criminal violence have been inconclusive. Blau and Blau (1982), for instance, in a widely cited study, found significant positive relationships between racial inequality and murder, robbery, and aggravated assault.

However, a subsequent reanalysis of their data by Blau and Golden (1986) revealed that racial inequality was significantly associated with robbery only. More recently, Balkwell (1990) reported a significant positive relationship between racial income inequality and homicide rates. In contrast, Corzine and Huff-Corzine (1992) dichotomized black homicide rates into felony homicide(killings that occurred while committing a felony) and nonfelony homicide. They detected a significant positive relationship between racial income inequality and nonfelony black homicide rates although the relationship for felony black homicide rates was not statistically significant. Moreover, Harer and Steffensmeier (1992) noted that, regardless of the measure used, economic inequality was a poor predictor of violent crimes by African Americans, even though economic inequality was a strong predictor of violent crimes by whites.

What accounts for the inconsistent findings? An analysis of racial inequality and violent crime by Golden and Messner (1987) disclosed that differences in the operationalization of racial inequality and model specification contribute to discrepant outcomes. More specifically, socioeconomic status-based measures of racial inequality are more likely than income-based measures to reveal strong positive associations between racial inequality and criminal violence. Additionally, by respecifying the model (i.e., changing the variables contained in the model), it is possible to alter the observed effects of racial inequality on violent crime.

Numerous criticisms of socioeconomic explanations of crime exist. First, the use of official statistics to support the theory that the lower class is disproportionately involved in crime suffers from a number of limitations, including the possibility that the figures may actually reflect differential law enforcement rather than differential criminality.[6] Second, economic deprivation theory and social class theory tend to ignore white-collar crime that is committed by higher-income persons and goes largely undetected in part because the typical crimes committed by higher-income persons (e.g., embezzlement, fraud, tax evasion, etc.) tend to be less visible to detection than the typical lower-class crimes (e.g., burglary, robbery, auto theft, etc.) and in part because the typical lower-class crimes are more likely than the typical middle- and upper-class crimes to be seen as a threat to society by the higher social classes. Third, crimes such as murder and rape are committed by people in all strata and cannot be accounted for by focusing exclusively on either social class or economic deprivation. Fourth, theories that emphasize a breakdown in family structure as a cause of deviance, particularly those connecting the broken home with delinquency, often lack strong empirical support. And finally, if racism is solely responsible for African American crime, this explanation leaves unanswered the question, Why don't *all* African Americans participate in illegal activities?

A critique of mainstream sociological theories. The criticisms directed at these theories should not be construed as a blanket condemnation of them. Nonetheless, each theory is inadequate as an explanation of African American crime in that each of the previously mentioned theories neglects to take into account the possibility that the laws themselves can be racially biased. An illustration of this can be found in Minnesota. A law recently passed in that state and subsequently declared unconstitutional established a 4-year prison sentence for first-time *crack cocaine* users but probation for first-time users of *powdered cocaine.* While on the surface the law does not appear to be discriminatory, its enforcement would be highly discriminatory. Based on 1988 statistics, 92 percent of those arrested for crack cocaine use were African American, but 85 percent of those arrested for the use of powdered cocaine were white (Lynch & Patterson, 1991, p. 3).

Additionally, those theories attributing greater delinquency to African American youths than white youths do not consider the likelihood that the physical appearance of many African American youths, which often corresponds to the stereotype of a juvenile delinquent, may increase an African American's chance of being apprehended by the police.[7] Furthermore, the assertive behavior of many African American young people, used to obtain status among black peers, may be misinterpreted by the police, thereby increasing one's risk of arrest (Pinkney, 1987).

Some of the previously discussed theories have alluded to a broken home-delinquency nexus. Statistics cited in chapter 2 indicated a substantial increase in the prevalence of female-headed households among African Americans. But to what extent is delinquency among young African Americans attributable to inadequate supervision resulting from the absence of one parent or to the increased chances of official intervention by legal authorities due to the *perception* that the single-parent family provides (by middle-class standards) a delinquency-producing environment (Pinkney, 1987)?

The preceding theories also tend to ignore the possibility that some of the discrepancy in black-white rates of offending may be due to differential patrolling by the police. Because many lower-class African Americans live in heavily patrolled areas of the city, any transgression of the law is more likely to result in a police contact than a similar violation of the law occurring in suburban or rural areas. Using arrest data for 1975, Hawkins (1983, p. 410) observed that African Americans living in rural areas comprised 10 percent of the rural population and 10 percent of the arrests for all types of crimes. African Americans living in suburbs were actually slightly *under*represented in arrest statistics (15 percent of the suburban population and 12 percent of all arrests). Only in the heavily patrolled urban areas were African Americans disproportionately arrested.

Coramae Mann (1993, p. 103), in commenting on mainstream theories of minority crime, notes the irony "that so many of the explanations of minority crime focus on minority violence when American history is filled with violence, particularly as directed against its minority citizens." And despite the preoccupation of some sociological theories with African American violence, Hickey (1991, p. 77) found that black serial murderers constituted only 10 percent of the offenders in his study. In fact, 97 percent of the female serial killers and 85 percent of the male serial killers were white (pp. 110 & 133).

A final general criticism of these theories is that many of the variables contained in the theories may differentially affect criminal behavior by race. LaFree, Drass, and O'Day (1992), using annual time-series data from 1957 to 1988, observed that opportunity variables typically associated with strain theory were generally in the predicted direction for whites but in the opposite direction for African Americans. More specifically, they reported that even after controlling for relevant variables, there was a significant positive relationship between median family income and the robbery and homicide rates for African Americans. Black robbery and burglary rates were positively related to educational attainment as well. And a negative relationship existed between percent female-headed households and robbery and burglary rates for African Americans.[8]

Conflict and Labeling Theories

Conflict theory. Conflict and labeling theories differ from the earlier sociological theories in that they examine societal forces that highlight minority crime and understate the extent of crime by the dominant group. Conflict theories assume that societies are characterized by conflict not consensus. If consensus exists, it is transient and cannot be easily sustained. Apart from a few shared suppositions, however, conflict theories vary considerably in their view of conflict. Williams and McShane (1988) contend that conflict theories can be placed along a continuum. On one end would be those theories subscribing to the view that society is made up of numerous groups that compete with one another for power. At the other end would be those theories that stress class conflict and assume the existence of two classes, each attempting to assert its domination over the other.

The radical conflict perspective includes a wide range of theoretical positions including political anarchism, Marxism, economic materialism, and value diversity (Williams & McShane, 1988). Nonetheless, most of these positions were influenced by Karl Marx (though Marx did not develop a formal theory of crime). As viewed by Marxist criminologists, the law is a tool of the ruling class in that what is defined as criminal reflects the interests and concerns of the dominant group (hence, the interest in strict enforcement of laws protecting private property). Likewise, offenses typically involving members of the dominant group are not likely to be defined as criminal, being either ignored in the legal code altogether or being placed within the rubric of administrative or regulatory law. Moreover, all crime in capitalist societies is attributed to class struggle. Thus, Marxist criminologists see the street crimes of African Americans and other minorities as the result of underemployment, unemployment, demoralization, capitalist exploitation, capitalist victimization, and racism. If the lower class engages in property crime, it is because social inequality has created the need to steal as a means of economic survival. Violent crimes and substance abuse are explained as being a consequence of the anger and frustration that persons in the lower class experience.

A critique of conflict theory is difficult given the variety of theoretical positions falling under this heading, thus some criticisms of this theory will *not* equally apply to all versions of conflict theory.

Nevertheless, one rather general criticism of the theory is that it tends to ignore the consensual basis of much criminal law (Hagan, 1990). Because investigations of police discretion, sentencing, and corrections have produced mixed results, some critics argue that the assumption that the criminal justice system benefits only the interests of the powerful is largely unfounded (Siegel, 1992). Shoemaker (1990) alludes to four limitations of conflict theory when applied to the study of delinquency: (1) it is unable to account for delinquency in socialist societies; (2) it has difficulty explaining the existence of middle-class delinquency; (3) the theory tends to overemphasize the importance of economic and social class variables in the development of delinquency, although various studies have revealed the importance of other factors in delinquency; and (4) conflict theory has been largely unable to demonstrate the presence of class-linked motives for behavior, both on the part of the adolescent and on the part of social control agents.[9]

Despite these condemnations of the theory, conflict theory (along with labeling theory) has helped criminology to overcome its preoccupation with criminal actors by redirecting its attention to the role of law enforcement in the creation of crime. It has also served the purpose of reminding criminologists of the fallacy involved in assuming that laws always reflect a consensus in society. Moreover, there is some empirical support for the basic tenets of the theory. Jackson and Carroll (1981), for example, examined the relationship between race and police expenditures for 90 nonsouthern U.S. cities. Because conflict theory asserts that the law is an instrument of oppression used by the dominant group against subordinate groups, they hypothesized that "the amount of resources devoted to policing will vary directly with the threat posed by subordinate to dominant groups" (p. 293). If African Americans (the subordinate group) are viewed as a threat by whites (the dominant group), then conflict theory would predict that expenditures for police should be related to the racial composition of the city, the number of race riots during the 1960s, and the level of civil rights mobilization activity. The authors found general support for their hypotheses.

Labeling theory. Labeling theory has its intellectual foundation in the symbolic interactionist perspective (Williams & McShane, 1988). According to labeling theory, no act is intrinsically deviant (Schrag, 1971). An act becomes deviant only *after* being defined as such. In other words, deviance is a relative concept since what is defined as deviant by one society may not be similarly defined by another society. Moreover, as evidenced by self-report studies of deviance, virtually everyone at some time has violated society's norms or, to use the terminology of labeling theory, participated in **primary** deviance. Most primary deviants, however, do not come to see themselves, or to become seen by society, as deviants. Only a fraction of primary deviants come to be labeled as (**secondary**) deviants. Labeling theory thus attempts to describe the process by which some people come to be designated as deviants by their society.

Power is an important ingredient in the ability to ascribe a negative label to others (Garfinkel, 1956). Because power is differentially distributed in American society, labeling theory asserts that offender characteristics, such as race, age, and social class, become relevant in criminal justice decision making (Schrag, 1971). Given that African Americans and other minorities tend to have little power in society, their ability to successfully rebut accusations of illegal conduct is considerably weaker than that of nonminorities. Hence, labeling theory predicts that African Americans will be more likely than whites to be officially labeled deviant.

Once labeled, the individual may find it difficult to avoid being re-labeled. As Williams and McShane (1988, p. 88) explain:

> those who are in deviance-processing occupations (criminal justice agencies) closely watch individuals once they have come to the attention of their agency. In a sense, those labeled are the clientele of the criminal justice system and, like any other good business, the system keeps close tabs on its customers. It is difficult for the once-labeled, such as probationers, parolees, or ex-offenders, to escape the attention of this audience, and subsequent behavior is likely to be identified and relabeled.

This view receives support in the literature reporting that African Americans and other relatively powerless minorities, many of whom are poor, are more likely than whites to be arrested, prosecuted, and incarcerated for longer periods of time. Moreover, recidivism rates of young parolees (ages 17 to 22 years) reveals that, compared to whites, African Americans are more likely to be rearrested, reconvicted, and reincarcerated (U.S. Department of Justice, 1988, p. 111). Furthermore, Quinn and Downs (1993), after investigating police perceptions of local gangs in 79 municipal police departments, note that the race of the largest gang was significantly related to police perception of the severity of the gang problem in their city. Black gangs were perceived as posing the most severe problem for the police, despite the fact that race was unrelated to the size of the gang, the gang's organizational sophistication, and length of operation in the city.

Critics of the labeling perspective point out a number of weaknesses of the theory. A general criticism of labeling theory is that it is not a theory but a "sensitizing perspective" that makes criminology cognizant of its use of middle-class values in assessing criminality (Williams & McShane, 1988). Akers (1968) is critical of the theory for being excessively deterministic and not allowing for the active rejection of a negative label by the deviant actor. Wellford (1975) takes exception to labeling theory's assumption that no act is intrinsically deviant, pointing out that this might be true of minor offenses but not major ones. The theory has also been criticized for paying too little attention to the causes of initial deviance (Hagan, 1990).[10]

Additional shortcomings of the theory are suggested by Martin, Mutchnick, and Austin (1990). They note that much research fails to corroborate labeling theory's assertion that known delinquents and criminals possess deviant self concepts. Additionally, the persistence of a negative label would appear to be called into question by the aging-out process in delinquency, which occurs at about 16 years of age. A third criticism, and a common one for criminological theories, is that labeling theory is conceptually ambiguous and is consequently difficult to test empirically.

Shoemaker (1990) notes an additional limitation of the theory. His summary of empirical investigations of the effects of labeling on delinquency suggests that those juveniles who are the least delinquent are the ones most likely to experience changes in identity or attitude as a result of official labeling. They are also the ones most likely to undergo behavioral changes. It would thus appear that official labeling has rather minimal effects on the more advanced delinquent.

Regardless of its limitations, a major contribution of labeling theory lies in the fact that it shifted our attention away from a preoccupation with the causal factors in deviance to the processes that amplify and sustain deviant behavior. Labeling theory has also been the impetus for various diversion programs in existence today.

PSYCHOLOGICAL AND BIOLOGICAL THEORIES OF CRIME

Psychological Theories

Frustration-aggression theory is the most widely accepted of the psychological explanations of homicide (Mann, 1993). According to the theory, aggression results from frustration, or the inability to achieve a goal. Applied to African Americans, frustration stems from the discrimination and caste status accorded to blacks in America. The resultant anger manifests itself in arguments, verbal abuse, and physical aggression directed toward others of one's own race (Mann, 1993).

Other psychological theories have attributed various personality traits to criminal behavior. One such personality trait is self-esteem. For a number of years many researchers have argued that African Americans typically have lower self-esteem than whites, making them more vulnerable to criminogenic influences. However, Ross (1992) contends that there are two major problems with this research which limit its generalizability. First, his review of the literature on self-esteem disclosed a lack of consensus regarding the conceptualization of self-esteem: over 200 different measures of self-esteem exist in the literature in psychology. Second, definitional problems of self-esteem are common. For example, there is disagreement over whether the concept is multidimensional or unidimensional. Moreover, some studies ignore the possibility that the sources that influence self-esteem vary by race. Leonard Bloom (1971) further warns against attributing any particular personality trait, such as low self-esteem, to minority status because this tends to create a stereotype and there is not a single African American personality any more than there is a single white personality. In addition, many of the studies of personality have chosen to attribute as normal or preferable only those values of the dominant group.

A psychological-political explanation for black-on-black homicide has been advanced by Alvin Poussaint (1983). He argues that murderers and their victims (who are usually African American, too) are psychologically impaired due to the psychology of the black experience in America. Oppression has resulted in psychological scarring in many impoverished African Americans. Murderers and their victims tend to have a poor self-image and a low threshold for violence. The black experience has also led to self-hatred. Institutional racism (the discrimination that occurs when the traditional practices of social institutions result in one race receiving more favorable treatment than another race) has taught African Americans that whiteness is a positive attribute and blackness is a negative attribute. The end-result of institutional racism is that many blacks have no respect for the criminal justice system. Because much violence is victim precipitated (i.e., brought on in some way by the victim), the individual characteristics that lead one to commit murder are the same ones that increase one's chances of becoming a victim.

Although other psychological theories of crime could be mentioned, those discussed here are particularly germane to African American crime. Still, psychological explanations as a whole have limited applicability because only a small proportion of all criminals have mental, emotional, or personality disorders. Moreover, investigators have been unable to confirm the presence of a substantive correlation between minority crime and these psychological factors (Flowers, 1990).

Biological Theories

The earliest explanations of criminal behavior focused on the physical makeup of offenders. Cesare Lombroso (1835-1909), an Italian physician, was the first to systematically explore this view. It was his contention that a number of criminals were atavistic individuals who were less fully evolved than noncriminals. These "born criminals" possessed many ape-like physical features such as protruding jaws, flattened noses, and strong canine teeth (Siegel & Senna, 1991). Although Lombroso's ideas were later discredited by Charles Goring (1913), biological explanations of crime continue to flourish.

Another biological theory connected body type to delinquent behavior (Sheldon, 1949). William Sheldon identified three body types: (1) the endomorph, (2) the ectomorph, and (3) the mesomorph. According to Sheldon, the mesomorph, a person with an athletic build, tends to be aggressive and is the most likely to be involved in delinquency.

Intelligence has frequently been determined to be associated with delinquent and criminal behaviors. A number of investigators have reported that low intelligence is related to involvement in illegal activities (Hirschi & Hindelang, 1977; Kirkegaard-Sorensen & Mednick, 1977; West & Farrington, 1973; Wilson & Herrnstein, 1985). Further, after analyzing data from several earlier investigations, Hirschi and Hindelang (1977) concluded that IQ was a more important indicator of delinquency than either race or socioeconomic status. They contend that the effect of IQ on delinquency is *indirect* in that low IQ adversely affects school performance, and poor school performance increases the likelihood of delinquent behavior.

Because African Americans typically score lower than whites on IQ tests, this explanation would lead one to hypothesize that African Americans should be more likely than whites to be involved in illegal activities. Whether or not this explanation is a biological one depends upon the source of the difference in IQ scores. If, for instance, the black-white differential is primarily attributable to environmental factors associated with the subordinate position of minorities in society, then the difference is an artifact of sociological factors and is not biologically based. Moreover, this interpretation suggests that intelligence can be modified through manipulation of the sociological factors causing the differences to exist. On the other hand, should the racial differences be largely innate, then the explanation is primarily a biological one. Given that biological interpretations of intelligence have periodically surfaced, the IQ-crime relationship is discussed under the heading of biological explanations of criminality.

Herrnstein and Murray's 1994 book, *The Bell Curve: Intelligence and Class Structure in American Life*, has renewed interest in the debate over racial differences in intelligence. Impressive in length (the book is 845 pages long and contains seven appendixes), the authors argue that success today is defined by the ability to use and manipulate information, an ability enhanced by high intelligence. They further contend that intelligence (or cognitive ability) is differentially distributed across ethnic groups. Carefully documenting black-white differences in IQ scores, Herrnstein and Murray state that these differences are substantial since the typical white score is higher than approximately 84 percent of all black scores, while the typical black score is higher than only about 16 percent of the white scores (p. 269). The authors additionally assert that intelligence is not very malleable.

They then proceed to demonstrate how low IQ tends to be correlated with various social ills such as criminality and welfare dependence.

Despite the book's length and frequent references to tables and graphs, critics have been quick to point out its flaws. Coming under scrutiny are the sources of data employed in the authors' discussions. Charles Lane (1994) observes that many of the cited works have been published in *The Mankind Quarterly*, an anthropology journal in Edinburgh that promotes the view that the white race is genetically superior. Many authors mentioned in the book also have ties with the Pioneer Fund, a New York foundation that has racist roots and that, as recently as 1989, advocated the abandonment of integration in the United States because, it argued, it is beyond our capabilities to enhance the intelligence of African Americans.

Stephen Gould (1994) questions the legitimacy of using a single intelligence score to measure cognitive ability. He shares the view that multiple intelligences (e.g., verbal, mathematical, spatial, etc.) exist and the use of a single general measure of intelligence may therefore be meaningless for comparison purposes. Gould further notes that even if one accepts their hypothesis that IQ is related to various social behaviors, the percent of explained variance is very small (usually < 10 percent). Additionally, if one accepts their claim that about 60 percent of one's intelligence is inherited, then the extent to which the genetic component accounts for social behavior is further diminished (i.e., explained variance is 60 percent of a figure that is typically less than 10 percent).

Herrnstein and Murray are also chastised for confusing correlation with causation (although the authors indicate that correlation does not prove causation, they commonly approach their correlations as if a cause-and-effect relationship existed). Additional criticisms include the omission of relevant facts not supportive of their views and an apparent unwillingness to recognize the true consequences of what their book appears to be documenting (Gould, 1994; Kamin, 1995).

Finally, Leon Kamin (1995) has commented on the wisdom of comparing the IQ scores of blacks from Africa to those of African Americans as a way of ascertaining whether slavery and discrimination has artificially depressed the IQ scores of American blacks. He contends that this comparison fails to take into account the historical fact that African blacks have also been the victims of prejudice and discrimination and should consequently have low IQ scores as well.

Not all biologically oriented theories rely exclusively on biological factors to explain crime. **Integrated theories** borrow ideas from several different theoretical models to develop a more comprehensive explanation of criminal behavior. Typical of these theories is Wilson and Herrnstein's (1985) explanation of property and violent crimes that incorporates elements of biology, psychology, and sociology. Using the notion of rational choice, they argue that individual factors (e.g., low intelligence, mesomorphic body type, impulsivity, etc.) may be more important than social factors (e.g., family background, school failure, etc.) in decisions to commit crime as the individual factors may make it difficult for one to resist temptation and defer gratification. Before any behavior occurs, however, the individual will weigh the potential rewards of crime (e.g., material gain, sexual gratification, peer approval, etc.) against the potential costs of crime (e.g., guilt feelings, peer disapproval, possible punishment, etc.). Rewards associated with noncriminal behavior (e.g., a favorable self-image, freedom, etc.) will also be considered before a decision is reached. Overall, individuals who are biologically and psychologically impaired will be more likely than others to engage in criminal behavior.

Biological explanations of crime, as applied to the understanding of racial differentials in offending, suffer from many weaknesses. Perhaps the most significant shortcoming of biological theories of crime is that they assume that race is a biological concept when, in fact, it is a social concept. As Roberts and Gabor (1990) indicate in their critique of genetic explanations of crime, many years of interbreeding have resulted in mixed ancestry. Moreover, according to Mann (1993), those explanations of homicide that subscribe to the view that the higher rate of homicide for African Americans is biologically determined fail to take into account those studies that have found that blacks in Africa tend to have lower homicide rates than blacks in America. Further, those studies tend to suggest that African blacks have homicide rates that are lower than those for the general population in the United States.

Flowers (1990) mentions some additional shortcomings of biological explanations of minority crime. First, biological explanations tend to ignore fluctuations in crime rates over time. Second, these theories are unable to explain the decline in criminal activity that frequently occurs after the early twenties. Third, typically the theories ignore the role played by the environment in generating criminal behavior. Fourth, the impact of discriminatory criminal justice policies on crime is overlooked. Fifth, biological explanations cannot satisfactorily account for crime committed by people without these biological traits. And finally, these theories help to perpetuate a racist ideology.

MINORITY VIEWS ON CRIME

Largely absent from the literature are minority interpretations of criminality (more is said about this in Chapter 7). Despite the paucity of the literature, it is possible to identify some recurring themes in this area. According to Young and Sulton (1991), the research of African American scholars has generally emphasized the effect of structural inequality on the opportunity structure and subsequent pressure on the individual to engage in criminal behavior. Therefore, an explanation of delinquency and crime should *not* focus on the characteristics of individual offenders or groups of offenders. Instead, the researcher interested in understanding black crime should concentrate on such problems as poverty, illiteracy, unemployment, selective law enforcement, discrimination, segregation, inadequate housing and nutrition, etc.

A minority perspective on crime also questions the validity of the scientific method in the social sciences (Takagi, 1981). By limiting our understanding of crime to phenomena that are observable and quantifiable, Takagi contends that we fail to completely comprehend the reasons for the criminal activity: "The etiology of crime in minority communities cannot be understood by a science that does not take into account thoughts and experiences of the people in the community (p. 50)." Takagi further argues that to understand the behavior of oppressed minorities, one must examine how a history of discrimination might affect an individual's present behavior, a view echoed by Mann (1993).

An exemplary theory of the minority perspective is the **internal colonial model** of crime and delinquency. Offering a socio-psychological interpretation of criminality, this theory views African Americans and other minority groups as victims of social, economic, and political oppression. As a result of this oppression, minorities are likely to experience alienation. Several forms of alienation are possible, including alienation from an individual's own racial group. Feelings of alienation, in turn, can lead to one of three adaptive forms of behavior, one of which includes crime and delinquency. Thus, the theory tries to explain criminality by changing the focus of the analysis from the individual who has committed a crime to the exploitative structural system in which the individual has resided (see Tatum [1994] for an expanded discussion of this theory).

According to Becky Tatum (1994), the internal colonial model's strength lies in its use of a historical perspective. By examining the historical antecedents of oppression, the researcher develops a more complete understanding of current conditions and perceptions of minority groups. Nonetheless, as presently developed the model contains a number of shortcomings. As Tatum (1994) acknowledges, there are both theoretical and empirical limitations of this model, five of which are enumerated below.

- The model lacks specificity. It does not, for instance, provide answers as to why some individuals engage in crime and delinquency as an adaptive response to alienation while others choose other behavioral options.

- Although the significance of race is evident in the model, it does not adequately address the issue of social class. While it would seem that the impact of structural oppression on minorities is likely to vary along social class lines, it is unclear how race and social class interact to produce various behavioral responses.

- The theory tends to ignore the issues of alienation and class differences among whites.

- Internal colonial theory does not take into consideration the variability of structural oppression among different minority groups. Probably all minorities have experienced some of the same forms of oppression. Yet their relationships to the white power structure are not identical and consequently require further elaboration.

- It is difficult to operationalize the variables thereby complicating the empirical testing of the model.

A different view of black male crime is presented by Willie Dantzler, Jr. (1991), an African American prisoner in Illinois. In a paper written in partial fulfillment of a course offered by Roosevelt University, Dantzler enumerates five factors that contribute to the failure of African American men in the inner-city. First is an inadequate and distorted definition of manhood. African American males get their definition of manhood primarily from television and the local community. Regardless of the source, the definition of manhood revolves around sex, violence, and athletics. Intelligence, compassion, and understanding are qualities that are not highly valued.

A second factor is the absence of a positive male role model in the family and school. Dantzler argues that a father is needed to help the young male to learn how to resolve differences in a peaceful manner, the failure of which has contributed to a high homicide rate among African American men. Moreover, the father would teach his son cooperation and discipline, two traits missing from many inner-city black men.

Third, is a preoccupation with a superficial view of blackness. According to Dantzler, a lack of positive role models helps to perpetuate this view. It is this superficial view of blackness, along with its depreciation of education, that prevents the African American male from assimilating.

The last two factors include a basic mistrust of American institutions (e.g., the police, the courts, the government, big business, etc.) and the perception that many conventional avenues to success that are open to whites are closed to African Americans. Collectively, these aspects of inner-city black culture make it difficult for African American men to succeed in life.

CONCLUSION

Numerous theories have been advanced to explain racial disparity in crime. For the most part these theories suffer from a monolithic view of black culture based on stereotypes. Many can be criticized for relying on official measures of crime to validate their conclusions. Biological and psychological theories are particularly suspect in that they assume biological and psychological traits that are not present in most black offenders.

Minority theorists have been critical of mainstream criminological theories and have faulted them for neglecting such factors as selective law enforcement, discrimination, and unemployment. Minority theorists have also questioned the validity of the scientific method for ascertaining the truth because of its inability to measure the thoughts and experiences of African Americans.

To address the concerns of minority theorists, future theoretical explanations of African American crime should ideally explain both the distribution of crime (epidemiology) and why a specific individual engages in criminal behavior (etiology). To understand the distribution of crime, historical and structural factors that account for the overrepresentation of African Americans in official crime statistics must be identified. Some questions that need to be raised are: (1) To what extent do laws (e.g., drug legislation) differentially impact the African American population?, (2) Under what structural conditions are African Americans more (or less) likely than whites to be officially processed by the criminal justice system and receive stiffer sentences?, and (3) What effect does institutional racism have on the distribution of crime in America? In addition to macrotheoretical concerns, a full accounting of African American crime will need to explain why some African Americans become involved in crime while others refrain from that activity. Toward this end, microtheories stressing the role of individual and group factors in African American criminal behavior will need to be developed.

NOTES

1. Cohen (1955) does briefly address middle-class male delinquency, although his comments are speculative and not well developed. He hypothesizes that middle-class male delinquency primarily results from sex-role anxieties. Because middle-class fathers are likely to be extensively involved with their work and away from the family much of the time, Cohen asserts that children develop an identification with their mothers. This is acceptable for girls who are supposed to eventually assume the role of a mother but unacceptable for boys who are expected to be masculine like their fathers. To reassure himself of his own masculinity, the middle-class boy may reject the conduct norms associated with his mother and engage in delinquent behavior.

2. Cloward and Ohlin (1960, p. 7) define a delinquent subculture as "one in which certain forms of delinquent activity are essential requirements for the performance of the dominant roles supported by the subculture." This represents a tautology in that "the existence of dominant subcultural roles is supported by the occurrence of certain forms of behavior, which, in turn, are explained by the existence of subcultural roles" (Martin, Mutchnick, & Austin, 1990, p. 288).

3. In defense of differential opportunity theory, however, Martin, Mutchnick, and Austin (1990) acknowledge that Cloward and Ohlin's plan was to be a preventive measure and was not intended to convert delinquents. Secondly, Cloward and Ohlin never contended that providing more legitimate opportunities to a segment of the population would eliminate crime. The authors further contend that it is possible that these programs as modified to fit the whims of bureaucrats did not constitute an adequate test of the theory.

4. It should be noted that Miller does attempt to address the issue of middle-class delinquency in a subsequent work (Kvaraceus & Miller, 1967). In that work Walter Miller and William Kvaraceus contend that middle-class delinquency is due to the absorption of lower-class values into the middle class. They further state that this diffusion is primarily the result of the popularity of music which emphasizes the focal concerns of the lower class.

5. An interesting extension of Merton's theory has been advanced by Robert Agnew (1985). Although Merton argues that strain occurs because the lower class cannot realize middle-class goals, Agnew proposes that the desire for unlimited and unattainable goals means that even members of the middle class may feel strain and therefore engage in deviance.

6. Differential law enforcement can have a self-perpetuating quality. Because police surveillance is typically concentrated in the less affluent sectors of an urban area, law-violating behavior of the lower class is more likely than law-violating behavior of the more affluent classes to come to the attention of the police. Moreover, police discretion may lead to the greater chance of arrest for lower-class individuals who look "suspicious" to the police simply because they are in a known high-crime area. Consequently, more deviance will be discovered in lower-class areas than in higher-class areas, thereby justifying the increased patrolling of lower-class areas of the city. Since African Americans are disproportionately poor and therefore more likely to live in these areas, they are disproportionately likely to be arrested.

7. That the police often act on the basis of stereotypes and that African American youth are more likely than white youth to match this stereotype are illustrated by the following example provided by Piliavin and Briar (1964, p. 212) in their study of police encounters with juveniles. When a police officer was quizzed as to why he apprehended a particular African American youth, the officer stated that the youth "looked suspicious" because "He was a Negro wearing dark glasses at midnight."

8. While in the opposite direction to that predicted by strain theory, the amount of variance explained in black robbery, burglary, and homicide rates by the three opportunity variables and four control variables was rather modest. The adjusted R^2 for black robbery was .25; for black burglary, .19; and for black homicide, .00.

9. The danger involved in criticizing conflict theory on the basis of sweeping generalizations about the theory is indicated by the second criticism. Although generally true that conflict theory is unable to account for the presence of delinquency among juveniles in the middle

class, power-control theory, a version of conflict theory, does predict middle-class delinquency (see Hagan, Gillis, & Simpson, 1985).

10. However, Howard Becker (1963), a leading proponent of the labeling perspective for many years (although he never actually considered himself a labeling theorist), stresses that the perspective never claimed to explain the etiology of deviance.

CHAPTER 4
AFRICAN AMERICANS,
THE POLICE,
AND THE JUDICIAL SYSTEM

Studies of satisfaction with the police have consistently disclosed that African Americans are less satisfied with police performance than whites. Bayley and Mendelsohn's (1969) investigation of Denver, Colorado, for example, revealed that African Americans were less satisfied with the police than whites and the strongest predictor of views of the police was one's ethnicity. Additionally, Peek, Lowe, and Alston (1981) identified 19 studies published between 1953 and 1975 that found African Americans hold less favorable opinions of the police than whites. Smith, Graham, and Adams (1991) also reported that individual attitudes toward the police vary by race and are influenced by characteristics of the neighborhood. More specifically, even after controlling for variables such as crime rates, poverty levels, and individual characteristics, nonwhites residing in predominantly nonwhite areas of the city had less favorable opinions of the police than nonwhites residing in racially mixed areas of the city. In their analysis of data from a 1973 Gallup Poll, Peek, Lowe, and Alston (1981) concluded that black and white Americans differentially perceive the police, with blacks perceiving the police as being pro-white.[1]

Attitudes of individuals toward the police are more complex than first thought. Two studies employing factor analysis (Scaglion & Condon, 1980; Sullivan, Dunham, & Alpert, 1987) revealed racial differences in the patterns of attitude structures of African Americans and whites. Data from Pittsburgh disclosed that components of satisfaction with the police varied by race: whites were more concerned with police politeness and laziness, whereas African Americans were more concerned with perceived brutality and impartiality of the police (Scaglion & Condon, 1980). The authors conclude

> It is apparent that, regardless of Black and White evaluations of certain variables, the elements that comprise general satisfaction differ. It would thus be overly simplistic to merely report differences for Blacks and Whites on individual attitudinal items, since their overall attitudes are not determined in the same way (p. 281).

Similarly, an investigation of African Americans, Cubans, and whites in Miami revealed that attitudes toward the police were not unidimensional and were structured differently from one group to the next (Sullivan, Dunham, & Alpert, 1987). Moreover, there were differences in attitudinal structures between adolescent and adult African Americans. The significance of these two studies is suggested by Sullivan, Dunham, and Alpert (1987, p. 177): "When members of the group being studied do not share the same abstract notions about the police, using composite scales may lead to faulty interpretations and may measure something other than what is described."

MINORITY STATUS AND LIKELIHOOD OF ARREST

In carrying out their duties, the police have considerable discretion in determining the appropriate actions to take in police-citizen encounters. Some determinants of police discretion include community attitudes and values; police departmental policies, customs, and procedures; peer pressure; individual perception; and the circumstances surrounding the police encounter with the suspect (Flowers, 1990, p. 150). A controversial issue within criminology and criminal justice is whether police discretion results in racially selective arrests. We will now pursue this topic by looking first at black juveniles and then at black adults.

Black Juveniles and Decisions to Arrest

Numerous studies have reported racial bias in police arrests of juveniles (e.g., Cicourel, 1968; Ferdinand & Luchterhand, 1970; Goldman, 1963; Gould, 1969; Piliavin & Briar, 1964; Thornberry, 1973; Werthman & Piliavin, 1967). Nonetheless, some researchers have concluded that the higher probability for black juvenile arrests is due to the dispositional preferences of complainants (Black & Reiss, 1970; Lundman, Sykes, & Clark, 1978).[2] Additional studies from the late 1960s/early 1970s report no evidence of arrest bias based upon the race of the suspect once relevant variables (e.g., offense seriousness) are controlled (Green, 1970; Terry, 1967; Weiner & Willie, 1971).

More recent evidence corroborates the view that racial bias exists in the police processing of black juveniles. Dannefer and Schutt (1982) observed in their examination of six police juvenile bureaus in New Jersey that (1) African Americans were less likely than whites to be released by the police, (2) the race of the suspect was a more important determinant of police dispositions than juvenile court dispositions, and (3) the effect of race on police dispositions was stronger in the county with a higher concentration of African Americans. Sampson's (1986) investigation of data from the Seattle Youth Study revealed that being black was significantly (p < .05) and positively related to lifetime measures of police contacts, independent of actual involvement in delinquency (as indicated by self-reported delinquency). However, race was not significantly related to court referrals.

African Americans and Arrest Decisions

There is less agreement as to the effect of race on arrest decisions for adult African Americans. Numerous variables have been proposed as possible explanations for the disproportionately high arrest rates for African Americans. Some of the more commonly analyzed variables are suspect demeanor, type of offense, complainant's race, complainant's preference for arrest, neighborhood characteristics (e.g., poverty level), and police department characteristics (e.g., degree of bureaucratization). The evidence remains inconclusive, however, despite a number of investigations into this topic.

For instance, Smith and Visher's (1981) examination of 742 police-citizen encounters in three American cities revealed that African Americans were more likely than whites to be arrested, even after controlling for the effects of such variables as suspect demeanor and offense seriousness. A subsequent analysis of the same data found that the importance of race in arrest decisions varied according to the type of encounter (Smith, Visher, & Davidson, 1984). In encounters with no complainant, the suspect's race was directly related to police decision to arrest for females but not for males. In encounters with suspects and complainants, the suspect's race was not directly related to police decision to arrest, although the complainant's race was directly related to police arrests (the police were more likely to arrest the suspect when the complainant was white than black). Further analysis of the data disclosed that in cases of interpersonal conflict, nonwhites were significantly more likely than whites to be arrested if they had had prior contact with the police (Smith, Graham, & Adams, 1991). These three studies, though only a small sample of the research, indicate the complexity of the relationship between race and arrest.

POLICE USE OF FORCE AGAINST AFRICAN AMERICANS

Police violence directed at African Americans is not a recent development. This form of violence and repression existed during slavery as slave patrols were employed to whip, intimidate, and murder slaves. During the post-Reconstruction period, moreover, the police were responsible for enforcing Jim Crow laws. Some were also involved in black lynchings (see Taylor Greene, 1994a).

Given the adversarial quality of police-black relations that characterized the early history of America, it is important to raise the question whether police today continue to use excessive force in their dealings with African Americans. Prior to a discussion of this issue, however, it is necessary to recognize the weaknesses of this research. Studies of police shootings typically suffer from one or more of the following weaknesses: (1) samples are too small to produce statistically significant findings, (2) samples are limited to a single geographic area, and (3) reliance on preexisting records provided by police or coroners (Geller, 1982). The last shortcoming is particularly problematic in that police records may contain "reporting bias" (i.e., the records are written to make the officer look good), and the use of these data precludes an assessment of situations where officers in potentially violent encounters refrained from shooting. In addition, comparisons of police behavior in multiple cities may result in distortions because reporting categories may vary by police department, the organizational characteristics of police departments may vary, etc. (Geller, 1982). Despite these shortcomings, it is possible to identify the "typical" police shooting:

> The most common type of incident in which police and civilians shoot one another in urban America is one involving an on-duty, uniformed, white, male officer and an armed, black, male civilian between the ages of 17 and 30 and occurs at night, in a "public" location within a "high-crime" precinct, in connection with a suspected armed robbery or a "man with gun" call (Geller, 1982, p. 158).

Sorensen, Marquart, and Brock (1993) note that African American police officers are disproportionately involved in police shootings of African American felons. However, this is not tantamount to saying that African American police officers are involved in a larger *number* of shootings than their white counterparts. What it does mean is that the *rate* of shootings is higher for African American police officers. Moreover, Fyfe (1981) suggests that the relationship between officer race and police shootings is a spurious one resulting from racially differentiated patterns of assignment, socialization, and residence.[3]

How much more likely are African Americans to be shot by the police than whites? Geller (1982, p. 158) found in his review that, depending on the location of the study, anywhere from 44 percent to 89 percent of the civilians shot by the police were black. Meyer (1980, p. 102) reported that 55 percent of the suspects shot at by the Los Angeles police between 1974 and 1978 were African American.

To account for the racial disparities in police shootings, researchers have frequently examined arrest rates. For example, a study conducted in seven cities by the Police Foundation found that African Americans comprised 73 percent of the arrests for Index Crimes and 79 percent of the civilians shot by the police (reported in Geller, 1982, p. 163). Examined this way, the overrepresentation of African Americans in police shootings is diminished. Caution should be exercised, however, in using arrest rates to justify black shootings by the police.

> If police systematically discriminate against minorities
> in   making   arrests   (arresting   minorities   in
> circumstances where whites are not arrested or
> charging minorities with more serious offenses), then
> a high correlation between the rate at which
> minorities are arrested for serious offenses and the
> rate at which they are shot would be far from
> reassuring. Indeed, national victimization studies
> have been interpreted as suggesting that blacks may
> be arrested out of proportion to their involvement in
> certain offenses (Geller, 1982, p. 164).

It should be recalled that Petersilia (1983) noted that in California African Americans were more likely than whites to be arrested without sufficient evidence to support criminal charges. Further, Meyer's (1980) analysis of the Los Angeles Police Department from 1974 to 1978 suggests possible racial bias in the processing of blacks. Unarmed blacks, for instance, were at greater risk of being shot at by the Los Angeles police than were either unarmed Hispanics or unarmed whites. Additionally, the shooting of unarmed black suspects was less likely to elicit administrative disapproval than the shooting of unarmed white or Hispanic suspects.

An empirical examination of two explanations of why police disproportionately shoot and kill minorities[4] was conducted by Sorensen, Marquart, and Brock (1993). The **conflict hypothesis** proposes that police use of deadly force is a function of the social status of the suspect. Minorities and the lower class are more likely to be singled out by the police because these segments of society are most likely to be seen as a threat to the status quo which favors the dominant group (in particular, upper-class whites). In contrast, the **community violence hypothesis** argues that police use of deadly force corresponds to actual or perceived threats. Therefore, "the level of police violence in any community is a function of the level of violence in that community (p. 418)." Using cities as their unit of analysis, the authors found consistent support for the conflict explanation. For example, economic inequality was the best predictor of the rate of felony killing by the police. The racial composition of the city (percent black) was also significantly and positively related to the rate of felony killing by the police even after controlling for the violent crime rate.

RACIAL COMPOSITION OF THE CITY
AND POLICE EXPENDITURES

A conflict perspective was also used by Pamela Jackson and Leo Carroll (1981) to predict the effect of race on police expenditures. Since this perspective sees the law as an instrument of oppression used by the dominant group against subordinate groups, "the amount of resources devoted to policing will vary directly with the threat posed by subordinate to dominant groups" (p. 293). Consequently, the racial composition (percent black) of a city's population should be positively related to policing expenditures. The model contained a number of other variables (including the crime rate) that have been found to be related to expenditures on police services. The authors further hypothesized that the number of race riots during the 1960s and the level of civil rights mobilization activity should have influenced expenditures for police in 1971. Their analysis found support for the notion that police expenditures increase as economic inequality between blacks and whites increases. Moreover, the relationship between racial composition of the city and per-capita police expenditures was curvilinear: from 10 to 50 percent black, the per-capita police expenditures increased; once blacks became a statistical majority, there was a precipitous drop in per-capita police expenditures. Jackson and Carroll interpret this finding as evidence that blacks "may have translated their numbers into political power, thus becoming the dominant group in city politics" (p. 300). They conclude that general support exists for a conflict explanation of police expenditures.

Whereas the study discussed above analyzed 90 nonsouthern U.S. cities, a more recent study by Jackson (1986) examined 442 cities from southern and nonsouthern regions. She investigated the hypothesis that in smaller cities the presence of a black population may be perceived as less of a threat to the established order due to the greater effectiveness of informal social control mechanisms. Using a model containing seven independent variables, Jackson observed that the impact of the size of a city's black population on expenditures for police is considerably stronger in large cities ($\geq$ 50,000 population) than in small cities ($\geq$ 25,000 but < 50,000 population), even after controlling for the crime rate and region.

AFRICAN AMERICANS AND
THE JUVENILE JUSTICE SYSTEM

Dannefer and Schutt (1982) contend that racial bias in the processing of juveniles should be less evident in the juvenile court than with the police. For one thing, the juvenile court can devote more time to getting the facts surrounding the case than can the police officer who frequently must take action without benefit of all the relevant facts. Moreover, in comparison with the police, the juvenile court over the years has become more formal and bureaucratic in its operation thereby diminishing the amount of discretion of the juvenile court judge. The overall result should be more uniform decisions by the juvenile court judge. Further, decision making by the juvenile court is more visible than decision making by the police. Since many police-citizen encounters are not officially reported, police decisions are less subject to public scrutiny than are the decisions of the juvenile court judges.

Does this mean that racial bias is nonexistent in the juvenile court system? Not necessarily. An investigation of racial disparity in juvenile court processing in 159 counties in the U.S. for 1985 and 1989 found some alarming trends:

- While referrals to juvenile court for whites increased modestly (a 4.3 percent increase), nonwhite referrals increased rather dramatically (a 38.5 percent increase).

- Increases in nonwhite detentions, petitions, and placements exceeded the increase in nonwhite referrals to juvenile court. At the same time white detentions, petitions, and placements remained relatively stable (McGarrell, 1993).

The researcher examined the possibility that increases in nonwhite youth involvement in the juvenile court could be attributed to an increase in the nonwhite youth population. His analysis suggested that only a small proportion of the increase in nonwhite cases could be attributed to nonwhite youth population increases. However, the existence of racial disparities alone does not confirm the presence of racial bias. Without evidence to the contrary, it remains a possibility that the greater involvement of nonwhite youth in the juvenile court system reflects the greater involvement of nonwhite youth in illegal activities.

Although McGarrell (1993) did not address this issue, an earlier study by Huizinga and Elliott (1987) revealed that differences in delinquent behavior were unable to account for the racial differences in incarceration rates. Using data from the National Youth Surveys for 1976 to 1980, they demonstrated that neither the prevalence nor the incidence of delinquency for black juveniles could satisfactorily explain the racial differences in incarceration rates. When the data were examined for differences in the proportion of chronic offenders by race, the researchers concluded that with the exception of 1976, there was no support for the notion that the black youth population contained a higher proportion of chronic offenders than the white youth population.

Despite these findings, research analyzing the impact of race on juvenile court decision making does not disclose a consensus. An extensive review of the literature by Tittle and Curran (1988, p. 25) identified 35 studies published between 1967 and 1986 that examined the effect of race on decision making in the juvenile court. Fourteen of those investigations (40 percent) concluded that race had some effect on juvenile court decision making. Phrased another way, 60 percent of the investigations did *not* detect any appreciable effect of race on juvenile court decisions.

Why do researchers fail to agree on the role of race in juvenile court decision making? At least four factors account for the different findings (Bishop & Frazier, 1988). First, many researchers limit their analyses to a single stage of the juvenile justice system, especially the dispositional stage. This may produce discrepant outcomes in that limiting research to the last stage of processing may conceal the indirect effects of race resulting from the relationships between race and decision making at earlier stages of the juvenile justice system. When investigators confine their research to one stage of the juvenile justice system the importance of race in decision making may be minimal. Yet, the *cumulative* effect of race on decision making may be substantial.

Second, some studies do not control for relevant legal factors (e.g., prior record and offense seriousness) that might explain apparent racial disparities in juvenile justice processing. This omission is particularly common in the early research.

A third factor involves the failure to use multivariate models and to examine possible interaction effects between race and other variables. Studies published prior to 1980 frequently relied on bivariate analyses and first-order partial correlation techniques to examine racial effects on decision making. Ignoring possible interaction effects between race and other variables can cause the researcher to prematurely reject race as unimportant.

And finally, Bishop and Frazier (1988) assert that the imprecise measurement of the dependent variables precludes a reconciliation of the divergent findings. More specifically, the authors point out that many investigators use measures that are too simple to reflect the complexity of the decision making process. Further, because operationalization of the dependent variables varies from study to study, it is virtually impossible to account for discrepant findings.

Recognizing the limitations of the research, let us now examine the relationship between race and juvenile justice decision making by examining various stages. To minimize some of the problems discussed above, the studies to be examined are limited primarily to more recent investigations.

Intake Screening and Detention Decisions

Intake screening is important because at this stage a decision is rendered to do one of the following: dismiss the case, process the case informally (i.e., through extralegal channels), or handle the case formally. Therefore, a formal hearing represents the most severe decision at this juncture of the juvenile justice system. Early investigations of intake screening decisions may distort current practices as a result of changes occurring after the passage of the **Juvenile Justice and Delinquency Prevention Act.** Passed in 1974, this Act made receipt of federal funds for juvenile justice programs contingent on the removal of status offenders from secure confinement. Numerous states complied by changing their juvenile codes to emphasize community-based treatment, along with the removal of juveniles accused of status offenses from institutions (Siegel & Senna, 1991, p. 547).

The findings of Bortner, Sunderland, and Winn (1985) suggest that the Juvenile Justice and Delinquency Prevention Act had an impact on the processing of African Americans. Their research examined changes in intake decisions resulting from compliance with this act. The study focused on one juvenile court located in an affluent midwestern county of approximately one million people. Comparing juvenile cases processed during the predeinstitutionalization period (1973-1974) with cases processed during the postdeinstitutionalization period (1976-1977), they found that the Act had an overall effect of decreasing the use of formal hearings for both white and African American youth, although the only substantial reduction in use of formal hearings occurred among African American youth. Nevertheless, African Americans continued to have a greater likelihood of being formally processed than whites.

Although researchers cannot agree on the importance of race in intake screening, researchers generally find that legal factors are important in decisions made at intake. For example, Bell and Lang's (1985) analysis of 533 male juveniles in Los Angeles County in 1982 revealed that race was not consistently related to the type of intake disposition received although prior record was. Similarly, Pope and Feyerherm (1981) found that intake determination was most affected by legal factors. More recent investigations using data from juvenile courts in the southeast have disclosed that both race and legal factors were directly related to intake disposition (Bishop & Frazier, 1988; McCarthy & Smith, 1986). The latter study further found that race had direct and indirect effects on intake disposition.

Detention decisions are important in that detaining a juvenile may influence decisions at later stages of the juvenile justice system. Returning to the earlier research by Bortner, Sunderland, and Winn (1985, p. 40), we find that the effect of the Juvenile Justice and Delinquency Prevention Act of 1974 on detention varied by offense and race. For all offenses combined, there was a decrease in use of detention for whites and African Americans (although African Americans continued to be substantially more likely than whites to be detained). For status offenses (which should be most directly impacted by the Act), however, the percent of whites detained *dropped* (from 26.6 to 22.9 percent) while the percent of African Americans detained *increased* (from 31.3 to 36.6 percent). Moreover, 1983 data from a juvenile court in a western state disclosed that decisions to detain were influenced by the race of the juvenile (Fagan, Slaughter, & Hartstone, 1987). In contrast, Bishop and Frazier (1988) reported no statistically significant relationship between race and detention decisions for Florida juveniles.

Adjudication and Disposition Decisions

Bishop and Frazier's (1988) analysis of Florida juveniles revealed an interaction between offense severity and race on adjudicatory outcomes. Their results indicated that black minor offenders were dealt with more harshly than whites charged with minor offenses. For more serious offenses, blacks and whites were treated similarly. This finding illustrates the importance of examining interaction effects as discrimination will not be evident if an additive model is used. They also found that black youth were significantly more likely than white youth to be either incarcerated or transferred to criminal court. Nevertheless, the impact of race was less than the impact of legal variables at both the adjudication and disposition stages. Additionally, McCarthy and Smith (1986) detected direct and indirect effects of race on adjudication decisions for youths in a juvenile court in the southeast.

Race was also observed to be an important determinant of decisions to adjudicate and punish youth in Fagan, Slaughter, and Hartstone's (1987) investigation of a juvenile court in a western state. An examination of the juvenile court system in a six-county region of New Jersey disclosed that, compared to whites, African Americans were *less* likely to receive probation and *more* likely to be institutionalized (Dannefer & Schutt, 1982). It should be noted, however, that part of the sample was drawn from juvenile court cases before the enactment of the Juvenile Justice and Delinquency Prevention Act. They further reported that legal factors also influenced juvenile court dispositions.

McCarthy and Smith's (1986) examination of a cohort of juveniles through three stages of the juvenile justice system disclosed that the importance of legal factors diminished as one progressed through the juvenile justice system. Concomitantly, social factors became increasingly more important in decision making. For adjudicated youths, race had a significant direct effect on disposition while none of the legal factors affected the disposition outcome.[5]

Not all researchers have detected racial bias in juvenile court dispositions. Kowalski and Rickicki (1982), for example, examined a representative sample of adjudicated male delinquents in Alabama. After controlling for relevant variables (including number of past offenses and committing offense), the investigators determined that race was not significantly related to type of disposition.

Other investigators have found that the effect of race on disposition is offense specific. A comparison of juvenile court dispositions both before and after the Juvenile Justice and Delinquency Prevention Act revealed that the Act had the overall effect of reducing the likelihood of institutionalization for African American and white youth. But when status offenses were examined separately, the authors found that the rate of institutionalization for black males increased over the 5-year period (Bortner, Sunderland, & Winn, 1985). Tittle and Curran (1988) also noted that the effect of race on severity of disposition varied by type of offense. Although they reported no significant relationship between race and severity of disposition for status offenses, there was a significant relationship between race and severity of disposition for drug/sex offenses and for other misdemeanors. Moreover, the researchers concluded that racial disparity in dispositions was greatest when there were relatively large proportions of nonwhites and young people living in the county. The authors speculate that "this is because nonwhites and youth symbolize to white adults resentment-provoking or fear-provoking qualities like aggressiveness, sexuality, and absence of personal discipline" (p. 52). However, contradictory results were obtained by Frazier, Bishop, and Henretta (1992) who reported that, even after controlling for the effects of various legal and extralegal variables, the lower the percent of African Americans in the general population, the harsher the dispositions for African American youth.

Another study compared adolescents referred to a correctional school to adolescents referred to a state psychiatric hospital (Lewis, Shanok, Cohen, Kligfeld & Frisone, 1980). Both groups were equally violent and psychotic symptoms were prevalent in both groups, yet black males were significantly more likely to be incarcerated than hospitalized. Their analysis disclosed that while 67.3 percent of the incarcerated males were black, only 18.2 percent of the hospitalized males were black (p. 1215). Further, in three of four multiple regression analyses, race was the best predictor of disposition outcome.

Judicial Waiver Decisions

Judicial waiver to criminal court represents the most severe punishment one can receive from the juvenile justice system. If race is an important determinant of the judicial waiver decision, then this could account for some of the overrepresentation of African Americans in criminal court and prison. Recent literature suggests racial bias in waiver decisions varies by jurisdiction.

Fagan and Deschenes (1990) examined the role of race in waiver decisions to transfer violent juvenile offenders to criminal court. Violent juvenile offenders from courts in Boston, Detroit, Newark, and Phoenix were analyzed. Race was an important determinant of the judicial waiver decision in Detroit only. Even in that juvenile court, race was the weakest predictor of the waiver decision of the five discriminating variables in the model. In an earlier investigation of those same courts, Fagan, Forst, and Vivona (1987) found that race had an indirect effect on the waiver decision. Minorities, being more likely to be charged with murder and to be initially arrested at an earlier age than whites, were more likely to be waived to criminal court because murder and age at onset of delinquency were both predictive of transfer to criminal court.

Another study investigated use of the youthful offender designation in New York State. In this state all juveniles 16 to 18 years of age are tried as adults. With some exceptions, once an individual this age is convicted, but before sentencing, the individual may be considered for youthful offender status. If granted, this designation substantially lessens the penalties that can be assessed. Investigating 6,453 cases involving 16- to 18-year-old defendants in New York State's felony courts in 1981, Peterson (1988) observed geographic differences in use of the youthful offender designation. In New York City, the impact of race on type of conviction was minimal. Conversely, in jurisdictions other than New York City, the impact of race on type of conviction was substantial. In those jurisdictions, African Americans were 14.4 percent less likely than whites to be designated youthful offenders (p. 121). However, regardless of jurisdiction, black youthful offenders were more likely than white youthful offenders to be sentenced to confinement.

AFRICAN AMERICANS AND
THE CRIMINAL JUSTICE SYSTEM

Before proceeding to discuss the research in this area, it is necessary to recognize some problems associated with demonstrating discrimination in the criminal justice system. William Wilbanks (1987, pp. 40-52) provides an excellent critique of the extant literature and the reader desiring more information should refer to his book, *The Myth of a Racist Criminal Justice System*. He contends that researcher bias and problems associated with direct proof prohibit any definitive statements about racial discrimination in the legal system. Researcher bias may be reflected in the researcher's choice of topic, methodology, and interpretation of the results. The issue involving direct proof of discrimination is more complicated. For example, more severe sentences for minorities are typically interpreted as evidence of racial discrimination, yet more lenient sentences for minorities may also be indicative of discrimination. Wilbanks (1987, p. 43) offers the following illustration:

> If a judge considers murders of blacks to be less important than murders of whites, he or she may sentence the killers of blacks to lesser terms than the killers of whites. Since murders are predominantly intraracial (black on black and white on white) the more permissive attitude toward the killing of blacks would result in more lenient sentences for black killers. Thus it is not clear what would constitute racial discrimination, in that in some cases a lenient sentence might be based on racial discrimination.

Wilbanks is also critical of much research examining racial discrimination in the criminal justice system because (1) spurious relationships are frequently reported as the "cause" of the outcome, (2) the unexplained variance after controls are introduced is often assumed by the investigator(s) to be the result of race, although some unmeasured variable(s) may be responsible for some or all of this variance, (3) statistical significance is commonly confused with practical significance[6], and (4) the use of aggregate data can mask differences in the importance attached to race in decision making across jurisdictions and criminal justice personnel and at different time periods. For these reasons he concludes that the perception of the American criminal justice system as racist is an unsubstantiated assertion (i.e., a myth).

Discrepant findings in the research may also be the result of misspecified models (Miethe & Moore, 1986). Many investigators have relied on **additive models** to examine racial disparities in criminal justice processing. These models assume "that no systematic variation exists within racial groups *and* that between-race differences are constant across levels of other social, case, and legal attributes" (Miethe & Moore, 1986, p. 230 [italics in original]). An alternative, the **interactive** or **race-specific model**, allows one to examine the possibility that race interacts with other variables in determining judicial outcomes. A comparison of these two models by Miethe and Moore (1986) revealed that the additive model tended to conceal and suppress racial differences in criminal processing whereas the interactive models demonstrated that differential criminal processing existed both between and within the racial groups.

Moreover, Samuel Myers (1985) argues that regression techniques commonly employed in investigations of racial discrimination may be inadequate. He contends that use of conventional regression techniques may result in wrongly accepting the null hypothesis of no racial differences when, in fact, discrimination is present. To remedy this potential problem he suggests using residual discrimination methodology, a procedure borrowed from labor economics, to measure discrimination in punishment.

Theoretical Explanations of Racial Differences

Two of the theories most frequently used to explain racial differences in criminal processing are the conflict and labeling perspectives. As indicated in Chapter 3, **conflict theory** assumes that the powerful members of society use social institutions (such as the legal institution) to protect their own interests. Because minority crime is likely to be seen as threatening to the status quo and because minorities have little power and few financial resources, they are more likely than members of the dominant group to receive harsher treatment by social control agents.

Labeling theory also attempts to explain the differential processing of minorities. However, it focuses on societal reaction to illegal behavior. Because crimes by minorities are typically more visible than crimes by whites (particularly, white-collar crimes committed by middle- and upper-class whites), they are more likely to be officially detected and labeled as deviant. Although originally no more likely to engage in crime than nonminorities, minorities come to accept this negative label and eventually engage in secondary deviance (see Chapter 3). Thus, the agents of social control produce a self-fulfilling prophecy.

Of the two perspectives, the tenets of conflict theory are more amenable to empirical investigation. And while research is not always supportive of conflict theory, there is a growing body of literature that is supportive of at least some of the ideas contained in that theory. For instance, if the dominant racial group (especially upper-class whites) manipulates the legal system to its own advantage, then minorities accused of victimizing whites should be most likely to incur the wrath of the law. Rape is an offense that should be seen as particularly threatening to the dominant racial group if it involves an African American assailant and a white victim. An analysis of 881 sexual assault cases in a large, midwestern city disclosed that African American men charged with sexually assaulting a white woman were more likely than other defendants to be charged with a serious offense, to be given a longer sentence, and to have their case filed as a felony. They were also more likely to receive an executed sentence and to be incarcerated in the state prison. However, African American men who sexually assaulted a white woman were *no* more likely than other defendants to be arrested or to be found guilty (LaFree, 1980).

In addition, conflict theory would suggest that the racial composition of an area should be related to crime control. More specifically, as the proportion of the total population composed of a minority group increases, the political clout of that minority group should also increase. The overall result should be a less punitive legal system for members of that group. Two recent studies provide some support for this assertion. Liska and Chamlin's (1984) investigation of 76 cities revealed that the racial composition of the cities significantly affected arrest rates. As the percentage of nonwhites in a city increased, there was a decrease in the arrest rate of nonwhites. Further, this relationship remained even after controlling for police size and reported crime rates. Similarly, Bridges and Crutchfield (1988) examined racial disparities in imprisonment. After controlling for differential involvement in crime, they found that racial disparities in imprisonment were greatest in those states where African Americans represented a small proportion of the total state population and where African Americans were highly visible due to their heavy concentration in urban areas. While neither study fully substantiates the claims of conflict theorists that minorities are differentially processed by the criminal justice system as a result of their limited power and influence, these studies (and others to be cited later) suggest that the social structure is at least partly responsible for the racial disparities observed in the criminal justice system.

Presentencing Decisions

African Americans and other minorities may be disadvantaged in ways that are not readily apparent in investigations of racial disparities in the criminal justice system.

> For example, decisions to release defendants on their own recognizance or on unsecured bonds are based primarily on the strength of community ties, determined largely by steady employment and home ownership. Such indicators tend to favor middle-class whites over poorer whites and minorities. Also, financial resources become important where attempts at acquittals or dismissals require delaying case processing until the evidence stales or public interest in the case dissipates. . . . Finally, the wealthy executive who is "an upstanding pillar of the community" may be viewed as having "suffered enough" if conviction results in loss of position, wealth, or reputation, but these same losses are apparently not sufficient for the poor and minorities who fill our prisons (Zatz, 1987, p. 84).

As the above quotation suggests, differential processing of African Americans can occur *prior* to sentencing. When Farnworth and Horan (1980) examined court cases in North Carolina, they concluded that if racial differences in court processing occurred, they were more likely to appear at the stages preceding final sentencing. We therefore now turn to a discussion of some of these early stages.

Bail decisions are important for two reasons. First, if the criminal defendant is unable to post bail and is later found innocent, then the defendant has been punished without proof of guilt. Second, research suggests that, for various reasons, a defendant who is unable to make bail is more likely than one making bail to be found guilty (Patterson & Lynch, 1991). These statements indicate that African Americans may be at a disadvantage because they are more likely than whites to be of low income, but what about differentials in bail amounts based on race? Admittedly, it is difficult to separate the effects of race and social class on differential treatment in criminal processing. Nevertheless, an analysis of 335 felony arrests in Florida by Patterson and Lynch (1991) suggests that race of the offender is still important in bail amount decisions. The county studied had a bail schedule to use in determining bail amounts. In theory, this should have the effect of minimizing discrimination based on extralegal factors since rules based on offense seriousness are already established. After controlling for relevant factors (including social class), the researchers found evidence of racial disparities in bail amount decisions. Although nonwhite suspects were no more likely than their white counterparts to receive high bail, nonwhite suspects were *less* likely than white suspects to receive *low* bail. Moreover, whereas white female suspects were more likely than white male suspects to receive low bail, black female suspects were treated similarly to black males.

Prosecutorial discretion in the handling of criminal cases represents another instance where race can potentially influence outcomes. Radelet and Pierce (1985) analyzed over 1,000 homicide cases in Florida, comparing the police department's classification of the case to that of the prosecutor's. Three categories of homicide were used: (1) nonfelony homicide, (2) possible felony homicide, and (3) felony homicide. Concentrating on cases where police and prosecutorial classifications differed, the investigators found that in cases involving white victims, black defendants were more likely than white defendants to have their cases upgraded (e.g., treating a possible felony homicide as a felony homicide) and less likely to have their cases downgraded (e.g., treating a possible felony homicide as a nonfelony homicide).[7] The researchers caution against attributing these differences to conscious racial discrimination by the prosecutors, however, as bureaucratic and political variables may enter into the decision making process.

Prosecutors also have the discretion of rejecting or dismissing charges against alleged offenders. A study of alleged felons in Los Angeles revealed that black and Hispanic males were less likely than white males to have their cases rejected (either by dropping the charge entirely or by reclassifying it a misdemeanor) at the initial screening, although there was no evidence of discrimination in later decisions by prosecutors to dismiss felony charges (Spohn, Gruhl, & Welch, 1987). Thus, earlier studies reporting no discrimination at the dismissal stage may be misleading if undetected discrimination occurred at the initial screening.

Holmes, Daudistel, and Farrell (1987) investigated courts in Delaware County, Pennsylvania, and Pima County, Arizona. The influence of race on charge reductions varied by jurisdiction. While race had no significant effect on charge reductions in Arizona, black defendants in Pennsylvania were more likely than white defendants to receive a charge reduction. On the surface this would seem to imply preferential treatment of African Americans. However, the authors conclude that the charge reductions probably reflect the initial overcharging of black defendants by the police.

Sentencing Decisions

> After fifty years of research on whether or not there are racial or ethnic disparities in sentencing, there is only one generalizable finding: Sometimes judges discriminate and sometimes they don't (Unnever & Hembroff, 1988, p. 53).

The ambiguity of the research on race and sentencing is reflected in the above passage. Two frequently mentioned reviews of the literature on race and criminal sentencing are Hagan (1974) and Kleck (1981). Both authors contend that differential sentencing by race is not widespread with the strongest evidence of discriminatory sentencing being found in the South. And although interracial crimes involving black defendants are typically punished more harshly than crimes involving other racial combinations, Kleck (1981) argues that this is largely attributable to legal factors associated with the offenses. He does acknowledge that for noncapital cases there is evidence of scattered discrimination by jurisdiction, judge, type of offense, etc. More recently, Kempf and Austin (1986) reexamined some commonly cited studies of racial bias in sentencing that reported limited support for the discriminatory sentencing hypothesis. They also examined over 2,500 cases from Pennsylvania. The researchers concluded that there is more evidence of widespread racial bias in sentencing than previously recognized by Hagan (1974) and Kleck (1981).

Part of the confusion lies in the type of bias that one is attempting to identify. Zatz (1987) differentiates overt bias from subtle bias. **Overt bias** occurs when race is *directly* related to court outcomes. According to Zatz (1987) this type of bias was more common in the past and is easier to detect. Conversely, **subtle bias** exists when race, either *indirectly* or in *interaction* with other factors, affects the outcome of court decisions. Because subtle bias has become institutionalized, it is less obvious and more difficult to detect. Her review of four "waves" of research on race and sentencing suggests that subtle bias persists and typically occurs *prior* to the sentencing stage.

It may also be the case that under certain conditions African Americans receive more lenient treatment in the criminal justice system than whites. Kleck (1981) enumerates six factors that may result in black leniency in criminal processing. The first factor focuses on the devaluation of black lives by the larger society. If African Americans are devalued by white society, then intraracial crimes involving black offenders may be dealt with less harshly. A second factor considers the possible effect of white paternalism on sentencing. If whites view African Americans as more childlike and irresponsible than whites, then African Americans may not be held as accountable for their actions as whites are. Another factor, which Kleck (1981) refers to as sociology-based tolerance, looks at the effect of the environment on black behavior. Since many of the sociological factors responsible for black crime (e.g., poverty and racism) are beyond the control of African Americans, then black crime may be treated more leniently than white crime.

A fourth factor attributes the preferential treatment of black defendants to affirmative action in the courts that stems from the guilt of liberal white court officials over *past* discrimination. According to Kleck (1981), these officials compensate for their guilt by treating black defendants with less severity than white defendants. The fifth factor recognizes that *institutional racism* may make receiving an equitable sentence more problematic for African Americans. Because African Americans may have lower incomes and longer prior criminal records than their white counterparts, they may be treated more severely by the criminal justice system for similar offenses. Thus, the more lenient treatment accorded some African Americans may be the result of an attempt by court officials to "adjust" the sentence to reflect the handicaps that low income and prior records have on black defendants. Finally, the last factor is similar to the fourth, except for the absence of white guilt over past discrimination. According to this explanation, the greater leniency shown African Americans may be the result of judges trying to compensate for any unconscious prejudice that *they* might have against that minority group.

The importance attached to each of these factors may vary over time. Kleck (1981) contends that factors 1 and 2 may largely explain the less harsh treatment of African Americans found guilty of intraracial crimes in the South prior to the 1950s. In contrast, the more lenient treatment accorded African Americans since the 1960s may be the result of any combination of factors 3 through 6.

Because sentencing actually involves two decision points (a decision as to whether or not the defendant should be incarcerated and a decision as to the length of the incarceration), the remaining discussion focuses separately on the decision to incarcerate (the in/out decision) and the decision regarding sentence length. Although earlier research often lumped the two decisions together, more recent investigations have treated these decisions as discrete stages in sentencing as it is conceivable that racial factors might affect one decision without affecting the other.

The in/out decision. A plethora of studies have focused on the relationship between race and sentencing outcome. It is beyond the scope of this chapter to analyze all of these investigations. Instead, some of the more recent studies are discussed in this section. Let us first examine research that investigated the influence of race on the decision to incarcerate. Given the history of slavery in the past, the South may be more likely than other regions to be influenced by the race of the defendant in criminal cases. For this reason recent studies using southern jurisdictions are examined initially. Unless otherwise noted all studies mentioned controlled for at least some of the relevant legal factors that could result in differential sentencing.

Women arrested in Atlanta on felony charges were examined by Mann (1984). She observed no evidence of racial discrimination in the sentencing of black women. However, her sample was small (N=217) and her analysis was restricted to chi-square tests. An earlier examination of over 1,000 cases in an Atlanta court also found that race was not related to sentence severity at the *aggregate* level. But when the researcher disaggregated the data according to individual judges, he discovered that black defendants were sometimes the beneficiaries of discrimination and sometimes the victims of discrimination by individual judges (Gibson, 1978). Thus, his findings suggest aggregate level data (which are typically used) may mask important differences in sentencing.

In North Carolina, Clarke and Koch (1976) analyzed data on almost 800 burglary and larceny cases. They determined that race was not significantly related to the decision to incarcerate after controlling for the effects of other variables. Their data, however, were limited to the Charlotte area. More recently, Darnell Hawkins (1986) examined statewide data to ascertain the extent to which arrest data for one year were related to prison admissions for the subsequent year in North Carolina. The researcher found that the arrest data were least able to explain racial differentials in prison admissions for drug offenses, forgery, and driving under the influence. In other words, sentencing disparities were offense specific. Myers and Talarico (1986) also reported offense specific racial differences in sentencing. Their examination of convicted felons in Georgia revealed that African Americans convicted of robbery were more likely than their white counterparts to be sentenced to prison. However, African Americans convicted of aggravated assault and theft were *less* likely than whites convicted of the same offenses to be sentenced to prison. They speculated that the differences may be due to the fact that robbery is more likely to be interracial (i.e., an African American robbing a white) than aggravated assault and theft.

Three studies (Unnever, 1982; Unnever, Frazier, & Henretta, 1980; Unnever & Hembroff, 1988) examined offenders in Florida. An investigation in one unidentified Florida court disclosed that race had a moderately strong direct effect on sentencing outcome. Evidence also suggested that racial disparities began at earlier stages of the criminal justice process and were passed on through sentencing recommendations in the pre-sentence report (Unnever, Frazier, & Henretta, 1980). An examination of convicted male drug offenders in Miami revealed that African Americans were 2½ times more likely than whites to be incarcerated even after controlling for legally relevant variables (Unnever, 1982). The same data were used by Unnever and Hembroff (1988) to test a **status characteristics and expectation states** explanation of racial disparities in sentencing. This theory posits that racial disparities in sentencing will be least likely to occur when the characteristics of the case are consistent (i.e., all the characteristics suggest prison or probation). Conversely, racial disparities in sentencing will be most likely to be present when the characteristics of the case are inconsistent (i.e., some characteristics indicate prison while others indicate probation).[8] It is in this context that judges will turn to extralegal factors to assist in resolving the inconsistencies. The data provided general support for the theory.

Two studies (Holmes & Daudistel, 1984; Humphrey & Fogarty, 1987) compared jurisdictions in different regions of the United States. Holmes and Daudistel (1984) examined defendants convicted of burglary or robbery in El Paso, Texas, and Tucson, Arizona. Only in the South (El Paso, Texas) were African Americans more likely than whites to be incarcerated. (Although the interactive model revealed that judges in Tucson more severely punished black defendants who insisted on jury trials instead of plea bargains.) An investigation of plea bargained outcomes in five jurisdictions, two of which are in the South (Norfolk, Virginia, and New Orleans, Louisiana), found that race substantially increased the chances of incarceration in southern jurisdictions only (Humphrey & Fogarty, 1987).

In summary, studies of southern criminal courts suggest that racial disparities in criminal sentencing cannot be accounted for solely by legal factors. The extent to which these disparities manifest themselves, however, varies by jurisdiction, type of offense, and context.

Investigations of the in/out decision in nonsouthern courts also reveal evidence of racial disparities in sentencing. Once again the disparities are not uniformly distributed across all jurisdictions. For instance, an examination of defendants arrested in New York State in 1985 and 1986 disclosed that minorities (African Americans and Hispanics) were more likely than whites to be incarcerated, although the disparities in sentencing varied by county. The importance of using *disaggregated* data is demonstrated by the fact that disparities were not evident at the state level because sentencing differentials by county tended to cancel one another out when using statewide data (Nelson, 1992). An investigation of female prostitutes in New York City disclosed that for this class B misdemeanor, race was related to the probability of incarceration (Eterno, 1993). Although a limited number of variables were examined, the researcher found that black females were more likely than either white or Hispanic females to be sentenced to jail regardless of prior misdemeanors. However, as the number of prior misdemeanors increased, the strength of the association between race and incarceration diminished. Another study conducted in the northeast revealed that race was both directly and indirectly related to the decision to incarcerate male defendants charged with felonies. Overall, black defendants had a 20 percent greater chance of being incarcerated than white defendants (Spohn, Gruhl, & Welch, 1981-1982).

Two studies investigating in/out decisions in Pennsylvania at different times allow us to determine what effect determinate sentencing guidelines have had on racial disparities in that state. Kempf and Austin (1986) analyzed sentencing decisions in Pennsylvania in 1977. Since determinate sentencing guidelines did not go into effect until 1982, the data represent the predeterminate sentencing period. The researchers reported that race was directly related to decision to incarcerate in urban areas only. There was also a significant interaction between race and offense seriousness. In all areas African Americans convicted of a serious crime were more likely to be incarcerated than their white counterparts. A more recent investigation by Kramer and Steffensmeir (1993) used data on over 61,000 convicted felons in Pennsylvania between 1985 and 1987. These postdeterminate sentencing data disclosed that race continued to exert an effect on the decision to incarcerate. After controlling for relevant factors it was found that African Americans were approximately 8 percent more likely than whites to be incarcerated. Upon further examination the researchers discovered that the reason for this disparity was that whites were more likely than African Americans to receive a "departure" sentence that deviated from the sentence guidelines.[9]

Analyses of criminal defendants charged with armed robbery or burglary in Milwaukee between 1967 and 1977 were conducted by Pruitt and Wilson (1983). They detected racial disparities in incarceration decisions for the 1967-68 period, although race was not related to type of sentence during either the 1971-1972 or 1976-1977 periods. The researchers attributed the decreased importance of race in the 1970s to (1) changes in the composition of the judiciary (more liberal judges had been appointed to the bench by the 1970s), (2) the greater bureaucratization of the felony court system in Milwaukee, and (3) the development of more formal rules governing case disposition.

Another investigation in the midwest examined convicted violent felons in Detroit (Spohn & Cederblom, 1991). Controlling for 12 relevant variables, the researchers observed a significant relationship between race and decision to incarcerate only in the less serious felony cases. They also found support for an interactive model of sentencing as the additive model misspecified the relationships among the variables.

An extensive investigation of 11,553 convicted felons in California in 1980 revealed that race was not related to type of sentence once relevant variables were examined first (Klein, Petersilia, & Turner, 1990). This finding is indeed curious as an earlier analysis of 1980 data from the same state by Petersilia (1983, pp. 27-28) demonstrated that African Americans convicted of felonies were *more* likely than whites to be sentenced to prison even after relevant legal controls (e.g., prior record and probation/parole status) were introduced. However, the earlier investigation utilized data from California's Offender-Based Transaction Statistics (OBTS), while the more recent investigation relied primarily on data collected by the California Board of Prison Terms (CBPT).

Another western state was analyzed by Bridges, Crutchfield, and Simpson (1987). These investigators, using data from the state of Washington, found that nonwhites from urbanized counties with large minority populations were more likely than whites to be sentenced to prison. Moreover, this relationship remained intact even after controlling for racial differences in arrests for serious and violent crimes. Interviews with criminal justice officials suggested that fear of crime and perceived dangerousness of black offenders may be behind the differential processing of nonwhites.

As with studies of southern jurisdictions, the investigations of nonsouthern jurisdictions reveal the presence of sentencing differentials along racial lines. These findings suggest that the degree to which race appears to be a factor in decisions to incarcerate varies according to characteristics of the county (e.g., racial composition and degree of urbanization) and the offense (e.g., type and seriousness of offense). It also appears that the influence of race in in/out decisions can change over time. Moreover, evidence from Pennsylvania indicates that even with determinate sentencing guidelines some racial differentials persist.

Sentence length. Because similar results were obtained using southern and nonsouthern jurisdictions, this section does not organize research according to geographic areas. Instead, we are first going to examine investigations reporting racial differences and then examine investigations reporting no racial differences. The section will conclude with a brief summary of the discrepant findings.

One of the most frequently cited studies reporting racial disparities in sentencing is Petersilia's (1983) research on prison inmates from California, Texas, and Michigan. Based on the Rand Inmate Survey (RIS), her study found that after controlling for defendant's age, conviction crime, and prior record, African Americans received longer court-imposed sentences in all three states (although the 7.2-month black-white differential in Michigan was the only case where the difference was statistically significant).

While Petersilia's research analyzed prisoners in state prisons in 1978, Myers' (1985) research focused on over 2,000 prisoners released from federal prisons in 1972. Using a residual discrimination procedure, he determined that African Americans served almost 6 more months in prison than comparable whites. Further, this discrepancy could not be rationalized empirically on the grounds that African Americans were more likely than whites to engage in crime or to become recidivists.

Thomson and Zingraff (1981) examined data from a single state in the southeast. Limiting their analysis to males sentenced for armed robbery in 1969, 1973, and 1977, they found that race had a significant direct effect on sentence length in 1977 only. The researchers interpret this finding as a reflection of "get tough" policies in criminal justice and the fact that armed robbery is becoming less intraracial today.

Analyzing data from Chicago criminal courts, Alan Lizotte (1978) concluded that, other things being equal, laborers and nonwhites were given longer prison sentences than the higher social class groups. Nevertheless, race was not directly related to sentence severity. Most of the disparity was the result of the indirect influence of race and social class on inability to make bail and the legal counsel's degree of success in sentencing.

An investigation of males committed to Kentucky prisons in 1980 disclosed that African Americans received longer prison sentences than whites (Crew, 1991). The researcher also noted that African Americans were charged with more serious crimes than whites engaging in similar crimes. However, the results of this study must be viewed as more suggestive than definitive as the small sample (N=228) precludes generalization to other prison populations.

Historically, prison staff have been white. At the time of the Attica prison riot in 1971, only 2 of the more than 500 employees were minorities, yet 63.5 percent of the prison population was African American (Carroll, 1990, p. 512). Moreover, white prison guards have typically had limited exposure to African Americans (Carroll, 1974) and commonly exhibit tendencies toward racial prejudice and discrimination (Carroll, 1974; Mann, 1993; Marquart, 1986). White guards frequently view African American inmates as more threatening and dangerous than their white counterparts (Carroll, 1990; Flowers, 1990; Mann, 1993). This results in closer surveillance of African American inmates (Carroll, 1990; Flowers, 1990; Mann, 1993). Poole and Regoli (1980, p. 933) explain how these circumstances can culminate in differential treatment of inmates.

> First, perceptions of inmate behavior based on racial stereotypes may foster a more oppressive disciplinary posture among guards in their response to blacks. The greater visibility of black inmates may also evoke greater attention to and concern for their actions; i.e., their behavior may be viewed more suspiciously. The black inmate is then more likely to be scrutinized and therefore to be observed in any rule violations, which will in turn reinforce the prior stereotypic expectations. Similarly, if black inmates perceive that they are being differentially treated (e.g., subject to stricter rule enforcement), they may react more defiantly or with greater hostility toward guards. This too simply supports the expectations of the guards as well as their pattern of closer surveillance and control of these types of inmates. To the extent that guards either implicitly or explicitly incorporate such racial stereotypes into their decision making, black inmates face a greater probability of being dealt with less favorably.

The differential treatment of inmates based on racial membership may also be a reflection of the use of "building tenders" or inmate guards. Before the dismantling of the building tender system in Texas, handpicked inmates were selected by prison guards to serve as inmate

Data on male prisoners (N = 412) from Maryland revealed that race was significantly related to sentence length. Even after controlling for relevant variables, African Americans received longer sentences than whites (Jendrek, 1984). However, African Americans did *not* receive longer sentences than whites under all conditions. The interactive model used by the researcher disclosed that, compared to African Americans, whites received longer prison sentences when they were charged with more serious offenses and when they used more court resources.

Contradictory results were obtained by Kempf and Austin (1986). Using 2,578 cases from Pennsylvania, these researchers noted that race had no direct effect on sentence length, although African Americans convicted of a serious crime were more likely than their white counterparts to be given a longer sentence. This interaction between race and offense seriousness was strongest in suburban areas. As with many other studies, their results demonstrate the necessity of utilizing an interactive model to ferret out possible obscured relationships.

Not all researchers report significant relationships between race and sentence length. Unlike the in/out decisions, the literature on race and sentence length is more inconclusive. Investigations in New York City (Eterno, 1993), Pennsylvania (Kramer & Steffensmeir, 1993), and California (Klein, Petersilia, & Turner, 1990) detected no substantive relationship between race and sentence length once relevant factors were controlled. It should be recalled that two of these studies (Eterno, 1993; Kramer & Steffensmeir, 1993) had observed a relationship between race and the in/out decision (see earlier section). In addition, a large scale examination of convicted felons in Georgia by Myers and Talarico (1986) found that after offender and county characteristics were controlled, African Americans actually received *shorter* sentences than comparable whites.

Spohn, Gruhl, and Welch (1981-1982), examining 2,366 African American and white defendants charged with felonies in a large city in the northeast, concluded that race did not have a direct effect on sentence length. Race did, nevertheless, exhibit an indirect effect on sentence length. For example, African Americans were less likely than whites to be represented by a private attorney and having a private attorney increased one's chances of pretrial release which, in turn, was related to the length of the sentence. Overall, however, African Americans sentenced to prison received *shorter* sentences than similarly situated whites, a finding that corroborates the Georgia study by Myers and Talarico (1986).

An examination of 1,512 criminal defendants in Milwaukee over three time periods illustrates the importance of time (Pruitt & Wilson, 1983). When the data were disaggregated by year, it was found that black defendants were more likely than white defendants to be given longer sentences during the earliest time period only. As indicated in the in/out decision section, the investigators attributed this to changes in the judicial system.

So what can we conclude about the importance of race in decisions on sentence length? First, there is considerably *less* support for racial bias in decisions on sentence length than in decisions to incarcerate. This conclusion is buttressed by the findings of Eterno (1993) and Kramer and Steffensmeir (1993) who, after reporting a relationship between race and type of sentence, found no evidence supporting a similar relationship between race and sentence length. Second, where racial disparities cannot be explained by legal factors, it appears that race is more likely to influence sentence length indirectly and/or through interaction with other variables. And finally, the failure to find evidence of racial discrimination at this stage of the criminal justice system does *not* preclude the possibility that discriminatory factors were operative earlier in the processing. Because the population of criminal defendants becomes increasingly homogeneous as it proceeds through the stages of processing, one would expect (unless overt bias is present) that racial differences should become less apparent.

AFRICAN AMERICANS AND CAPITAL PUNISHMENT

As of 1991, 36 states had statutory provisions for sentences of death (Flanagan & Maguire, 1992, pp. 146-147).[10] Although a majority of the states allow defendants to be tried for capital crimes, the death penalty is infrequently imposed. A survey of state prison inmates in 1991 revealed that only .5 percent of the white inmates and .3 percent of the black inmates were sentenced to die (U.S. Department of Justice, 1993, p. 6). These figures belie the significance of death penalty statutes, however, as historically these statutes have been differentially applied to black and white offenders. For example, in the

1830s Virginia had only 5 capital crimes for whites compared to 70 capital crimes for black slaves. Then in 1848 Virginia mandated the death sentence for any black committing a crime that would result in at least three years imprisonment for a white (Radelet, 1989). Moreover, it should be recalled that during the antebellum period the southern slave codes typically did not permit a black to testify against a white in a court of law, making it virtually impossible to prosecute a white who committed a crime against a black. Laws such as these tended to inflate the number of African Americans eligible for the death penalty while limiting the number of whites who could be accused of crimes punishable by death.

Historically, the law has not accorded black victims the same protection as white victims. Examining almost 16,000 executions in the United States dating back to the eighteenth century, Radelet (1989) found only 30 cases where a white was executed for a crime against an African American. An analysis of those 30 executions disclosed that, in those rare instances where whites were executed for crimes against African Americans, the cases typically involved economic crimes (e.g., the murder of a slave was an economic crime in the sense that the slave was the "property" of a white slave owner) or white defendants who were disliked, poor, or seen as threatening those in power. In only 4 cases were whites executed for crimes against African Americans primarily because their actions offended the moral sentiments of white society.

The death penalty was temporarily suspended in 1972. In *Furman v. Georgia* the United States Supreme Court invalidated death penalty statutes using the argument that the Eighth Amendment was being violated because the statutes were too arbitrary. However, the decision did *not* declare the death penalty unconstitutional; it merely asserted that the sentencing procedure under capital statutes was unsatisfactory (Inciardi, 1990, pp. 498-499).

In *Gregg v. Georgia* in 1976, the Supreme Court upheld as constitutional Georgia's new capital statute thereby reinstating the death penalty in America. By a 7-to-2 majority the Court ruled that (1) punishment by death was not cruel and unusual punishment and (2) a bifurcated trial (i.e., separate proceedings for determining innocence or guilt and, if guilty, the type of punishment) in first-degree murder cases met the objections raised in *Furman v. Georgia* (Inciardi, 1990, pp. 499-500).

The Supreme Court placed additional restrictions on the death penalty in 1977 when it ruled in *Coker v. Georgia* that imposing a death sentence in a nonlethal adult rape case was a violation of the Eighth Amendment (Bohm, 1991). Removing rape from capital statutes eliminated a major source of racial disparity in death sentences. Between 1930 and the early 1970s, 89.5 percent of the persons executed for rape had been nonwhite (Wolfgang & Riedel, 1973).

Nevertheless, the conservative orientation of the Supreme Court was evident in *McCleskey v. Kemp* (1987). Despite a wealth of data indicating racial bias in sentencing (in particular, that African Americans accused of murdering a white are considerably more likely to receive a death sentence than whites accused of murdering an African American), the Court ruled that the death penalty was not unconstitutional (Siegel, 1992, pp. 461, 543).

That racial disparities in death sentences exist is not proof of racial bias, however. Only if it can be demonstrated that African Americans and whites committing similar capital crimes under similar circumstances receive dissimilar sentences can it be said that racial bias is evident. To examine this possibility, a sample of empirical studies are examined. The investigations are dichotomized according to whether the data are from the pre-*Furman* or post-*Furman* time periods.

Pre-Furman *Studies of the Death Penalty*

Research on race and the death penalty conducted during the pre-*Furman* period tends to suffer from methodological problems that restrict its utility. One weakness of much of this research is the absence of control groups. Another weakness stems from its use of unsophisticated statistical techniques. Although many of today's more robust statistical techniques were unavailable then, the use of cross-tabular analysis and bivariate statistical techniques such as chi-square precludes the investigation of conditional relationships. A third methodological problem is that researchers relied on limited data. All of the research was conducted in a total of 15 states. Moreover, few studies before 1972 controlled for other variables that could have affected the outcome (Ralph, Sorensen, & Marquart, 1992).

One of the more frequently cited investigations of the pre-*Furman* period was conducted by Wolfgang and Riedel (1973). They gathered data on persons convicted of rape in southern states where rape constituted a capital crime. Spanning a 20-year period beginning with

1945, the data included information on offender and victim characteristics, the victim-offender relationship, and circumstances of the offense and trial. Their results indicated that (1) African Americans were almost 7 times more likely than whites to be sentenced to die and (2) black offenders whose victims were white were 18 times more likely than other offender-victim combinations to be sentenced to die. Nonetheless, the inability of their statistical analyses to detect possible interaction effects places severe limitations on their findings.

A more recent examination by Ralph, Sorensen, and Marquart (1992) benefits from the more robust statistical procedures utilized today. These researchers analyzed death-sentenced and prison-sentenced male murderers in Texas between 1942 and 1971. Including legal and extralegal variables, the study employed a multivariate analysis to determine the relative importance of race in sentencing. The researchers concluded that both legal and extralegal factors influenced sentencing. The best predictor of the death sentence was type of homicide. Holding other variables constant, murders committed during a felony had a 29.4 percent greater chance of receiving the death sentence than nonfelony murders. Nevertheless, the *victim's* race emerged as the strongest extralegal determinant of the death sentence. Other things being equal, defendants who murdered whites had a 25.2 percent greater chance of receiving the death sentence than killers of nonwhites. The defendant's race, however, was not of primary importance in determining type of sentence. Further, an interaction was observed between the race of the offender and victim. After controlling for other factors the researchers found that nonwhite killers of whites were slightly more likely than white killers of whites to be sentenced to die.

Because this chapter is concerned with what effect(s) the *Furman* decision has had on capital sentencing, the greater volume of discussion focuses on post-*Furman* studies. Let us now turn to an analysis of those investigations.

Post-Furman *Studies of the Death Penalty*

At first glance it would appear that the *Gregg* decision reinstating the death penalty under the new "guided discretion" statutes had the desired effect of reducing racial disparity in capital cases. Between January 17, 1977 and September 21, 1990, 56 percent of the persons executed were white while 39 percent were African American (Bohm,

1991, p. 75). This figure is considerably lower for African Americans and higher for whites than had been the case historically. When we focus on the South, where 88 percent of the executions in the U.S. since *Furman* have occurred, it also appears that racial disparities in executions have improved. But, as Bohm (1991) suggests, the improved black-white execution ratios may be an illusion, not a reality. The initial flood of white executions in the South after *Furman* has receded and black executions are once again on the rise. When we divide the 123 post-*Furman* executions in the South into half, some intriguing findings emerge. During the first 61 executions, 57 percent involved whites and 43 percent involved African Americans and Hispanics. But during the last 62 executions, only 45 percent involved white offenders while 55 percent involved African American and Hispanic offenders (p. 76).

Georgia is a southern state that has been extensively researched (e.g., Baldus, Pulaski, & Woodworth, 1983; Baldus, Woodworth, & Pulaski, 1985; Barnett, 1985; Heilbrun, Foster & Golden, 1989). Baldus et al. (1983), after examining data from Georgia for the years 1973 to 1979, concluded that race of the victim remained an important determinant of the death penalty. They found that cases involving black homicide victims were considerably less likely to result in the death penalty than cases involving white homicide victims. A more recent examination by Baldus et al. (1985) revealed that racial disparities in the death penalty were concentrated in cases that were neither the most nor the least serious. Arnold Barnett (1985) also detected some racial disparities in the administering of the death sentence in homicides that were moderately serious. However, he further found that white victims were disproportionately likely to be involved in the more serious homicides which could account for the typically harsher punishment accorded crimes with white victims.

The Heilbrun et al. (1989) study warrants a more intensive discussion not because of its findings but because of the way in which the researchers confirmed their hypotheses. Let us begin by stating their findings. First, as many researchers before them have noted, African American men in Georgia tended to receive the death penalty when their victim was white but life imprisonment when their victim was another African American. However, using an index of dangerousness composed of scores from an antisociality measure and an intelligence test (the researchers argue that studies have disclosed a relationship between low IQ and antisociality and violent behavior), the investigators concluded that racial bias was *not* evident in cases in Georgia involving the death penalty because, regardless of race, the more dangerous criminals received death sentences and the less dangerous criminals received life sentences. The problem with their methodology is that many of the criteria used to measure dangerousness may have been influenced by racial discrimination at earlier stages of the criminal justice system. For example, one of the nine measures of an antisocial personality is problems with the police (e.g., multiple arrests). But since African Americans are more likely to be arrested than whites, this criterion could be an artifact of selective arrest patterns by the police. Thus, black offenders may only *appear* to be more antisocial than their white counterparts. Moreover, other measures of an antisocial personality (e.g., school problems, poor work history, marital difficulties, etc.) could be the result of a history of racial discrimination. In other words, these researchers may unwittingly be "blaming the victim."

Several investigations of capital punishment conducted in Kentucky reveal a pattern of racial bias in sentencing (Keil & Vito, 1989, 1990; Vito & Keil, 1988). Using data from 1976 to 1986, these researchers found that, after controlling for seriousness of the homicide, prosecutors in Kentucky were more likely to classify a homicide a capital crime if it involved an African American assailant and a white victim than other assailant-victim combinations. Additionally, Keil and Vito (1989, 1990) concluded that, regardless of offense seriousness, African Americans who murder a white are more likely than other offender-victim combinations to be sentenced to die.

Evidence from South Carolina also suggests racial bias in sentencing (Paternoster, 1983, 1984). Analyses of data from 1977 to 1981 disclosed that race of the victim was significantly related to the prosecutor's decision to seek the death penalty in death-eligible cases. Cases involving a white victim were more likely than cases involving a black victim to be subjected to the death penalty even after controlling for a number of relevant factors. Moreover, Paternoster (1984) observed that the effect of victim's race on the prosecutorial decision to request the death penalty was dependent on the number of statutory aggravating felonies accompanying the homicide. As the number of statutory aggravating felonies increased, the treatment of blacks and whites became increasingly similar. The investigator interprets this finding as evidence of the devaluation of black lives.

> The value or sanctity of white lives may be seen by white-dominated communities or by prosecutors (who in South Carolina are all white) to be higher than the value of black lives . . . . If a community or its prosecutors are more offended (or threatened) when whites are killed than when blacks are, the murder of a black will have to be accompanied by more seriously aggravating circumstances before a death sentence is demanded (Paternoster, 1984, p. 473).

In Florida, Radelet (1981) examined 637 homicide cases. Race of the victim was significantly related to imposition of the death penalty. Defendants accused of murdering a white were more likely to receive a death sentence than defendants accused of murdering an African American, due to the higher probability that persons accused of murdering a white will be indicted for first-degree murder. After controlling for race of the victim, race of the offender was not significantly related to the type of sentence. Bowers and Pierce (1980) also analyzed data from Florida and found that in offenses involving a black offender and a white victim, prosecutors were likely to "upgrade" the cases. One hundred percent of the black offender-white victim cases reported by the police as *suspected* felony homicides became felony homicide cases, whereas almost 69 percent of the black offender-white victim cases reported by the police as *nonfelony* homicides became felony homicides.

Texas provides us a chance to see what effect the changes in capital statutes resulting from the *Furman* decision had on another southern state. After the *Furman* decision, Texas revised its guidelines making them more restrictive in capital punishment cases than the post-*Furman* statutes of such states as Georgia, South Carolina, and Florida. These states permit more discretion in capital cases than does Texas. Consequently, one would expect race to be *less* important in capital cases in Texas than in states with greater discretion. Sheldon Ekland-Olson (1988), analyzing death-eligible homicide cases in Texas from 1974 to 1983, observed that the death sentence was more likely in cases involving a white victim than in cases involving either an African American or Hispanic victim. Moreover, this finding was consistent throughout the three types of capital offenses examined.[11]   In comparison to statewide homicide rates, African American and Hispanic offenders were *under*represented on death row while white offenders were *over*represented.   The researcher attributes the underrepresentation of minorities and overrepresentation of whites to the intraracial quality of many homicides.

The death penalty in Louisiana has also been studied (Smith, 1987). An examination of 504 homicide cases between 1977 and 1982 revealed that, although race of the offender was not significantly related to the likelihood of receiving a death sentence, race of the victim was. Cases involving a white victim were almost twice as likely as those involving a black victim to receive death sentences. Nevertheless, the inability of the seven-variable model to explain much of the variance in death sentences (only 7 percent of the variance was explained) led the researcher to conclude that the decision making process in capital cases in Louisiana is characterized by much capriciousness.

Keil and Vito (1992), rather than concentrating on death sentences, examined actual executions of African Americans and whites in the South from 1900 to 1987. Their data suggested that the new statutes reduced the disparity in black-white executions in the South. In fact, after *Gregg* more whites than blacks were executed. However, the race of the victim remained important in capital sentencing. Despite the changes in state statutes, the death sentence was still more likely to be given to killers of whites than blacks (especially in cases where a black offender killed a white victim).

What can we conclude from the various empirical studies of race and capital punishment? First, it can be stated that historically African Americans have been disproportionately represented among those receiving death sentences. A second conclusion is that the *Furman* and *Gregg* decisions did not completely eliminate racial disparities in capital sentencing. The research suggests that white victims are valued more highly by the criminal justice system and black offenders who victimize a white are more likely than other offender-victim combinations to receive death sentences. Nonetheless, it does appear that the *Furman* and *Gregg* decisions (along with the *Coker* decision which made rape a noncapital offense) did substantially alter the importance of race of the offender in death-eligible cases. And finally, it must also be recognized that legally relevant variables have played a role in determining who receives the death penalty.

CONCLUSION

This chapter analyzed various components of the criminal justice system in relation to their contributions to racial disparities. Statistics suggest that the police are more likely to arrest black juveniles than white juveniles, although it is unclear how much of this differential can be attributed to differences in black-white offending patterns. Adult African Americans also have disproportionately high arrest rates. Undoubtedly *some* of the difference in black-white arrest rates is the result of the greater visible presence of African Americans in criminal activities. However, anecdotal evidence suggests that the police are often more suspicious of blacks than whites and that at least part of the difference in arrest rates stems from selective law enforcement.

An illustration of selective law enforcement can be found in Homestead, Pennsylvania, a town of approximately 5,000 residents ("Black Males Line Up," 1987). The police had been looking for a black man who had been raping elderly women over a 4-year period. (Because the attacker would throw a sheet over the victim's head, none of the victims had been able to determine what the rapist looked like.) The Police Chief asked the black community to assist in locating the attacker by having black men voluntarily submit to fingerprinting. At the time of the arrest, about 100 black men had been fingerprinted. The alleged assailant was finally arrested when he attempted to sell a gun owned by one of the victims (voluntary fingerprinting had not been responsible for his arrest). This example raises an important issue: Would the police have asked all *white* men in their community to voluntarily submit to mass fingerprinting if the attacker had been identified as a white male? This author thinks that it is extremely doubtful that the police would have resorted to such harsh measures if the attacker had been white.

An examination of the juvenile court revealed that nonwhite referrals have increased sharply in recent years at the same time that white referrals have increased rather modestly. Although the Juvenile Justice and Delinquency Prevention Act of 1974 reduced the use of formal hearings for blacks, African Americans still have a greater chance than whites of being formally processed. Moreover, evidence suggests that in some jurisdictions, black juveniles are more likely than comparable white juveniles to be waived to criminal court. That there is support for the notion that race has an important effect on outcome decisions in the juvenile court is further demonstrated by a review of the literature, cited by Pope and Ross (1992), which found approximately two-thirds of the research disclosed evidence of direct or indirect race effects.

At the criminal court level, some studies have indicated that racial differences in court processing are more likely to occur at the earlier stages than at final sentencing. For instance, bail amount decisions may be influenced by the race of the defendant. Additionally, prosecutors may be less likely to reject or dismiss charges against African Americans than against whites.

Sentencing outcomes may also be differentially affected by race. Racial disparities in the in/out decision show considerable variation by jurisdiction, type of offense, and context. There is, however, noticeably less support for the contention that racial bias exists in decisions on sentence length. Studies of capital sentencing consistently report that race of the victim is more important than race of the offender. Crimes involving a white victim (particularly those with a black offender) are more likely to be prosecuted as a capital crime than crimes involving a black victim.

NOTES

1. For some personal accounts of why many African Americans are less satisfied with the service provided by the police, see Jerry Watts (1983) and Don Wycliff (1988).

2. These investigators contend that black complainants are more likely than white complainants to request the police to arrest the suspect.

3. For example, Fyfe (1981) points out that minorities tend to be assigned to areas that are characterized by high concentrations of minorities and high levels of violent crime, thus increasing the likelihood that they will be called upon to use their firearms. This situation is exacerbated by the fact that, unlike white officers, many minority officers live in these same areas and may encounter violent situations during their off-duty hours.

4. In Los Angeles, for instance, 50 percent of the suspects fatally shot by the police between 1974 and 1978 were African American (Meyer, 1980, p. 102). Nationally, between 1976 and 1988, 45.6 percent of all felons killed by the police were black (Sorensen, Marquart, & Brock, 1993, p. 428).

5. The authors do not necessarily attribute racial bias to their findings. They note that the same actors were involved in earlier decisions and since legal factors were more important initially, there is little reason to assume that extralegal factors would become more important later. Moreover, they contend that it is conceivable that some unmeasured legal factors were influencing the outcomes.

6. Wilbanks (1987, p. 47) notes that statistical significance, or the likelihood that the results occurred by chance alone, is a function of sample size and strength of the correlation between the variables. If a study contains a large number of cases, then even a weak relationship may be statistically significant.

7. Upgrading and downgrading, as used by Radelet and Pierce (1985), do not refer to changes in formal charges. Instead, these terms are used to refer to situations where the prosecuting attorney "presents the case to the court as if it were more or less serious with respect to accompanying felonies than the police originally perceived it to be" (p. 599).

8. An "inconsistent" case is perhaps best illustrated by an examination of the components of a "consistent" case. Consider two scenarios in which a judge has knowledge of the following factors: the defendant's prior criminal record, seriousness of the most recent offense, the defendant's employment status, the defendant's occupation, and the defendant's race. A consistent case pointing to the probable use of probation would include a defendant with no prior criminal record who has been charged with a nonviolent offense. Further, the best candidate for probation would be currently employed in a professional or semiprofessional occupation. In contrast, a consistent case suggesting the need for incarceration would be a defendant with a lengthy prior criminal record who has been repeatedly charged with violent offenses and who is currently unemployed. According to the status characteristics and expectation states thesis, to the extent that each scenario contains some elements of the other, the case is inconsistent, and judges are free to use extralegal factors such as race to resolve the inconsistency.

9. Although the sentencing guidelines are based on legally relevant criteria, departures from these presumptive sentences are permitted if the judge provides written statements justifying the departure. The sentencing departures examined in this study (which were limited to the in/out decision) more typically favored white defendants.

10. The following states did not have statutory provisions for sentences of death: Alaska, Hawaii, Iowa, Kansas, Maine, Massachusetts, Michigan, Minnesota, New York, North Dakota, Rhode Island, Vermont, West Virginia, and Wisconsin (Flanagan & Maguire, 1992, pp. 146-147).

11. The three types of capital offenses examined were robbery homicide, burglary homicide, and aggravated sexual assault homicide.

CHAPTER 5
INCARCERATED
AFRICAN AMERICANS

At the outset the reader should recall that racial disparity does *not* necessarily indicate the presence of racial discrimination. According to Petersilia and Turner (1988, p. 92):

> Racial *discrimination* occurs if system officials make ad hoc decisions based on race rather than clearly defined standards. Racial *disparity* occurs when legitimate standards are applied but have different results for different racial groups (italics in original).

That racial disparity exists in the prison population cannot be refuted. Moreover, there has been an increase in the disparity as evinced in Table 5.1. As the table clearly shows, the difference between the proportion of prison admissions that are black and the proportion of the U.S. adult population that is black has steadily increased between 1926 and 1982.

More recent data suggest that the disparity has remained relatively constant over the past several years (U.S. Department of Justice, 1993, p. 3). In 1986, for example, African Americans comprised 45 percent of the state prison population. Five years later, 46 percent of the state prison population was African American. Since 12.1 percent of the U.S. population is African American (U.S. Bureau of the Census, 1992, p. 17), this represents a disparity of 33.9 percent in 1991, a figure comparable to that of 1982 using prison admissions.

When the racial distribution of prisoners is broken down geographically, some interesting results emerge. After disaggregating the racial distribution of prisoners by state, William Sabol (1989) observed that, for the period 1850 to 1980, relative to their numbers in the general population, African Americans were *more*

Table 5.1
Disparity Between Blacks as a Percentage of Prison Admissions
and Blacks as a Percentage of the U.S. Adult Population
for Selected Years, 1926 to 1982

Year	Disparity*
1926	+ 13.9%
1930	+ 15.1%
1935	+ 18.4%
1940	+ 20.5%
1945	+ 24.0%
1950	+ 21.3%
1960	+ 24.9%
1964	+ 26.3%
1977	+ 29.5%
1980	+ 31.9%
1982	+ 34.7%

* Calculated as the percent of prison admissions represented by blacks minus the percent of U.S. adult population that is black for each year. Therefore, a positive figure reflects an excess of blacks in prison.

Source: Langan, P. A. (1985). Racism on trial: New evidence to explain the racial composition of prisons in the United States. *Journal of Criminal Law & Criminology, 76*, adapted from Table 1.

disproportionately imprisoned in the North than in the South. More recently, however, the trends have started to converge.

Scott Christianson (1981) notes a relationship between the recent racial disparity in imprisonment and the rapid expansion of prisons in the United States commencing in the early 1970s. He points out that black-white differences in incarceration rates substantially increased during the 1970s. In 1973, for instance, the African American incarceration rate for state prisons was 368.0 per 100,000 black civilian population, compared to a white rate of 46.3 per 100,000 white civilian population (a difference of 321.7). By 1979, the incarceration rates for both groups had increased: 544.1 per 100,000 black civilian population for African Americans and 65.1 per 100,000 white civilian population for whites. Thus, by 1979 the racial disparity had grown to 479.0 per 100,000 civilians, an increase of 157.3 per 100,000 civilians in just six years (p. 366). Moreover, 47 of 51 jurisdictions (Washington, D.C. was counted as a jurisdiction) reported increases in the disparity between black and white incarceration rates (pp. 366-367).

The costs associated with monitoring large numbers of people including minorities under the control of the criminal justice system is rather substantial. It is estimated that $2.5 billion is spent annually to house and supervise African American men who fall under the jurisdiction of the criminal justice system (Mauer, 1990, p. 3).[1]

EXPLANATIONS OF RACIAL DISPARITY IN PRISON

Unquestionably the most frequently cited study of racial disproportionality in prison was conducted by Alfred Blumstein (1982). Using aggregate arrest data from the 1970s, he concluded that 80 percent of the black overrepresentation in state prisons was attributable to their greater involvement in crime as indicated by arrests. Although one can question the wisdom of using police arrests as an indicator of illegal behavior (see Chapter 1), the investigation suggests that much of the overrepresentation of African Americans in state prisons can be explained by a legal variable (arrests).

While Blumstein (1982) used aggregate arrest data, Hawkins and Hardy (1989) examined state-level arrest data for 1979 and imprisonment data for 1980 for the 39 states in the continental U.S. with at least 1 percent African American population. Their analysis revealed that the extent to which arrests of African Americans for serious crimes explain the black-white imprisonment rate differences varies considerably by state. Four states (New Mexico, New Jersey, Arizona, and Washington) had less than one-third of the variance explained by black arrests. On the other hand, 6 states (Oklahoma, North Carolina, Tennessee, Mississippi, Indiana, and Missouri) had over 80 percent of the variance in black-white imprisonment rates accounted for by arrest data. Overall, this study suggests that the 80 percent explained variance in imprisonment rates noted by Blumstein (1982) may actually *overstate* the extent to which arrests account for

racial disparities in prison. Further, these findings allude to the need
to disaggregate data prior to analysis.

Unlike the two previous investigations which relied on police
arrests as a measure of criminality, Langan (1985) used victimization
data to estimate African American involvement in crime. Examining
data for 1973, 1979, and 1982, the researcher observed that black
involvement in crime accounted for all of the black admissions to state
prisons in 1973,[2] 84 percent of the black admissions to state prisons
in 1979, and 85 percent of the black admissions to state prisons in
1982. He concluded, as did Blumstein (1982), that black
overrepresentation in state prisons is primarily due to their
disproportionate involvement in crime.

Critical of aggregate measures of criminality, such as that used by
Blumstein (1982) and Langan (1985), Sabol (1989) disaggregated arrest
data for 1960, 1970, and 1980 by state and region. His analysis
disclosed that aggregate data tended to conceal meaningful variations
in arrest and incarceration data.

> . . . the aggregate data hide the fact that while
> overall there is an *appearance* of improvement, as the
> increase from 66 to 72 percent in the proportion of
> the variation in the racial disproportionality of prisons
> explained by the racial distribution of arrests, for the
> U.S. between 1970 and 1980, in actuality each
> region's experience was the opposite, that is, in each
> region we were able to explain *less* of the
> disproportionality (p. 426, italics mine).

AFRICAN AMERICANS IN
JUVENILE CORRECTIONAL FACILITIES

From the start juvenile reformatories treated black and white
juveniles differently. Alexander Pisciotta (1983), examining racial
discrimination in reformatories between 1825 and 1900, found that
some reformatories excluded African Americans altogether. The effect
of this exclusion was that black children continued to be housed in adult
jails. In those juvenile institutions that did house African Americans,
black children were treated differently from white children. For

instance, reformatory managers in the South frequently admitted black children because of their utility as laborers.   Though economic exploitation of African Americans was less evident in the North, reformatory managers shared the southern view of black children as inferior to white children.   This attitude was reflected in the de-emphasis on education for black children.   Moreover, compared to white children, black children received less desirable apprenticeships.[3]

Nineteenth-century penologists justified the differential treatment of African Americans and whites on theoretical grounds (Pisciotta, 1983).   It was thought that biological factors were relatively unimportant as causes of deviance in whites.   If a white child was engaging in deviant behavior, it was largely attributed to environmental causes.   In contrast, black inferiority was viewed as a primary determinant of deviance in African Americans.   Consequently, reform efforts were seen as being wasted on black children since they had limited reform potential.

As indicated in Chapter 1, African American juveniles tend to be overrepresented in juvenile correctional facilities today.   The U.S. Department of Justice (1990, p. 81) reports that 41.4 percent of the juveniles in long-term state youth correctional facilities in 1987 were African American.   How do black youths respond to this institutionalization?   According to Bartollas and Sieverdes (1981), African American juveniles find confinement to be *less* disturbing than their white counterparts.   Their investigation of six juvenile correctional institutions in a southeastern state revealed that white juveniles were more likely than black juveniles to be victimized by other residents of the institution.   In particular, white female juveniles were more likely than white male juveniles to experience high levels of victimization. Bartollas and Sieverdes (1981, p. 541) explain white victimization in cultural terms.

> As part of the southern culture, whites are used to a position of greater superiority in the free society relative to minority groups than are youths elsewhere in the United States.   To become part of a juvenile correctional system, in which half the residential staff members are black and six of every ten residents are black, is not an easy task for them.   The dominance and exploitation by black youths make incarceration

an even more disturbing experience for white youths
than might be the case in a situation with less racial
conflict.

The dominance of African American youths in juvenile correctional
facilities is not due simply to race. Sieverdes and Bartollas (1982)
assign the dominance of African American youth to differences between
African Americans and whites in previous institutional experience,
impression management skills, age, and physical size. The findings
that both male and female African Americans are aggressive and tend
to dominate life within the institution are echoed in French's (1983)
review of the literature on incarcerated black females. The literature
revealed that delinquent black females who are incarcerated are more
likely than their white counterparts to be accorded high social status,
engage in pseudo-masculine roles, and be influential within the
correctional facility.

MISCONDUCT IN PRISON
AND DISCIPLINARY REPORTS

Most of the literature examining incarcerated African Americans
has focused on adult males in prison. Many of these investigations
have analyzed decision making by correctional personnel. An
important decision which can potentially influence parole outcome is
whether or not observed rule infractions will be formally documented.[4]
Because prison guards have considerable latitude in this area, an
understanding of the relationship between race and disciplinary reports
is essential.

A review of the literature on race and disciplinary reports revealed
mixed results (Goetting, 1985). The researcher found 7 studies
reporting no significant differences between African Americans and
whites in number of disciplinary writeups, 9 studies reporting that
African Americans received more disciplinary writeups than whites,
and 1 study reporting that whites received more disciplinary writeups
than African Americans. Nevertheless, an interesting pattern emerges
if one analyzes only the most recent studies (i.e., those published in the
1980s). A breakdown of these 9 studies reveals that only 2
investigations noted no significant racial differences in number of

disciplinary writeups, while 6 investigations observed that African Americans were more likely than whites to be officially reported for misconduct. Additionally, one study detected a higher rate of disciplinary writeups for whites. Overall then, two-thirds of the studies from the 1980s disclose racial differences unfavorable to African Americans.

Racial disparity in number of disciplinary reports does not, however, constitute racial discrimination unless it can also be shown that African American and white inmates engage in similar misconduct. An examination of a medium security prison in the South revealed that black inmates were more likely than white inmates to be cited for disciplinary infractions, even though black and white inmates were equally likely to report violations of prison rules (Poole & Regoli, 1980). Further evidence of racial bias was found when the researchers analyzed separate models of disciplinary writeups. For white inmates the only variable directly related to disciplinary reports was their self-reported rule infractions, thus suggesting that the inmate's own misconduct was the main determinant of disciplinary writeups. In contrast, *prior* disciplinary record (which itself is influenced by the race of the inmate) was the main direct determinant of disciplinary reports for black inmates. Prior disciplinary records explained 48.8 percent of the variance in disciplinary writeups for blacks, whereas self-reported rule infractions accounted for a meager 2.4 percent of the variance.

Two studies (Poole & Regoli, 1983; Ramirez, 1983) investigated disciplinary writeups in federal correctional institutions. Poole and Regoli's (1983) examination of a minimum security federal prison disclosed evidence of racial discrimination. Although African Americans and whites reported similar involvement in rule breaking at the prison, African Americans were more likely to receive disciplinary writeups for their behavior. John Ramirez (1983) observed the same thing at a medium security federal prison. He ascribes much of the disparity to the disproportionate number of African American inmates receiving multiple disciplinary writeups (especially, 6 or more citations). The researcher further noted that, in comparison to white inmates, African American inmates were more likely to be written up for misconduct that involved *definitional discretion* on the part of the staff.[5]

The racial composition of prison staff accounts for some of the differential treatment of African American and white prisoners.

guards. These elite inmates were given considerable power over other inmates. In Marquart and Crouch's (1985) investigation of a maximum security prison in Texas prior to the elimination of the building tender system, the researchers found that prison guards, being composed largely of rural whites, disproportionately chose white inmates for these positions. Although 47 percent of the inmates were African American, only 3 of the 18 head building tenders (16.7 percent) were African American. However, 14 of the building tenders (77.8 percent) were white, despite white inmates comprising only 36 percent of the prison population (p. 567). Since building tenders are used to monitor the activities of other inmates, the preponderance of white building tenders may further contribute to the likelihood that minority infractions will be brought to the attention of prison staff.

PRISON LIFE

Two Explanations of Inmate Social Organization

Two theoretical models have been used to explain inmate culture and social organization. The **deprivation** (or **functional theory**) **model** emphasizes the structural conditions within prisons (Anson & Cole, 1984; Carroll, 1974). According to this model, inmate culture and social organization are the result of collective functional responses to the deprivations (e.g., loss of freedom, loss of autonomy, etc.) prisoners experience while incarcerated. Prisoners are able to allay the pain felt by these deprivations through inmate solidarity. Because the inmate culture evolves through the interaction of incarcerated offenders, new inmates must learn these norms during the course of imprisonment. Thus, this model views the prison as a closed system (i.e., one that is unaffected by forces operating in the noninstitutionalized population).

In contrast, the **importation model** stresses the importance of factors external to the prison (Anson & Cole, 1984; Carroll, 1974). The model posits that the prison culture is shaped by participation in groups outside the institution. Within the prison, inmates develop primary groups and cliques based on past experiences. This view of the prison as an open system (i.e., one that is affected by forces operating in the noninstitutionalized population) suggests that there will be a limited amount of inmate solidarity, since allegiance is to the primary groups and cliques in which one had previous membership (e.g., street gangs).

Although typically conceptualized as competing models of inmate culture and social organization, Carroll (1974) contends that the two explanations may actually be complementary. He speculates that whether the deprivation model or the importation model better explains prison culture is dependent upon the degree to which the institution deprives and controls its inmates. According to Carroll (1974, pp. 5-7), the greater the deprivation and control of inmates, the more likely that a normative code of solidarity (as suggested by the deprivation model) will evolve. Conversely, when the level of deprivation and control exercised by the institution is minimal, there is less need for a normative code of solidarity and the importation model may be more appropriate.

This book takes the view that both perspectives contain some merit. Implicit in this view is the assumption that, while pre-prison socialization contributes to inmate culture and social organization, life in correctional institutions can exacerbate previously existing tendencies thereby resulting in behavioral changes in inmates.

Adaptation to Prison

Summarizing the literature, Carroll (1990) contends that African American prisoners are better equipped to deal with the stresses of institutionalization than white prisoners. He notes that research has found that African American prisoners have more self-esteem than white prisoners and, unlike their white counterparts, do not experience a decline in self-esteem the longer they are incarcerated. Additionally, African American prisoners are less likely than white prisoners to report symptoms of general psychological distress. They also feel safer in prison and are less likely than white inmates to contemplate suicide.[6]

What accounts for this adaptability to prison? According to Carroll (1990) the black urban ghetto subculture facilitates adjustment to the prisoner role. Because the ghetto reinforces blacks' views of themselves as victims, it is easier for them to blame society for their behavior. Life on the street has made them feel less vulnerable to the whims of others and better able than whites to become involved in peer groups that collectively enhance their power in prison. Moreover, their orientation to the present makes "doing time" easier since they become involved with the prison rather than being preoccupied with life outside the institution.

Not all researchers concur with these conclusions. Kevin Wright (1989), analyzing over 900 inmates at 10 New York State correctional institutions, observed that, although black inmates were significantly less likely than white inmates to inflict injury on themselves, black and white inmates adapted to prison life in similar ways. While he also found modest support for the notion that an economically disadvantaged background facilitates adjustment to prison, the relationship was not race specific. His findings would seem to call into question the common theme of black male superiority in adapting to prison. However, two shortcomings of his study preclude an unqualified acceptance of his results. The more critical shortcoming involves the way in which he operationalized race. The category "whites" included whites, Hispanics, and Native Americans which could conceivably make blacks and whites *appear* to be more similar than they really are. Moreover, the sample was flawed in that African American and less educated inmates serving time in the 10 institutions were undersampled.

Goodstein and MacKenzie (1984) studied over 1,600 black and white inmates at prisons in Connecticut, Minnesota, Missouri, and Illinois. All the correctional institutions were medium, maximum, or a combination of medium and maximum security and contained adult male offenders. Contrary to much research, they discovered that whites did not indicate a greater fear for their physical safety than blacks. Further, the data did not suggest that blacks are better prepared for life in prison and have fewer coping problems than whites. Overall, there were no racial differences on scales measuring anxiety and depression. Although one should be cautious of generalizing the results from a single study to the larger population, it is plausible that these divergent findings reflect a similarity in black and white acculturation once whites become enmeshed in the criminal justice system.

Black Solidarity in Prison

According to Flowers (1990) African American prisoners experience stronger feelings of group solidarity than their white counterparts. Three explanations for the greater group solidarity of incarcerated African Americans are suggested by Goodstein and MacKenzie (1984, pp. 274-275). First, their shared cultural and social class backgrounds may enhance in-group identification. Coming predominantly from the inner city, African Americans may also bring with them a similar set of experiences with which to identify. Because they have fewer employment opportunities than whites, African Americans are also more likely to come from the same (low) social class. These backgrounds combine to produce cohesiveness in black inmates. Second, African Americans in general are more uniformly committed to involvement in large-scale social, political, and religious groups, thus possibly facilitating the establishment of complementary groups in prison. Finally, their common exposure to racism and discrimination may strengthen their feelings of unity.

One illustration of racial solidarity is provided by prison gangs.[7] Membership in prison gangs (also known as "organizations" by inmates) has experienced a phenomenal rise in recent years. In 1986, for example, two black gangs--the Black Disciples and the Vice Lords-- organized at Parchman penitentiary in Mississippi. Within two years, their combined membership was estimated to be about 500 (Branson, 1988). In Illinois, where prison gangs are quite common, Jim Thomas (1991, p. 143) estimates that perhaps 80 to 90 percent of the prison population are members of gangs. Most of the powerful gangs in Illinois prisons are African American. While acknowledging the potentially coercive nature of these gangs, Thomas (1991) asserts that these gangs meet some important needs of inmates by providing security from other prisoners and by increasing the power of individual prisoners against the perceived discriminatory behavior and policies of white prisoners and correctional staff.

Despite these rather impressive statistics, gang members often constitute a small fraction of all inmates. Although figures on gangs should be viewed as somewhat speculative and subject to revision, data from the 1991 state prison population indicate that only about 6 percent of all inmates belonged to criminal gangs prior to entering prison (U.S. Department of Justice, 1993, p. 20).[8] The significance of this figure becomes apparent when one realizes that the greatest increase in numbers of gang members in prison has resulted from the incarceration of members of street gangs such as the Crips, the Bloods, and similar groups (Trout, 1992). According to Fong (1990, p. 37) the most recent national census of prison gangs discloses prison gangs in 32 states and the federal prison system. The estimated membership of these gangs is 12,634, or approximately 3 percent of the total federal and state prison population. The available figures on gangs in prison suggest that the significance of African American gangs varies by jurisdiction. As previously mentioned, in Illinois most of the powerful gangs are African American. However, in the Texas prison system, which is the second largest state prison system and contains the fourth largest number of gang members (Fong & Buentello, 1991, p. 67), none of the seven major gangs reported by Buentello (1992) are African American (they are either Hispanic or white). At the federal level, only one African American gang, the Black Guerrilla Family, is listed among the top five prison gangs (Trout, 1992). And the two most violent prison gangs in the federal system are the Aryan Brotherhood, a racist white gang that comprises less than .1 percent of the inmate population but was involved in 18 percent of all inmate homicides over a 10-year period, and the Mexican Mafia (p. 62).

Black Participation in Prison Programs and Work Assignments

An extensive study by Petersilia (1979), based on 1974 interview data from 10,400 inmates at 190 state correctional facilities in the United States, examined four needs of inmates: (1) alcohol rehabilitation, (2) drug rehabilitation, (3) job training, and (4) remedial education. The data revealed that race was not systematically related to participation in treatment programs. For instance, while white inmates having alcohol rehabilitation needs were significantly (p < .01) more likely than their African American counterparts to receive treatment, African American inmates requiring treatment for drug abuse were significantly (p < .01) more likely than their white counterparts to receive treatment. In contrast, whites and African Americans needing job training were equally likely to receive it. Moreover, African Americans with educational needs were slightly more likely than whites with similar needs to receive assistance. Although her results do not suggest racial bias, it is worthwhile noting the failure of prison treatment programs to address the special needs of inmates. African Americans having a need for alcohol rehabilitation had only a 12 percent chance of participating in a treatment program for alcohol abuse, whereas African Americans with drug rehabilitation, job training, and remedial education needs had approximately a 1-in-4 chance of receiving the needed treatment (p. 130).[9]

Another study conducted in 1978 analyzed 1,214 prisoners from California, Texas, and Michigan (Petersilia, 1983). Again, no apparent racial discrimination was found in either program participation or work assignments among the inmates. When prisoners were unable to work or participate in treatment programs, it was generally because the jobs or treatment programs were unavailable. An exception to this was Texas, where some African Americans complained that jobs were being withheld as a form of punishment.

A national study of inmates by Goetting and Howsen (1983) found that white prisoners were more likely than black prisoners to have a work assignment, but black prisoners were more likely than white prisoners to be taking classes or to be involved in training. An analysis of the work assignments disclosed no significant difference in the average number of hours worked. Although the type of work duties varied by race for 5 of the 9 job categories, it was unclear whether this was the result of racial discrimination. These mixed findings neither supported nor refuted the racial discrimination hypothesis.

More recently, a 1991 survey of inmates from state prisons reveals virtually no difference in participation rates of African Americans and whites in prison activities and programs. According to the survey, which included male and female inmates, 91 percent of the whites and 91 percent of the African Americans had participated in a program or activity after admission to prison. Furthermore, 81 percent of the whites and 80 percent of the African Americans were currently participating in a program or activity (U.S. Department of Justice, 1993, p. 27).

Failure to find evidence of racial discrimination should not be construed as suggesting that noninvolvement in prison programs similarly affects African Americans and whites. Petersilia's (1983, pp. 56-57) investigation of state prisoners revealed that a larger percentage of African Americans than whites had high needs for education and vocational training in the three sampled states. Moreover, given that African Americans outnumber whites in state prisons,[10] even if a similar percentage of whites and blacks do not participate in needed programs, a larger number of blacks than whites will fail to receive the needed training. According to Thomas (1991) cutbacks in these prison programs will more adversely affect black inmates as this will increase the probability of recidivism since after release blacks will continue to experience the problems that encouraged their illicit activities initially.

Black Victimization of Whites in Prison

According to Raymond Michalowski (1985, p. 241), the prison environment exacerbates the racial tensions found in the larger society in two ways. First, incarceration engenders frustration in inmates which can manifest itself in racial animosity and racial violence. The racial prejudices of African Americans and whites are intensified in prison as they compete for scarce goods and strive to retain their personal identity. Second, the racial mix of prisoners also encourages racism. Whites, no longer a numerical majority, may attempt to regain power over African Americans through racial segregation.[11] Conversely, African Americans, given their larger numbers and greater solidarity, may also assert themselves more and attempt to dominate the white inmates.

One consequence of the prison environment may be the victimization of whites by African Americans. Carroll's (1974, p. 182) study of a small state prison in the East revealed that at least three-fourths of the sexual assaults involved a black assailant and a white victim. Similarly, an investigation of incarcerated offenders in New York State found that the assailants were disproportionately black while the victims were disproportionately white (Toch, 1976).

Numerous explanations have been advanced to account for the tendency of African Americans to be aggressors in prison. Bartollas and Sieverdes (1981, pp. 535-536) suggest that black victimization of whites in prison may be due to (1) African Americans' hostility toward whites in general, (2) the greater solidarity of African American inmates permitting them to organize more effectively, (3) whites' fear of African Americans, (4) whites' lack of street sophistication and verbal aggressiveness, and (5) the greater confusion that whites experience resulting from role reversal in prison (in the free society whites hold an advantage over African Americans, but in correctional institutions whites are relegated to inferior positions). In addition, black aggressiveness is sometimes attributed to the subculture of violence in which many African Americans were raised (Goodstein & MacKenzie, 1984, p. 277).

Although the early studies of inmate violence suggested that whites were frequently victimized by African Americans, more recent evidence suggests that the issue is not yet fully resolved. For one thing, the dominance of black gangs in prison appears to vary by jurisdiction. It will be recalled that in Texas, none of the seven major prison gangs was African American (Buentello, 1992). Further, although a considerable amount of inmate violence appears to be gang related, much of the documented violence has been between members of the same race (Fong, 1990; Marquart & Crouch, 1985).

It may also be the case that black-on-white violence appears to be more common than other forms of violence because intraracial assaults are underreported. Walker (1985b) offers two explanations for this possibility. First, he notes that in the "free world" offenses committed by strangers are more likely to be reported than those perpetrated by acquaintances. He suggests that an analogous situation exists in prison in that an assault by a member of a different race (a "stranger") may be more likely to be reported than an assault by a member of the same race (an "acquaintance"). A second reason for the possible underreporting of intraracial assaults is that prison gangs, which are organized along racial lines, frequently require as a price of admission the sexual submission of a member to one of the more dominant members of the gang. Sexual advances of this nature are therefore likely to be interpreted by the submissive party as consensual.

AFRICAN AMERICAN WOMEN IN CORRECTIONAL INSTITUTIONS

Studies of African Americans in correctional institutions have focused primarily on African American men. This is unfortunate as, like their male counterparts, African American women are overrepresented at all levels of the criminal justice system (French, 1983). Although women of all races constituted only 5.2 percent of the state prison population in 1991, they represent a rapidly expanding inmate population. For a five-year period ending in 1991, the female state prison population outpaced their male counterparts: the female inmate population experienced a 75.2 percent increase, compared to a 52.9 percent increase for males (U.S. Department of Justice, 1994c, pp. 1-2). Since African American women are overrepresented in the female inmate population, let us now turn to an examination of incarcerated African American women.

A Profile of Incarcerated Black Women

Studies from the 1980s suggest that African American women in prison tend to be younger than incarcerated white women and tend to have less formal education (French, 1983). They also are more likely to have been reared in a father-absent family and to be on welfare or to be employed in a low-paying job requiring few skills (Bresler & Lewis, 1983). Although less is known about African American women in jail, an investigation of the population of a San Francisco jail indicates a similar profile. Compared to white women in jail, incarcerated black women are less likely to be a high school graduate, more likely to be a single mother, less likely to have ever had a job, more likely to be on welfare, and more likely to have been raised in a father-absent welfare family (Bresler & Lewis, 1983). The most common offenses that imprisoned black women are charged with are drug-related crime, murder, robbery, and larceny (Flowers, 1990, p. 172). In contrast, the two most frequent offenses for which African American women are serving time in the San Francisco jail are property crime and prostitution (Bresler & Lewis, 1983).

A similar profile emerges from 1991 data on women in state prisons recently released by the U.S. Department of Justice (1994c). Based on the most comprehensive survey of women inmates in state facilities to date (approximately 1 of every 11 women in state prisons was interviewed), the statistics reveal that in 1991 African American women accounted for 46 percent of the 39,917 incarcerated women, a figure unchanged from 1986. However, the percentage of white (non-Hispanic) women dipped slightly from 39.7 percent of all incarcerated women in 1986, to 36.2 percent in 1991 (p. 2). For *all* women (the statistic was not disaggregated by race), incarceration for drug offenses soared over the five-year period covered by the data. In 1986, drug offenses comprised only 12 percent of the current offenses. But by 1991, drug offenses accounted for virtually one-third (32.8 percent) of the current offenses (p. 3). A comparison of the family backgrounds of African American and white women in state prisons in 1991 further corroborates the earlier data: African American women were more likely than their white counterparts to have lived in a single-parent family headed by the mother (46.1 percent of all African American women versus 29.3 percent of all white women).[12] In addition, African American women were somewhat more likely than white

women to have lived with their nonadult children prior to incarceration
(pp. 5-6).

The Social Organization of Prison Life

A study of female inmates at a minimum security facility in
Minnesota reveals that nonwhites are more likely than whites to report
engaging in aggressive behavior (Kruttschnitt & Krmpotich, 1990).
Another analysis of the same data discloses that nonwhites are more
likely than whites to be confined to a more secure facility within the
prison (Kruttschnitt, 1983). However, contrary to men's prisons,
conflict between white and nonwhite inmates does not appear to be a
prominent feature of prison life (Kruttschnitt, 1983; Kruttschnitt &
Krmpotich, 1990), although nonwhite inmates are more likely than
white inmates to perceive racial discrimination by the staff and
administration (Kruttschnitt, 1983). The absence of extensive racial
conflict among inmates is illustrated by the fact that 55 percent of the
white inmates have a close tie with at least one black woman and 75
percent of the black inmates have a close tie with at least one white
woman (Kruttschnitt, 1983, p. 583). Moreover, nonwhite inmates do
not generally view themselves as "political" prisoners (Kruttschnitt,
1983), further suggesting less racial animosity in female prisons than
in male prisons.

This view of race relations is also expressed by Joycelyn Pollock-
Byrne in her book, *Women, Prison, and Crime* (1990). In comparing
prisons for men and women, she contends that:

> . . . race does not seem to be the cause of animosity
> in the women's facility as it does in the male facility.
> Although there are complaints of racism by staff and
> discrimination against blacks in job assignments, and
> some women choose to isolate themselves from other
> races, there is very little evidence of violence caused
> by racial disharmony. Women tend frequently to
> develop relationships that cross racial boundaries, and
> certainly no racial gangs are to be found in the prison
> for women. . . . It may be the case that because
> women do not form large groups, there is a greater
> possibility for individual understanding and friendship

rather than group stereotyping and the creation of boundaries (pp. 142-143).

It appears that, like African American men, African American women are likely to emerge as leaders within the prison (French, 1983; Pollock-Byrne, 1990). Furthermore, with their common disadvantaged background, they may also share with their male counterparts a greater adaptability to the institutional environment (Pollock-Byrne, 1990).

CONCLUSION

Racial disparities in the prison population consistently increased between 1926 and 1982, although recent data indicate that the disparity between racial composition of the population and percent of the incarcerated population that is African American has remained relatively static over the past several years. The amount of variance in the black prison population explained by black crime varies according to whether the researcher uses aggregate data or disaggregated data. The latter discloses that arrest and victimization data do not uniformly account for racial disproportionality in prisons.

Like their adult counterparts, African American youths are overrepresented in the incarcerated juvenile population. Also paralleling adult African Americans, black juveniles appear to be more aggressive than white juveniles and tend to dominate the correctional facility.

A number of recent studies suggests that African American males are more likely to receive disciplinary writeups than white males. Evidence alludes to the possibility that the racial prejudices of white prison guards may account for some racial differences in the number of conduct reports. There is, however, little support for the notion that African Americans are discriminated against in prison programs and work assignments.

Research indicates that African Americans typically adapt better than whites to prison life. A frequently cited reason is that exposure to life in the inner city has prepared them for life in the correctional institution. Studies have also found that African American inmates exhibit greater solidarity in prison than their white counterparts.

The background of incarcerated black women is similar to that of incarcerated black men. Investigations of black women in correctional institutions suggest that, in comparison to white women, African American women tend to be more aggressive, a finding that mirrors that of male African Americans. Nevertheless, female aggression is less likely than male aggression to reflect racial tension, and interracial friendships appear to be more common in women's facilities than in men's facilities.

NOTES

1. This 1989 estimate includes costs associated with housing black men in federal prisons, state prisons, and jails. Also included in the figure are costs associated with probation and parole.

2. Although 609 more African Americans were admitted to state prisons than expected in 1973, the difference was not statistically significant.

3. This was due, however, to the weaker demand for black apprentices by whites outside the institution.

4. To the extent that African Americans are more likely than whites to have extensive disciplinary reports, they are less likely to be viewed favorably by parole boards. This is not, however, the only predictor of parole outcome. Shirley Brown (1979), for example, observed an interaction between race and type of correctional facility in parole hearing outcome. She determined that African Americans were less likely than whites to be granted parole at the higher custody institutions (i.e., the medium and maximum security facilities) than at the minimum security facility. Further, Carroll and Mondrick (1976) found that the criteria used for granting parole was related to the race of the inmate. In addition to the criteria used for granting parole to white inmates, black inmates were typically expected to have participated in institutional treatment programs. This additional requirement for parole resulted in 77 percent of the paroled black prisoners serving significantly longer proportions of their sentences than their white counterparts (p. 104).

5. Ramirez (1983) uses the term definitional discretion to refer to situations requiring an interpretation by the staff of the extent to which the actual behavior is a violation of prison rules. Conduct reports written for "hostility toward staff" encompass such situations. Because hostility can be direct (e.g., insolence) or indirect (e.g., feigning an illness, lying to a staff member, failing to perform assigned work, etc.), some interpretation of the extent to which the behavior reflects hostility toward the staff member must be made.

6. It should be noted that inmate suicides are infrequent occurrences for both whites and African Americans. Anson and Cole's (1984) examination of suicides in the state prison system in Florida disclosed only 12 suicides for the years 1978 through 1982. As suggested above, however, African American inmates were significantly less likely than white inmates to commit suicide.

7. The distinction between a prison gang and a street gang has become blurred (Trout, 1992, p. 64). Once released from prison, members of a prison gang are expected to continue assisting their members on the inside or else be killed. Thus, they become a quasi-street gang. In contrast, members of a street gang (e.g., the Bloods or the Crips) tend to remain a cohesive unit once incarcerated, thereby becoming a quasi-prison gang.

8. A criminal gang was defined as a group that engages in illegal activities and possesses at least 5 of the following characteristics: (1) formal membership with a mandatory initiation or rules for members, (2) a recognized leader (or leaders), (3) common clothing or group colors, symbols, tattoos, or jargon, (4) a group name, (5) the members live in the same neighborhood or attend the same school, and (6) a turf or territory.

9. A numerical minority of white inmates having special needs also received treatment. Of the white inmates with alcohol rehabilitation needs, only 22 percent participated in such programs. An even smaller proportion (16 percent) of whites needing treatment for drug abuse received assistance. The percentages of whites receiving needed job training (25 percent) and receiving needed remedial education (22 percent) were additionally rather low (Petersilia, 1979, p. 130).

10. In 1991, 35 percent of the state prison population was white, while 46 percent was African American (U.S. Department of Justice, 1993, p. 3).

11. Prisons have had a long history of formal racial segregation. However, court decisions between 1963 and 1974 prohibited racially segregated prisons in the District of Columbia and such states as Alabama, Arkansas, Georgia, Louisiana, Maryland, Mississippi, and

Nebraska (Goetting, 1985, p. 11). These court decisions had the effect of eliminating formal segregation.

12. Also of interest are the responses to the question asking if a family member was ever incarcerated. African American women responded in the affirmative 52.7 percent of the time. The comparable figure for white women was 38.9 percent (U.S. Department of Justice, 1994b, p. 5).

CHAPTER 6
AFRICAN AMERICANS
AS SOCIAL CONTROL AGENTS

In discussions of African Americans and crime, it is unfortunate that frequently overlooked is the fact that the vast majority of African Americans are *not* involved in criminal activities. To rectify this problem, this chapter examines African Americans who are serving as agents of social control. We will first look at black police officers. Next, we will examine African Americans who are employed as correctional officers. Finally, the chapter will conclude with an overview of African Americans in the judicial system, including an analysis of African American representation on juries.

MINORITY REPRESENTATION
ON THE POLICE FORCE

The first African American police officer was hired in 1861 in Washington, D.C. (Kuykendall & Burns, 1986, p. 4). Despite the early start, little progress was made in minority hiring until the second half of the twentieth century. An illustration of the limited hiring of African Americans for police positions can be found in data for 1930 and 1940. Although the *number* of black police increased during this time, the *percent* of police officers who were African American declined slightly from .97 percent to .90 percent (p. 5). Additionally, employment of African Americans by police agencies has varied considerably from jurisdiction to jurisdiction. Memphis, Tennessee and Atlanta, Georgia, for instance, did not hire their first black officer until 1948 (p. 8).

Discrimination against black officers has been very common. Kuykendall and Burns (1986) describe a number of discriminatory policies and practices including: (1) discrimination in appointments and testing procedures, (2) lack of acceptance by white citizens and white police, (3) denial of promotions, (4) assignment to African American areas of the city only, (5) unavailability of departmental facilities accessible to white officers, (6) discriminatory treatment by supervisors (including lower efficiency ratings), (7) lower salaries than their white counterparts, (8) reduced arrest powers (e.g., having to summon a white officer to arrest a white citizen), and (9) less desirable duty assignments.

It was not until the turbulence of the urban riots in the 1960s that the absence of African Americans and other minorities in police departments became conspicuous. Affirmative action programs aimed at increasing minority representation in this area often encountered the resistance of police unions which represented the interests of white police officers who were challenging these court actions (Walker, 1985a). It was typically the case that those within the police profession saw the hiring of minorities as a political necessity as opposed to an opportunity to take advantage of the contributions that minorities could make to the police profession (Maghan, 1993). This opposition probably reflects the fact that police officers were recruited from the white lower-middle and working classes and contained conservative, authoritarian, and racially prejudiced persons whose attitudes were reinforced by the police subculture (Walker, 1985a).

These early experiences notwithstanding, the presence of minority police officers has increased over the years. By 1991, 11.3 percent of the police and detectives in public service were African American (U.S. Bureau of the Census, 1992, p. 394). The employment of minority women by police departments, however, has proceeded more slowly than that of minority men. In 1978, for example, only 1.6 percent of all sworn personnel in municipal police departments serving populations in excess of 50,000 were minority women. By the end of 1986, this figure had improved only slightly to 3.5 percent. The dearth of nonwhite women in municipal police departments is revealed by the fact that nonwhite women constituted a scant 16 percent of all nonwhite personnel in those departments. Nonwhite women are also grossly underrepresented at the higher ranks where they comprised only 1 percent of the supervisors in 1986 (Martin, 1993, p. 328).[1]

The underutilization of minority women in law enforcement is even more pronounced in state police agencies. In 1986, fewer than 1 percent of all sworn personnel in state police departments were nonwhite women (Martin, 1993, p. 344). Illustrative of this underrepresentation is the case of the Texas Rangers. On June 7, 1994, Christine Nix became the first African American woman to be sworn in as a Texas Ranger since its formation in 1823 (McCormick, 1994).

Although there has generally been an upward trend in the employment of African Americans, the increases have not been uniform across police jurisdictions. Using national data William Lewis (1989, p. 258) analyzed 46 police departments in cities of 100,000 or more and found that from 1975 to 1985 six police departments experienced a decline in the percentage of African Americans in the sworn police officer ranks.[2] Moreover, 22 police departments reported only modest (< 5 percent) gains in black representation. Only 3 police departments reported substantial gains (> 15 percent) in percentage of African Americans in the sworn police officer ranks between 1975 and 1985. Indicative of this variability is the range of black participation on the police force in 1985: the percentage of African Americans on the sworn police force varied from a low of 1.1 percent in Lubbock, Texas, to a high of 47.2 percent in Atlanta, Georgia.

Uneven progress in the hiring of African Americans in police agencies has also been observed by Samuel Walker (1989). His survey of police departments located in the 50 largest U.S. cities disclosed that between 1983 and 1988 about half (45 percent) of the police departments had made substantial progress in attracting African Americans to the police force. Nevertheless, 17 percent of the departments experienced a decline in the percentage of black police officers (p. 1). Table 6.1 shows those cities reporting the greatest gains in black employment and those cities having the largest declines during this period.

To what extent, then, are African Americans proportionately represented in municipal police departments? To examine this question, Lewis (1989) developed an Equal Employment Opportunity Index (EEO Index) by dividing the percentage of African Americans in the sworn police ranks of each city by the percentage of African Americans in each city's labor force. Therefore, an EEO Index of at least 1.0 suggests racial parity. Although using the percentage of minorities in the work force as a standard of racial parity has been criticized for inflating the amount of racial parity (Walker, 1985a)[3], the EEO Index employed by Lewis disclosed that only 10 of the 46 municipal police departments had achieved racial parity by 1985.

Table 6.1
Police Agencies of the 50 Largest U.S. Cities
Reporting Greatest Changes in African American Employment
Between 1983 and 1988

5 Police Agencies Reporting Greatest Declines
in African American Employment

Rank	City	1983 Parity Index*	1988 Parity Index*	% Change
1	Washington, D.C.	.71	.59	-16.9
2	Toledo, OH	1.05	.90	-14.2
3	Denver, CO	.49	.43	-12.2
4	El Paso, TX	.63	.59	- 6.3
5	Tucson, AZ	.81	.76	- 6.1

5 Police Agencies Reporting Greatest Gains
in African American Employment

Rank	City	1983 Parity Index*	1988 Parity Index*	% Change
1	Jacksonville, FL	.24	.58	+141.6
2	Buffalo, NY	.37	.77	+108.1
3	Detroit, MI	.49	.90	+ 83.6
4	Tulsa, OK	.36	.66	+ 83.3
5	Birmingham, AL	.30	.51	+ 70.0

* The parity index compares the percent of African American employees in the police agency to the percent of African Americans in the local population. Racial parity has been achieved once the index equals 1.0.

NOTE: Data was unavailable for three of the largest cities: Cleveland, Honolulu, and San Antonio.

Source: Walker, S. (1989). *Employment of black and hispanic police officers, 1983-1988: A follow-up study.* Omaha, NE: University of Nebraska, Center for Applied Urban Research, p. 4.

As indicated by Helen Taylor Greene's (1994b) investigation of African Americans in police departments in 17 cities and counties in Virginia, racial disparity can vary widely among police departments within a single state. If the criterion of racial parity is that the percentage of black full-time sworn police officers should equal the black representation in the jurisdiction, then only three police agencies had achieved racial parity. Of the 14 remaining police agencies, the disparity between the percentage of blacks in the larger population and the percentage of black full-time sworn police officers ranged from 3.8 percent in Prince William County to 34 percent in the city of Portsmouth (p. 13).

What accounts for these differences? There appears to be a positive correlation between the presence of black public administrators (e.g., black mayors) and black participation in a city's police department (Lewis, 1989; Walker, 1985a). In addition, cities with administrative leaders who evidence commitment to the goals of equal opportunity hiring tend to have greater African American involvement in the police (Hochstedler, 1984; Walker, 1985a). Likewise, the presence of court-ordered plans to increase minority recruitment is associated with greater black representation in police departments (Lewis, 1989; Walker, 1985a). More to the point, Hochstedler (1984) reports that the single most important determinant of affirmative action success in recruiting minorities for police agencies is a hiring quota.

The use of racial quotas to achieve parity, however, has not always been declared constitutional by the Supreme Court. In *University of California Regents v. Bakke* (1978), for instance, the Supreme Court ruled that the special admissions program reserving 16 places for minorities at the University of California Davis Medical School was a violation of the Equal Protection clause of the Fourteenth Amendment (Dye, 1994, p. 593). In contrast, in *United States v. Paradise* (1987), the Supreme Court upheld an Alabama affirmative action plan that required the Alabama Department of Public Safety to promote equal numbers of qualified blacks and whites until 25 percent of each rank contained minorities (Siegel, 1992, p. 496). The Court justified its decision by noting the long history of racial discrimination in the department (Dye, 1994, p. 594).

Recently, some lower court decisions have imposed limitations on affirmative action programs with quotas. In *Middleton v. City of Flint* (1993), for example, the city's affirmative action plan requiring that one minority be promoted to police sergeant for each nonminority until 41.5 percent of the sergeants were minorities was upheld as constitutional because the city had shown that there was a compelling need to remedy past discrimination and the affirmative action plan was narrowly tailored to address that need. The court further ruled, however, that the affirmative action plan could remain intact only until such time that the quota of 41.5 percent minority representation at the rank of sergeant had been reached ("Promotion--Police Department," 1993). Another 1993 court decision (*Detroit Police Officers Association v. Young*) recently terminated the 19-year-old affirmative action program in Detroit because approximately half of the police sergeants are African American and the program was no longer seen as serving a compelling state interest ("Promotion--19-Year-Old," 1993).

Although the cases cited above suggest that each affirmative action program is evaluated separately by the courts, Thomas Dye (1994, p. 595) observes that, in general, affirmative action programs have a better chance of being held constitutional if they meet four guidelines. First, the program is to redress past racial inequities. Second, the program is "narrowly tailored" to address the problem of racial disparity. Moreover, the program does not absolutely prohibit whites from participating or competing. Finally, the program has an important social or educational goal.

Enhancing Minority Representation in Police Departments

Police recruits must typically undergo an extensive background investigation of their education, work history, criminal history, and personal references (Alpert & Dunham, 1988). A survey by the International City Management Association (ICMA) disclosed that 93 percent of the police departments require background investigations (Fyfe, 1986). As Reynolds and Flynn (1981) point out, however, these investigations can disproportionately affect minority recruits in negative ways. Their examination of seven police departments revealed that such criteria as poor credit rating and employment history are susceptible to biased evaluations that differentially affect minorities. They suggest a revision of the criteria used in background investigations. The authors further recommend that since minority applicants are more likely than their white counterparts to have some record of minor violations, having a criminal record per se should not automatically disqualify one from the police force. Instead, criminal records should be examined to ascertain the nature of the offense, the date of the offense, as well as evidence of acceptable conduct since the violation.

Psychological testing is commonly employed to screen applicants for law enforcement positions. The previously mentioned survey by the ICMA found that 71 percent of the police departments use psychological tests to determine the admissibility of police recruits (Fyfe, 1986). The two most frequently used nonprojective pre-employment personality tests are the Minnesota Multiphasic Personality Inventory (MMPI) and the California Personality Inventory (CPI) (Wright, Doerner, & Speir, 1990). The MMPI was originally based on "normal" behavior patterns of Minnesota residents in the 1940s. While the battery of questions was revised in 1991, there has been no significant revision of the test since its inception (Alpert, 1993). Moreover, a review of the literature by Wright, Doerner, and Speir (1990) revealed that the MMPI and the CPI are not consistently related to either subjective or objective measures of police performance. Their analysis of 131 probationary officers further disclosed that the psychological tests are not predictive of Field Training Officer Program evaluation scores.

Another test, the Multijurisdictional Police Officer Examination, used by approximately 100 jurisdictions to select entry-level police officers was analyzed by Barry Morstain (1984). His investigation of 194 incumbent officers disclosed that minority police officers (33 African Americans and 4 Hispanics) had an average score on the overall exam that was significantly ($p < .001$) lower than that of white police officers, yet there was *no* significant difference between the mean overall performance ratings of white and minority police. Although this study was limited to six police jurisdictions in Delaware which hinders its generalizability, the findings suggest that because minorities typically score lower than whites but are about equally productive on the job, the use of aptitude tests to determine admissibility of police applicants may unduly handicap minorities.

Because the interpretation of psychological test scores has serious ramifications for the hiring and promotion of minorities, police departments can implement several strategies to minimize any adverse impact these scores might have on minority employment and advancement. Two procedures which have been successfully employed are the use of separate lists of test scores and the normalization of test scores using statistical methods (Alpert, 1993). The former procedure entails the creation of a separate list for the protected categories of minority candidates. Candidates are then rank ordered on each list and selected from each list as needed to ensure the desired minority representation. The latter procedure requires the statistical transformation of scores (e.g., the use of z-scores) so that they can be expressed in terms of their standard deviation from the mean. Thus, scores on psychological tests can be viewed in relative terms rather than absolute terms.

At least two other possibilities exist. Instead of rank ordering the scores, a police department can employ pass-fail grading. This has the advantage of allowing the department to use an arbitrary cutoff point that varies depending on the desired size of the applicant pool. Another possibility, and one that is a variation of the pass-fail scheme, is the development of categories of applicants. For instance, candidates could be placed in broad categories, such as "desirable," "acceptable," and "unacceptable" on the basis of their test scores (Alpert, 1993).

Do Minorities Make a Difference?

A study by the Public Administration Service in 1978 found that the presence of minorities and females had a positive effect on police performance (Locke, 1979). Police departments containing higher levels of female and minority representation were usually more successful in apprehending alleged offenders than those departments with fewer females and minorities. Apprehension effectiveness was particularly influenced by the presence of minorities at the levels of detective and sergeant.

Stephen Leinen's (1984) interviews with 46 African American police officers in New York City disclosed that many of the officers expressed the view that African American officers were better able to deal with problems in black areas because African Americans better understand black culture and take a greater interest in community problems than do white officers. Additionally, most of the African American officers believed that black officers were less likely than their white colleagues to encounter problems arresting black suspects, although many of the African American officers conceded that the demeanor and approach taken by the officer was also a crucial determinate of the outcome. This investigation, however, suffers from several limitations. First, the effectiveness of the police officers is based on perceptions of police effectiveness; no empirical assessment of actual police effectiveness was provided. Second, the sample did not include a random selection of all African Americans on the New York City police force. (In fact, the researcher, a white police officer on the NYPD, admits that he had a difficult time getting black officers to consent to an interview.) Further, the sample was composed entirely of black males so the question of the effectiveness of black female police officers remains unanswered.

Helen Taylor Greene (1994a) suggests another contribution of African American police officers. She notes that many African American police since the late 1960s have been working to reduce police brutality by helping to revise policies on police use of force. Furthermore, national organizations, such as the National Black Police Association and the National Organization of Black Law Enforcement Executives (NOBLE), were organized in part to alleviate problems associated with police brutality and racial discrimination.

Although the preceding research suggests a positive relationship between minority representation on the police force and police effectiveness, increased minority presence in police agencies may not always have this effect. In fact, a case can be made that under certain conditions the increased visibility of African American police officers could have a negative impact on community relations. For instance, if an African American officer is patrolling an area largely inhabited by another disadvantaged racial or ethnic minority, the presence of this officer may further exacerbate the tension between the two groups. Any incident perceived as involving "excessive force" by the African American officer may elicit feelings of racial bias by the group being patrolled.[4]

Another situation in which minority representation on the police force does not have a positive effect on community relations is found in the city of Harrisburg, Pennsylvania, where 17 percent of the police force is African American, yet the African American police officers in that city account for 61 percent of all citizen complaints against the police (Georges-Abeyie, 1984a, p. 161). The Harrisburg Director of Public Safety, an African American, hypothesizes that the disproportionality results from some of the African American officers identifying with racially insensitive white officers who come from or currently live in rural areas with little cultural diversity.

A review of the literature by Samuel Walker (1985a) reveals that the available evidence does not show that the addition of minority police officers will improve police-community relations. Moreover, while acknowledging that excluding the use of deadly force by the police, black-white differences in policing have not been extensively studied, Walker contends that, after controlling for relevant variables, it does not appear that African American officers behave differently than white officers. This conclusion is echoed by George Felkenes (nd) who examined the one-year probationary period following graduation from the police academy in Los Angeles. His data revealed no significant difference in citizen complaints between African American and white rookie police officers.

Even if the presence of minority police officers does not substantially alter the effectiveness of the police, there may be other reasons to increase minority representation. One could argue that the presence of African Americans and other minorities on the police force is symbolically significant. By providing African American youth with role models, their presence in inner city neighborhoods could serve as a reminder that opportunities for legitimate employment exist for minorities. Additionally, the visibility of African Americans on the police force could help disintegrate the stereotypical view of African Americans as perpetrators of crime.

It could further be argued that racial parity is desirable because it legitimates the presence of the police in minority communities. When nonminorities patrol minority neighborhoods, the inhabitants of these areas may resent their intrusion. However, if the police officers are of the same racial or ethnic background as the inhabitants, they may be less likely to be regarded as intruders since many of them may live in these same neighborhoods. To that extent the minority community may feel that police surveillance is justified.

Moreover, Walker (1985a) speculates that the increased participation of minorities and females may have invalidated our notion of a police subculture. With some urban police departments approaching a black statistical majority, our view of a police subculture that is based on the assumption that police officers tend to be white, prejudiced, authoritarian males from lower-middle and working-class backgrounds may no longer be appropriate. Although the impact of minority and female employment on the police subculture is at present unknown, it is doubtful that the police subculture has remained immune from the changes within.

AFRICAN AMERICAN POLICE OFFICERS

Double Marginality of African American Police Officers

In *Black in Blue: A Study of the Negro Policeman*, Nicholas Alex (1969) contends that African American police officers experience "double marginality" because they must adhere to two sets of conflicting expectations. According to Alex, the role of the police officer and the role associated with minority status produce the double marginality. Conflict exists because the African American police officer is neither accepted by other African Americans nor accepted by white police officers (i.e., African Americans are not accepted by other members of their race because they represent white society and they are not accepted by white officers because they are members of a low status minority group).

Support for this view has been mixed. Michael Wubnig's (1975) examination of a sample of African American police officers in New York City found that they perceived an absence of acceptance by their white supervisors. African American officers also believed that they were excluded from higher ranks as a matter of policy. Similar results were obtained by Reynolds and Flynn (1981). Using data compiled by the National Urban League's Law Enforcement Minority Persons Project (LEMPP), the researchers reported differences between African American and white officers. Compared to white officers, African American officers perceived less supervisory support during their probationary period. Moreover, black officers were less likely than their white counterparts to indicate that they had received fair treatment. The LEMPP data are limited, however, to responses from 303 black and white police officers representing seven police departments.

Leanor Johnson's (1989) examination of 86 African American police officers from two departments on the East Coast also suggests that African Americans are not fully accepted by their white counterparts. Compared to white police officers, black police officers were more likely to perceive annoying and unfair treatment. For instance, African Americans were more likely than whites to perceive that they were informally barred from taking certain assignments because of their race. They also felt that they were more likely than white officers to be sanctioned for their mistakes and to be more closely supervised by their department. Further, African American officers were more likely than white officers to report feeling that other officers were trying to intimidate them.

An extensive investigation of the Los Angeles Police Department also noted evidence of racial bias in that agency (Independent Commission on the Los Angeles Police Department, 1991). A review of 182 days of transmissions sent to and from patrol cars between November 1989 and March 1991 found that some of the messages contained racial epithets (p. xii). For example, African Americans were sometimes referred to using an animal analogy ("sounds like monkey slapping time"). Further, minority officers were regularly subjected to racial slurs during roll call and racist jokes and cartoons appeared on the bulletin boards in the locker rooms (Larsen, 1991). Moreover, one female African American police officer reports receiving a Ku Klux Klan calling card from white officers (Mydans, 1991).

The typically strained relations between black and white police are aptly illustrated by this quote from an African American police officer in Washington, D.C.:

> You may be their partner on the job, but the minute you're off duty, it's a different story. It's like you'll find a bunch of white cops hovering in the locker room snickering at something, then when you walk in they stop. Now what are you supposed to think? (quoted in Williams, 1988, p. 1).

An investigation of attitude changes in police officers from the time they entered the police academy until 18 months after graduation provides additional support for the view that African American police officers are not accepted by their white peers (Teahan, 1975). The study examined police in a single city and included only 24 blacks so care must be exercised in generalizing these results to other jurisdictions. Nevertheless, the researcher concluded that the white officers' prejudice toward African American officers increased over time.[5] Further, white officers tended to see their African American counterparts as less professional in their police work than whites.

Two studies fail to confirm the concept of double marginality. Valencia Campbell's (1980) investigation of 576 black male officers in a large metropolitan area found limited support for this concept. The author was especially critical of the concept of marginality in that it implies "that being black is in itself a type of pathology that involves inner turmoil for the members of a lowly evaluated racial group" (p. 481). Campbell goes on to suggest that this view may be the result of whites' assessment of the black situation and may not reflect the actual situation of that racial group. The second study, by Bannon and Wilt (1973), disclosed that African American police officers did not perceive any loss of status in the black community as a result of their profession. On the contrary, African American officers believed that they had high status among the law-abiding black population.

Mixed support is provided by Leinen (1984) in his investigation of 46 African American police officers in New York City. When asked "In your opinion are black policemen treated the same as white policemen by the department?," 52.2 percent of the subjects responded that they felt that black officers are treated on an equal status basis with white officers (p. 39). Nevertheless, most of the 24 subjects attributed the improvement of the black position in the NYPD to forces *outside* the police department. In particular, black gains were attributed to (1) direct government intervention on behalf of minorities, (2) pressures from various civil rights groups and black organizations, and (3) changing police needs in the city (e.g., to improve police-minority relations). Furthermore, while many African American officers contended that they had the respect and trust of most African Americans, a few did express the view that African American officers patrolling black areas are still seen in a negative light (i.e., as an enforcer of laws favoring whites).

What do these studies tell us about the double marginality of African American police officers? Collectively, these investigations suggest that African Americans have yet to achieve full acceptance by the white members of their profession, although the level of acceptance probably varies somewhat from jurisdiction to jurisdiction. Moreover, it appears that the stigma attached to being an African American police officer in an African American community may be less today than in the past. As the number of black police officers continues to increase, one would expect even greater acceptance of the legitimacy of this profession in the black community.

African American Women on the Police Force

African American policewomen appear to be even less accepted by their colleagues than their male counterparts. Using case studies from police agencies in Washington, D.C., Birmingham, Detroit, Phoenix, and Chicago, Susan Martin (1994) interviewed black and white males and black and white females to better understand the experiences of African American women working as police. While her investigation was not confined to police officers (it also included mid-level supervisors as well as command staff and other administrators) and so may not be indicative of the views of women police officers who terminated employment or have been less successful in receiving promotions, her findings are suggestive of possible problems that African American women face as police.

A comparison of the experiences of African American men and women on street patrol disclosed that many white *and* African American men still harbor negative images of women as police officers. For example, men often express a preference for another man as a patrol partner. And, although racial segregation is still common at roll calls and during off-duty socializing, African American men are more likely than their female counterparts to be viewed as capable officers because they are males in a traditionally male-dominated occupation.

African American women also encounter problems on non-patrol assignments. Interviews allude to greater respect being shown to white females than black females by white males in the department. As one African American woman explains:

> White males generally have very little respect for black females, especially if they don't know you. . . . If a white female is around and they start their cursing, they'll say "excuse me." If a black female is around they don't stop (Martin, 1994, p. 392).

Their experiences with African American men are not always cordial either. Some interviews suggested that black men are more hostile toward black women than white women. Martin (1994) attributes this hostility to two factors: (1) African American men are frequently in direct competition with African American women for positions reserved for African Americans by affirmative action programs and (2) hostility toward a white woman (especially one with ties to a white male officer) may result in a reprisal.

Nor can African American women necessarily turn to white women for support. Several of the 31 black women in the study expressed the view that white women are as racist as white men in their beliefs about the inferiority of black women. Moreover, the existence of an affirmative action program with special privileges for minorities can erect a barrier between African American and white women.

Upward Mobility of African American Police Officers

While affirmative action has been relatively successful in increasing minority representation in police departments, it has been less successful in increasing minority mobility in those departments. Indicative of this is Ellen Hochstedler's (1984) investigation of 15 public police departments in 12 states. Her research disclosed that minority males were underrepresented in higher level positions.[6] In the New York City Police Department there is also an underrepresentation of African Americans, especially at the higher ranks. In a city that is over one-fourth African American (U.S. Bureau of the Census, 1992, p. 36), 10.9 percent of the officers and 11.4 percent of the sergeants in 1987 were African American. Even more revealing is the fact that only 3.4 percent of the lieutenants and 1.9 percent of the captains and higher ranks were black (French, 1987).

More recent data tend to corroborate the notion that African Americans are most underrepresented at the higher ranks of the policing profession. For example, in 1990 African Americans comprised 14 percent of the population of Los Angeles (U.S. Bureau of the Census, 1992, p. 36) and 13.7 percent of the Los Angeles Police Department in 1991 (Pope, 1991) suggesting racial parity. However, 939 of the 1,147 African Americans employed by the Los Angeles Police Department worked at the lowest rank (police officer). More to the point, 9.9 percent of the sergeants, 7 percent of the detectives, 6.2 percent of the lieutenants and above, and 7.1 percent of the commanders and above were African American (Pope, 1991). A similar situation exists in the Los Angeles County Sheriff's Department where 10 percent of the deputies are black, while only 6 percent of the sergeants, 6 percent of the lieutenants, and 5 percent of the captains are black (Stolberg, 1992).

There is also evidence that affirmative action programs do not always uniformly benefit male and female African Americans as is indicated by this case involving the Chicago Police Department. In 1973 the sergeant's promotional exam was found to be discriminatory and a judge imposed promotion quotas. After the quotas were implemented, white women in the department complained that black women were receiving double advantages since they were both black and female. They argued that all women should be treated as a single minority group. The judge ruled that African American women could not receive double advantages and asked the Afro-American Police League if, for the purpose of a quota, the African American women could count as women only. The legal representative for the Afro-American Police League concurred. Although on the surface this decision has the appearance of increasing black representation on the police force as only African American men now counted toward the quota for racial minorities, the actual effect was more complicated. On the one hand, it did enhance the promotional opportunities for African American men since they were no longer competing with African American women for the allocated promotions. However, it *decreased* promotional opportunities for African American women as they were now in direct competition with white women who typically had higher test scores (Martin, 1994).

Despite the fact that African Americans have generally had greater success in being hired as entry-level police officers than rising through the ranks, there have been some recent gains in the employment of African Americans as police chiefs. Going back to 1976 one can find only one black police chief of a major city. However, by 1990 there were black police chiefs in approximately one-fourth of the 50 largest cities, including New York City, Chicago, Philadelphia, Baltimore, Detroit, Washington, D.C., and Miami (Malcolm, 1990).

What factors account for the inadequate black representation at the higher ranks? Undoubtedly, some of the inability of African Americans to climb the police hierarchy is due to their lack of full acceptance by their white colleagues. A 1983 interview with Alfred W. Dean, an African American Director of Public Safety in Harrisburg, Pennsylvania, however, sheds light on two additional factors (Georges-Abeyie, 1984a, pp. 163-164). First, there is the inability to receive a good assignment that will provide the black officer with the skills necessary for upward mobility. Common minority assignments to narcotics, prostitution, and vice details fail to provide them with the needed skills for promotions. Further impeding their progress is the fact that, for whatever reasons, African American police officers are disproportionately disciplined compared to white police officers. Because African Americans are more likely than whites to receive disciplinary actions and because they are more likely than whites to receive severe penalties, they are at a distinct disadvantage when promotional opportunities arise.

Another factor attributed to inadequate black representation at the higher ranks is that African Americans typically score lower than whites on tests used in promotion decisions. Moreover, since many African Americans have only recently been employed in police departments, they typically have less seniority than white candidates. Still another obstacle to upward mobility stems from the fact that African Americans tend to receive average performance ratings regardless of their actual performance. Because performance ratings are considered in promotion decisions, blacks may be more likely than whites to be overlooked for higher level positions (Moore, 1983).

Given these hindrances to promotion, what can be done to enhance black representation at higher ranks? Robert Moore (1983), an African American state trooper from Illinois, offers some recommendations for improving racial parity. One possibility, mentioned earlier as a means for increasing the number of minorities on the police force, is to establish a minimum score for promotion and then equally consider all candidates receiving this score or higher. Another possibility is rank-jumping. This permits a police officer to be eligible for a higher position while skipping an intermediate position. A feasible alternative is to create exempt positions that allow African Americans and other minorities to be appointed to higher level positions.

Ultimately, according to Moore, African Americans must take an active role in their preparation for executive positions.

> Once the barriers are removed by the organizations, they can no longer depend on affirmative action for their upward mobility. They must become politically astute, use mentors, form study groups, and use educational institutions to gain upward mobility (p. 20).

AFRICAN AMERICAN CORRECTIONAL OFFICERS

Prison guards (today more commonly referred to as correctional officers) have historically been pulled from the white male population in rural areas where the prisons were located. Because many of the correctional officers had little, if any, previous experience with minorities, their conservative views of racial issues were mainly shaped by their interaction with minority inmates (Owen, 1985). Although the number of African Americans in correctional work has increased over the years, their representation among correctional workers remains less than their representation among the inmate population. In 1989, for instance, 26 percent of the total number of correctional workers in the United States was nonwhite (Wright & Saylor, 1992, p. 64), yet African Americans in 1991 constituted 46 percent of the state prison population (U.S. Department of Justice, 1993, p. 3).

At the outset, minority employees working in prisons faced many obstacles. According to Wright and Saylor (1992, p. 64), "as in other professions, the first minority employees among prison staff were threatened, relegated to less desirable areas, and frequently subjected to racial slurs." While blatant racism has been substantially reduced over the years, all vestiges of racism have not been eliminated. Barbara Owen's (1985) investigation of the prison guard subculture at San Quentin revealed that racial conflict and competition continue to exist among the staff. While overt racism is no longer tolerated today (e.g., racial slurs are formally prohibited), African American correctional officers still express some concern over racism. Racial tension is further aggravated by the perceptions of white correctional officers. The white staff perceive the use of racial slurs as acceptable since this is seen as merely reflecting everyday prison jargon. Moreover, many white officers feel that they are the recipients of discrimination since a white officer using a racial slur is more likely than a black inmate using a racial slur to be written up (Owen, 1985).

James Fox (1982) studied maximum security prisons in California, Minnesota, New Jersey, Oregon, and New York State. Although his data did not reveal strong anti-black sentiment on the part of white correctional officers, interviews suggested that many white officers either misunderstood African Americans or resented or distrusted them. For example, some white officers questioned the performance of their black counterparts. In particular, African Americans were sometimes seen as being less dependable than whites. Others believed that African Americans and other minorities were more likely than whites to provide contraband to inmates. These views, though not indicative of a majority of the white officers, indicate a continued lack of full acceptance of minorities by a segment of the white prison staff. On the other hand, African American officers were perceived as being more effective in handling volatile African American inmates and were frequently called upon to intervene in situations involving these inmates.

Job Satisfaction and Turnover Among African American Correctional Officers

Studies suggest that African American correctional officers are less satisfied with their work than their white colleagues. A study by Cullen, Link, Wolfe, and Frank (1985) found that race was related to job satisfaction. They speculated that the greater dissatisfaction of African Americans was due to their perception that they have restricted upward mobility and receive less supervisory support for their work. A similar finding is reported by Robert Rogers (1991) in his investigation of correctional officers at two federal prisons. By using the Job Descriptive Index (JDI) to measure job satisfaction, he was able to assess satisfaction with work, supervision, promotions, coworkers, and pay. His investigation disclosed that black correctional officers were less satisfied than white correctional officers on four of the five subscales of the JDI. Only on the pay subscale were black and white scores virtually the same. Racial differences were most pronounced on the issue of promotions, where African Americans were significantly (p = .0007) less likely than whites to be satisfied with promotional opportunities. Failure to control for the possible effect of other relevant variables (e.g., length of time employed in corrections), nevertheless, limits the utility of the results.

An investigation of front-line staff in a southern correctional system in the United States in 1983 disclosed that African American correctional officers were significantly (p < .05) more likely than their white counterparts to indicate dissatisfaction with their jobs (Van Voorhis, Cullen, Link, & Wolfe, 1991). However, contrary to much research, their study revealed that African American officers perceived greater support from their peers than did white officers. The researchers attribute this anomalous finding to the racial composition of the correctional work force. Because African Americans comprised almost half of the staff, it was conceivable that the peer support was being provided largely by other African American officers.

Additional support for the thesis that African American correctional officers receive less job satisfaction than white correctional officers comes from an examination of correctional officers at four maximum security prisons in an eastern state (Toch & Klofas, 1982). The prison with a substantial urban minority officer population (68.8 percent were African American and 15.6 percent were Hispanic) experienced greater work-related alienation. The researchers conclude:

> the majority of city-based officers, who are also minority officers, feel circumscribed, poorly supervised, unappreciated, arbitrarily managed and haphazardly informed, while white farm-based officers are relatively acceptant of organizational constraints, and therefore nonalienated (p. 43).

Not all researchers have reported a relationship between race and job satisfaction. Wright and Saylor's (1992) analysis of survey data from 45 federal prisons revealed no significant relationship between these two variables. Nevertheless, it should be noted that although black-white differences were not statistically significant, overall African Americans reported less job satisfaction than their white colleagues.

Moreover, two studies have found that African American correctional employees are more likely than white correctional employees to terminate employment (Jacobs & Grear, 1977; Jurik & Winn, 1987). Jacobs and Grear's (1977) examination of 55 former correctional officers disclosed that race was the most important determinant of turnover. They observed that young African American correctional officers, who as a group have the highest rate of involuntary turnover, also tend to be at odds with the predominantly white prison administrators. Further, Jurik and Winn's (1987) investigation of 179 correctional officers at a prison in the West revealed that race was the second best predictor of voluntary and involuntary turnover. Although nonwhites were more likely than whites to terminate employment, the observed differences were not statistically significant.

African American Correctional Officers' Attitudes Toward Inmates

Two views of the impact of increasing the number of minority correctional officers on the treatment of minority inmates are proffered by Jacobs and Kraft (1978). The first view assumes that the presence of minority correctional officers will result in the more humane treatment of minority inmates because minority correctional officers and minority inmates come from similar economic and cultural backgrounds. According to this perspective, their similar backgrounds enable minority correctional staff to relate more effectively to the minority prisoners.

In opposition to the first view which predicts a beneficial effect on the treatment of minority inmates, the second view hypothesizes no effect. Emphasizing the structured conflict between correctional staff and inmates, this perspective posits:

> that the role demands on the prison guard are both so encompassing and restrictive, that all guards, regardless of social background and prior beliefs, will inevitably develop hostile attitudes towards the prisoners (p. 305).

Supportive of this position is the research of Philip Zimbardo (1972). In the early 1970s Zimbardo designed a mock prison experiment at Stanford University in which college students with no history of past criminality were randomly assigned to either the role of "prisoner" or the role of "prison guard." The guards were allowed to formulate their own formal rules for maintaining order and respect. To enhance realism, the prisoners were picked up at their home by a police officer. They were searched, handcuffed, fingerprinted, and booked at the police station and taken blindfolded to the mock prison. Once there, they were stripped, deloused, and given a uniform. Within six days the experiment had to be terminated as the subjects had been engulfed by the role that they were playing. During this brief period of time, about one-third of the guards had become emotionally abusive of the inmates. Further, the nonabusive guards refused to challenge the activities of the abusive guards.

To determine the validity of these two contrasting views, an examination of the literature was conducted. The literature review disclosed that five recent studies provided some corroboration for the first proposition. Three of these investigations analyzed southern correctional systems. Cullen, Lutze, Link, and Wolfe (1989) and Van Voorhis, Cullen, Link, and Wolfe (1991) examined the same data set. The latter study investigated both main and interaction effects. Their sample contained 155 correctional officers from an unidentified correctional system in the South. Of this number, 67 (43 percent) were nonwhite. Their analyses revealed that black correctional officers were more likely than their white counterparts to support a rehabilitation ideology. Similarly, Whitehead and Lindquist's (1989) study of 258 line correctional officers (about one-third of whom were African American) employed by the Alabama Department of Corrections revealed that African American officers were significantly (p < .05) less likely than white officers to express a punitive orientation toward inmates. However, the security status of the facility influenced blacks' attitudes toward the prisoners. African American officers employed in work release centers expressed a greater preference for rehabilitation than African American officers employed in more secure facilities. In spite of the fact that this investigation corroborates the notion that African American correctional workers are more supportive of inmates than white workers, race and 10 other variables were able to account for only 4 percent of the variance in punitive attitudes. Overall, then, race was of minimal importance.

An investigation of 179 correctional officers from a prison in the West further suggests that the hiring of minorities alone will do little to accomplish the goal of improving staff orientations toward prisoners (Jurik, 1985). The study included only 21 African Americans and generalizability is further restricted by the grouping of African Americans with Hispanics and Native Americans. Nevertheless, minority correctional officers had more positive attitudes toward inmates than white correctional officers. But when the investigator analyzed organizational characteristics, she discovered that organizational attributes were about as important in predicting correctional officer attitudes toward inmates as individual characteristics. For example, length of time employed in the state department of corrections was negatively correlated with attitudes toward inmates. Additionally, level of security of facility was related to attitudes. Assignment to the less secure unit was associated with more positive attitudes toward inmates, paralleling a finding by Whitehead and Lindquist (1989) reported earlier.

Whereas the three previous studies analyzed state prisons, Wright and Saylor (1992) investigated correctional workers' attitudes in federal prisons. Data from 45 facilities yielded 3,325 usable surveys, of which 10.6 percent was from African Americans. They also collected data to control for the influence of other factors, such as length of time employed at the current facility and the length of time employed with the Federal Bureau of Prisons. Their analysis revealed that African Americans and Hispanics felt more effective in working with prisoners than did whites, though the relationships were relatively weak (beta-values of .09 and .14 for African Americans and Hispanics, respectively). However, both white and African American staff perceived that they were less effective in working with inmates as the proportion of African American inmates in the prison population increased. Generalizability of their results to other correctional officers is hampered, however, as their sample contained staff at all levels and in all job categories within the federal prison system. Further, differences between federal and state prison systems (e.g., inmates in federal prisons tend to be older and incarcerated for a different mix of offenses than their counterparts in state prisons) make comparisons problematic.

Other research has failed to find significant racial differences in attitudes toward inmates. An examination of three consecutive classes of prison guard recruits trained at the Texas Department of Corrections and a follow-up conducted six months later while employed as prison security officers disclosed that race was unrelated to both punitive attitudes toward criminals and aggressive attitudes toward prisoners (Crouch & Alpert, 1982). Moreover, a study of 231 in-service guards (including 66 African Americans) from two maximum security prisons in Illinois found no consistent differences in attitudes toward prisoners when black and white responses were compared (Jacobs & Kraft, 1978).

Two additional studies (Klofas, 1986; Toch & Klofas, 1982) analyzed survey data from 832 correctional officers at four maximum security facilities in New York State. Despite responses from 91 African American correctional officers, the relatively low return rate (47.8 percent) reduces the confidence one can place in their conclusion that adding minorities to the correctional officer work force does not necessarily improve correctional officer-inmate relations. Moreover, since only one of the prisons had a substantial minority correctional officer population, their results may be unduly influenced by conditions unique to that facility.

John Arthur (1994) randomly sampled 175 black correctional officers employed at minimum, medium, and maximum security state prisons in Georgia and detected no single dominant correctional philosophy among the black correctional officers. Instead, demographic factors appeared to be important in determining an individual's philosophy toward corrections. For example, older black correctional officers (i.e., those 40 years of age and over) were significantly (p=.05) more likely to subscribe to a correctional philosophy based on deterrence. Marital status was also related to correctional philosophy in that married black correctional officers were significantly (p=.011) more likely than their single counterparts to believe in a rehabilitation ideology. Additionally, two nonrelationships are worthy of mention. Neither gender nor length of service was related to any of the three correctional philosophies (retribution, deterrence, and rehabilitation).

What accounts for the apparent absence of black-white attitudinal differences? Jacobs and Kraft (1978) suggest three possible explanations for findings of no racial differences. First, the failure to detect differences may be the result of correctional officers' failure to give correct answers. Correctional officers may be wary of revealing their true feelings to "outsiders," choosing instead to give socially acceptable answers. Another possibility is that the findings may reflect the screening process during probationary service. That is, African American correctional officers who are sympathetic to inmates may be released prior to permanent service. A final possibility is that correctional officer may become one's dominant status, thereby nullifying any racial differences that originally existed.[7]

Given the absence of a consensus in the literature, any conclusions to emerge from these findings must be labeled speculative. It would seem, however, that some differences in attitudes between black and white correctional officers probably do exist, although organizational characteristics (such as security level of facility) also contribute to attitudes about inmates. Because race generally explains little of the variance in attitudes toward inmates even in those studies which report racial differences, it seems reasonable to conclude that adding minority correctional officers *alone* will probably have minimal effect on correctional officer-inmate relations. Does this mean that African Americans and other minorities should not be actively sought for these positions? The answer to that question is an unequivocal no. John Klofas (1986) contends that there are at least two reasons why minority representation among correctional officers should be increased. For one thing, minority recruitment expands employment opportunities for African Americans and other minorities in an area where they have traditionally been excluded. An additional justification for active minority recruitment in prison employment is that it contributes to the credibility of the prison in which minority inmates are overrepresented.

African American Women in Correctional Employment

Maghan and McLeish-Blackwell (1991) trace the recognition of African American women in correctional employment as modern-day pioneers to the late 1960s and 1970s. Today increasing numbers of African American women are employed in the corrections field. In 1990 in New York City, for example, 24.7 percent of the total correctional officer work force was composed of black women (Maghan & McLeish-Blackwell, 1991, p. 88). Black women in the New York City Department of Corrections included 1 warden, 3 deputy wardens, 9 assistant deputy wardens, and 100 captains as first-line supervisors.

Despite the increased visibility of African American women in correctional employment, women of all races frequently encounter resistance from male correctional officers. Joan Potter (1980) reports that female correctional officers working in prisons for men face a number of obstacles, including (1) harassment from their male colleagues, (2) resentment of their intrusion into a male-dominated occupation, (3) the perception by male correctional officers that female correctional officers are too weak to defend themselves or other officers in confrontations with inmates, and (4) being judged by higher standards than their male counterparts. Further, the acceptance of women in the field of corrections may not be easily remedied. A study of 96 prison officers from three Federal Bureau of Prison facilities revealed that organizational factors are more important in explaining the variance in attitudes toward female prison guards than demographic factors. More to the point, the effect of demographic factors (gender, age, and level of education) on attitudes toward female correctional officers was reduced to statistical nonsignificance once the security level of the facility was included in the regression equation (more secure facilities were accompanied by reduced acceptance of female correctional officers). Another organizational variable, years of service, was also significantly related to diminished support for female correctional officers (Simpson & White, 1985).

African American women in corrections face some problems not encountered to the same degree by white women. Because African American women are more likely than white women to be the head of their household,[8] they are more likely than white women to have to organize their personal life and familial responsibilities around such job requirements as shift work, etc. Moreover, African American women who have a spouse or partner may find that their significant other is unable to appreciate their circumstances.

> The vestiges of wearing a uniform, carrying a gun, being an authority figure, and having economic dependence on the female partner are but a few of the common frustrations expressed by the male partners of black female correctional officers (Maghan & McLeish-Blackwell, 1991, p. 93).

Promotional opportunities may also present special problems for African American women working in corrections. The case of black women in the New York City Department of Corrections is illustrative of this situation. Maghan and McLeish-Blackwell (1991) allude to at least five potential problems. First, the typical African American woman, having been hired more recently, often lacks the seniority to be selected for a supervisory position. Second, if an African American woman has been employed at a female facility, she may not possess the knowledge of rules applicable to male facilities. This limitation may place her at a disadvantage if the opening is in a facility for males.

A third area of concern centers on the mandatory civil service exam. To perform satisfactorily on this exam it is necessary to keep abreast of changes in rules and regulations. The studying required may be particularly difficult for an African American woman who is a single mother due to time constraints imposed upon her by her family.

The last two problems refer to the issue of the promotion itself. If an African American woman enjoys her present job and is now able to secure needed overtime hours, she may be reluctant to accept a promotion because it means starting at the bottom again which may disrupt her personal and family life.[9] Moreover, she may reject a promotion because her spouse or partner resents her having a higher salary and greater prestige than he does.

AFRICAN AMERICAN JUDGES

Appointed to Boston's Magistrates Court in 1852, Robert Morris became America's first African American judge (Smith, 1983, p. 2). There was only a trickle of black appointments to the bench for the next 100 or so years. By 1977, a scant 22 of the approximately 500 active federal judges were nonwhite. Four years later, the percentage of federal judges who were African American had risen somewhat from 4 percent to nearly 9 percent (Slotnick, 1984, p. 374). By 1989 there were almost 500 African American judges in the United States (Spohn, 1990b, p. 1197).

Michael Smith's (1983) investigation of the attitudes of 185 African American judges disclosed that the majority of the judges saw themselves as liberal rather than conservative. Further, the liberal black judges expressed a concern for equal rights. Because no assessment was made of the actual behavior of African American judges on the bench, however, it is impossible to determine if these liberal attitudes translated into more favorable decisions for black defendants.

Other researchers have examined the sentencing decisions of African American and white judges. The first extensive investigation of the effect of African American judges on decision making was conducted by Thomas Uhlman (1978). He analyzed decisions of 16 black jurists and 75 white jurists from 1968 to 1974 in Metro City. His results show that African American judges were slightly less likely than white judges to convict both African American and white defendants. In contrast, African American judges were slightly more likely than white judges to sentence African American and white defendants more severely. These findings notwithstanding, conviction outcome and sentence severity appeared to be more heavily influenced by individual judge differences than by judicial race. Uhlman thus concludes that race has little impact on judicial decision making.

Another investigation of data from Metro City provides evidence that refutes the earlier study. Using data from 3,418 male defendants convicted of a felony between 1968 and 1979 in Metro City, Welch, Combs, and Gruhl (1988) examined the sentencing decisions of 130 white and 10 African American judges. Contrary to Uhlman (1978), who neglected to control for defendant's prior criminal record, these researchers controlled for prior record and a number of other legal and extralegal variables. They also controlled for three attributes of the judges: gender, length of time on the bench, and prior prosecutorial experience. Their study detected two important differences in sentencing patterns of the judges. First, while white judges were more likely to sentence African Americans to prison, African American judges were about equally likely to sentence African Americans and whites to prison. Moreover, African American judges were more likely than white judges to give lighter sentences to African American defendants. Overall, then, race of the judge did make a difference in judicial decision making.

Two studies analyzed decisions rendered in trial courts in Detroit (Spohn, 1990a, 1990b). The first investigation focused on the decisions of African American and white judges in sexual assault cases. Race appeared to be unrelated to judicial decisions as (1) African American and white judges convicted and incarcerated offenders at similar rates, and (2) African American and white judges imposed similar sentences on offenders (Spohn, 1990a). In the second investigation Spohn (1990b) examined 4,710 cases involving defendants initially charged with a violent felony between 1976 and 1978. Controlling for the effects of 13 variables, she concluded that few racial differences existed. Overall, both African American and white judges were more likely to incarcerate black offenders than white offenders, although African American judges were less likely than white judges to sentence black male offenders to prison.

A few investigators have examined racial differences in decision making among judges in federal courts (Gottschall, 1983; Walker & Barrow, 1985). Jon Gottschall's (1983) study of African American and white judges appointed to the U.S. Courts of Appeals by former President Carter reveals some racial differences. African American judges were substantially more likely than their white counterparts to support the legal claims of prisoners and those accused of criminal wrongdoings. Nevertheless, there were no significant differences in voting between African American and white judges in the areas of sex and race discrimination. The researcher attributes the absence of racial differences in decisions involving race discrimination to the desire on the part of African American jurists for professional acceptance.

Walker and Barrow's (1985) investigation of African American and white judges on the U.S. District Court bench employed a "matched pair" technique. This procedure involved matching 29 African American U.S. District Court judges appointed by former President Carter with 29 white U.S. District Court judges appointed by the same president. The researchers reported no significant differences in their decisions.[10] They suggest that the lack of racial differences is probably due to similar legal socialization experiences and the selection process itself which filters out those candidates with unconventional views.

Given the presence of at least some racial differences in many of these studies, it is tenable that African American and white judges do differ slightly in their decision making. However, legal factors appear to be the primary consideration in decisions by African American and white judges. It is also conceivable that African American and white decision making are differentially influenced by the type of offense with which one is charged as well as other unidentified factors.[11]

AFRICAN AMERICAN JURORS

Legal Status of the African American Juror

The exclusion of African Americans from jury service has been evident throughout much of American history. After the Civil War, Congress passed the Act of 1875 to eliminate the all-white juries common in many states. Section 4 of the Act made it a misdemeanor for a public official to disqualify any person from service on a petit or grand jury due to "race, color or previous condition of servitude" (Colbert, 1990, p. 62). However, state public officials were still responsible for determining if the prospective jurors fulfilled all of the other qualifications required by law.

Racism in jury selection was first addressed by the United States Supreme Court in *Strauder v. West Virginia* in 1880 (Serr & Maney, 1988). In that case the defendant requested that his trial be moved to a federal court because West Virginia's statute prohibiting nonwhites from serving on juries was a violation of the 1875 Act. The state trial court refused his request and an all-white jury convicted him of murder. In overturning his conviction, the Supreme Court acknowledged the right of African Americans to use the federal remedy of removal in cases involving statutes excluding African Americans from jury duty (Colbert, 1990).

Another case pertaining to the constitutionality of the Act of 1875 was decided in 1880. In *Ex Parte Virginia* the Supreme Court upheld the federal conviction of a Virginia judge who had refused to select qualified African Americans as jurors. As a result, the judge was in violation of section 4 of the Act and was guilty of a misdemeanor (Colbert, 1990).

The applicability of the federal removal statute was at issue in 1880 in *Virginia v. Rives* (Colbert, 1990). In this case, Federal Circuit Court Judge Rives had moved a state court case in which the defendant had been found guilty by an all-white jury to a federal court. The Supreme Court ruled that the federal removal statute was not applicable in situations where black exclusions from jury service were the result of the practices of a subordinate state official in violation of state law. Consequently, this decision limited the use of the federal removal statute to cases where African Americans were excluded from jury duty by state constitution or state law.

In *Neal v. Delaware* (1881), the constitutionality of Delaware's practice of selecting for jury service only taxpayers who were "sober and judicious" was examined (Serr & Maney, 1988). This procedure had resulted in no African Americans being included on venire panels.[12] The state attributed the absence of African Americans on venire panels to their lack of intelligence, experience, and moral integrity. Unconvinced by the state's arguments, the Supreme Court concluded that the complete absence of African Americans on juries provided a prima facie case of intentional discrimination. The significance of this decision is not that it found Delaware to be in violation of the Equal Protection clause, but that the decision "established an insurmountable constitutional standard for establishing an equal protection violation" (Colbert, 1990, p. 69). According to this case, a defendant was required to provide evidence of the total exclusion of African Americans from juries over a substantial period in order to successfully demonstrate a violation of the Equal Protection clause.

The proof required to show purposeful discrimination was relaxed somewhat in 1935. In *Norris v. Alabama* the Court ruled that once it could be established by the defendant that the state had excluded all African Americans from jury service, the burden of proof of nondiscrimination shifted to the state (Colbert, 1990). The *Norris* decision, nevertheless, proved to be an ineffective remedy for the all-white jury. Token black representation was deemed adequate for compliance with this decision. This is aptly illustrated in *Akins v. Texas* (1945) and *Cassell v. Texas* (1950), where having a single African American on each grand jury was sufficient to avoid conviction of intentional discrimination (Colbert, 1990).

Proving racial discrimination in the jury selection process became even more problematic after *Swain v. Alabama* in 1965. In this case Robert Swain was convicted of rape and sentenced to death by an all-white jury in Talladega County, Alabama. In assembling the jury, the prosecutor had used six of the allotted peremptory challenges to strike the only African Americans eligible to serve. Despite the fact that no African American had ever served on a petit jury in the history of that county, the Supreme Court upheld the lower court's conviction of Swain because, according to the Court, the defendant had failed to demonstrate a pattern and practice of unconstitutionally disqualifying all minorities from jury duty (Shapiro, 1985). More specifically, the Court ruled that it was not a violation of the Equal Protection clause of the Fourteenth Amendment for a prosecutor to use peremptory challenges to exclude African Americans from a particular jury if the exclusion results from the belief that African American jurors would be more likely than nonblacks to favor an African American defendant. According to *Swain*, for a violation of the Equal Protection clause to be evident, the defendant had to show that a *specific* prosecutor had engaged in purposeful discrimination in *every* case tried. Substantiating racial discrimination in the defendant's case alone was insufficient to prove a violation of the Equal Protection clause (Bobbitt, 1993).

Twenty-one years later, in *Batson v. Kentucky*, the Supreme Court overturned the *Swain* decision. This case involved James Kirkland Batson, an African American who was convicted of stealing two purses by an all-white Kentucky jury. He was sentenced to 20 years in prison for his conviction as he had a prior criminal record. During *voir dire*, 4 of the 6 allotted peremptory challenges were used by the prosecutor to remove African Americans from the jury (Shapiro, 1985). The Supreme Court ruled that a prima facie case of purposeful discrimination in the use of peremptory challenges by the prosecutor could be shown if the defendant could demonstrate that he/she is a member of a recognized racial group and that the prosecutor had excluded potential jurors in his/her trial because they were members of that race (Bobbitt, 1993; Serr & Maney, 1988).

Two Supreme Court cases in 1991 extended the provisions of *Batson*. In *Powers v. Ohio* the Court ruled that the *Batson* decision did not mandate that the defendant and the stricken jurors be of the same race because the Equal Protection right of both the juror and the defendant was the issue (Bobbitt, 1993).[13] Moreover, in *Edmonson v. Leesville Concrete Company*, the Court ruled that discrimination in the use of peremptory challenges was unacceptable in civil cases as well (Bobbitt, 1993).

The *Batson* decision has not been a panacea, however, despite its requirement that once a prima facie case of intentional discrimination has been established by the defendant, the state must provide acceptable racially neutral answers for its elimination of minority jurors. According to Serr and Maney (1988), a number of racially neutral reasons exist to successfully rebut accusations of purposeful discrimination. Some of the racially neutral explanations that have been ruled by appellate courts to be acceptable are: (1) the juror had a relative who had been charged with or found guilty of a crime, (2) the juror had legal problems with the government in the past, (3) the juror was young, single, unemployed, or poor, (4) the juror subscribed to a pro-defendant African American newspaper, (5) the juror had a negative attitude, (6) the juror appeared to be unintelligent or confused, (7) the juror appeared to be hostile toward the prosecutor, (8) the juror avoided eye contact with the prosecutor, and (9) the juror was known to be anti-law enforcement (pp. 44-47). As this partial list indicates, it is relatively easy for a prosecutor to disguise racial discrimination with racially neutral explanations.

African American Underrepresentation on Juries

In federal and state trials, African Americans and other minorities are regularly underrepresented as jurors (Fukurai, Butler, & Krooth, 1993). For example, an examination of black representation on juries in eight southern states by Nijole Benokraitis (1982) revealed that as African Americans move through the various stages of jury selection, "a racially representative cross-section of the community becomes increasingly less likely" (p. 33). An analysis of the same data by

Benokraitis and Griffin-Keene (1982) disclosed that at the initial stage of jury selection (the jury list or jury wheel), African Americans are underrepresented in 7 of the 8 states. Later stages of jury selection also revealed substantial black underrepresentation. An investigation of jury composition in six large urban counties in North Carolina found that African Americans are consistently and substantially underrepresented in each county at the jury pool and jury box levels (O'Reilly, 1979). Although each study was conducted prior to the *Batson* decision, these findings should be relatively unaffected by that court case as minority representation on juries is only partially influenced by the use of peremptory challenges during *voir dire*.

African American participation on juries is affected by a number of practices both before and after the *voir dire* examination. Problematic for many African Americans is inclusion on the initial jury list. Reliance on voter registration and personal property tax lists tends to undercount the black population (Benokraitis, 1982; Benokraitis & Griffin-Keene, 1982; Fukurai, Butler, & Krooth, 1993; O'Reilly, 1979). In addition, because jury qualification surveys and jury summonses are typically sent by mail, the lack of a permanent residence and high residential mobility affect the likelihood of receiving a jury summons and returning a jury qualification survey. Since nonwhite minorities are more likely than whites to rent rather than own, and since they are also more likely to move frequently, nonwhites are more likely to be excluded from jury lists as a result of undeliverable jury summonses and jury qualification surveys (Fukurai, Butler, & Krooth, 1993).

Another problem is that personal and subjective criteria are often used to initially determine jury list eligibility (Benokraitis, 1982; Benokraitis & Griffin-Keene, 1982). For instance, Benokraitis (1982) observed that officials used criteria (e.g., intelligence, good moral character, etc.) that were not specified by statute in composing a jury list. Moreover, where statutes required that potential jurors be "honest," of "good moral character," or "intelligent," the characteristics were not specifically defined and the jury commissioners and district clerks assigned to developing a jury list had considerable latitude.

Excuses and exemptions can further diminish black participation on juries. Because African Americans and other minorities are more likely than whites to have modest incomes, they are more likely to be excused for reason of economic hardship (Fukurai, Butler, & Krooth,

1993).[14] In addition, research by McShane, Pelfrey, and Williams (1986) suggests that African Americans are disproportionately likely to be excluded from capital juries. Using survey data from 1,131 adults drawn from a list of licensed drivers in Texas, the researchers identified three groups that would not be seated on a jury involving a capital offense: (1) those who object to the use of the death penalty, (2) those who are unwilling to serve on a murder trial in which the death penalty might be considered, and (3) those who would automatically sentence a convicted defendant to death. Upon deleting individuals from each of these groups, 69.2 percent of the original sample remained. (Although admittedly the *voir dire* exam could result in the striking of even more potential jurors.) An important consequence of these exclusions was the reduction in representation of lower-income male and female African Americans in capital trials.[15]

Judicial discrimination against minorities as jurors can also inhibit African American participation on juries. Dating back to the time of the Republic when only propertied males were allowed to serve on juries, the "blue-ribbon jury," still found in some state courts, typically results in the systematic exclusion of minorities. Even if African Americans get seated on a jury, their influence can be diluted by placing them either on smaller juries (i.e., fewer than 12 people) where it is easier for a person (or persons) from the dominant group to influence decisions, or on juries where a unanimous decision is not required and minority opinions can be more freely ignored (Fukurai, Butler, & Krooth, 1993).

Improving African American Participation on Juries

Many suggestions have been offered to increase minority participation on juries. Some of the more frequently mentioned recommendations appear below.

- Statutes should be revised to provide for better supervision of those responsible for devising jury lists. These statutes should also eliminate vague qualifications (e.g., "sound judgment," "good moral character," etc.) that can be broadly interpreted (Benokraitis, 1982; Fukurai, Butler, & Krooth, 1993).

- Replace voter registration and personal property tax lists as a source of juror names with lists that contain a more representative sample of the population (Benokraitis, 1982; O'Reilly, 1979). Combining broad-based lists (e.g., city directories, telephone directories, lists of licensed drivers, etc.) and deleting duplications would generate a more representative list from which to draw prospective jurors.

- Reduce the likelihood of attrition due to economic hardship by (1) increasing juror pay to more realistic levels, (2) developing measures that ensure that jury service will not jeopardize one's job or result in loss of wages, and (3) reducing the length of time of jury duty (O'Reilly, 1979).[16]

- Courts should be required to routinely collect social and demographic data on jurors to increase the confidence that juries represent a cross-section of the population (Benokraitis, 1982; O'Reilly, 1979).

- Frequent updating of the master file used in jury selection is also necessary because racial differentials in residential mobility and in individuals reaching eligible age will have an effect on the population of potential jurors. For example, a 1986 survey conducted in California found that if updating occurs every four years, based on residential mobility patterns of different groups, 70.6 percent of African American and Hispanic prospective juror candidates under 30 years of age will be excluded from the master list. In contrast, 63.8 percent of white prospective juror candidates under the age of 30 will be excluded from the same list (Fukurai, Butler, & Krooth, 1993, p. 49).

CONCLUSION

This chapter on African Americans as social control agents has focused on black police officers, prison guards, judges, and jurors. Our examination of African American police disclosed that although 11.3 percent of the police and detectives in public service are African American, employment of African Americans in this field remains spotty. Racial parity in municipal police departments is still the exception rather than the rule. African Americans are even more underrepresented at the higher ranks. Further, it appears that many of the criteria used in selecting and promoting police officers differentially affect African Americans.

The job of prison guard has historically been the domain of white males from rural areas. While one-fourth of the total number of correctional workers today is nonwhite, African Americans are still underrepresented in comparison to the proportion of the state prison population that is African American. The overt racism of the past is no longer tolerated, but some racial tension remains between African American and white correctional officers. Data indicate that African American correctional officers at state prisons are less satisfied with their jobs than their white counterparts. Some evidence suggests that African American correctional officers may also be more likely than white correctional officers to terminate employment. Largely overlooked in the literature are female African American correctional officers who comprise a significant minority of the total correctional officer work force in some places.

The first African American judge was Robert Morris in 1852. By 1989 almost 500 African Americans were serving as judges. Some evidence can be found which indicates that African American judges differ slightly from white judges in their decision making, though legal factors are of primary importance in decision making for both groups.

Traditionally excluded from full participation on juries, African Americans continue to be underrepresented today. A number of factors account for black underrepresentation including use of peremptory challenges to remove African Americans from juries and use of lists (e.g., voter registration) which place African Americans at a disadvantage. Moreover, the use of vague qualifications (e.g., "good moral character") and excuses and exemptions to disqualify minorities can further diminish black participation on juries.

NOTES

1. Acceptance of white women by law enforcement agencies has also been slow. In 1978, only 2.6 percent of all sworn personnel in municipal police departments serving over 50,000 people were white women. At the end of 1986, this figure had risen somewhat to 5.3 percent. Moreover, only 2.3 percent of all supervisors in the municipal police departments were white women (Martin, 1993, p. 328).

2. The six cities experiencing a decline in the percentage of blacks in the sworn officer ranks are Lubbock, Texas (-.2), Oxnard, California (-.5), Reno, Nevada (-.6), Newport News, Virginia (-.7), Norfolk, Virginia (-2.8), and Rockford, Illinois (-3.7).

3. Using this figure tends to inflate the amount of racial parity because African Americans are more likely than whites to be unemployed. In 1991, for example, the unemployment rate for civilians 16 years old and over was 6 percent for whites and 12.4 percent for African Americans. The difference is even more pronounced when comparing young whites and young African Americans. For instance, the unemployment rate for 20-to-24 year-old whites in 1991 was 9.2 percent, compared to 21.6 percent for their African American counterparts (U.S. Bureau of the Census, 1992, p. 399).

4. An illustration of this can be found in Compton, California, where on July 29, 1994, an African American police officer repeatedly struck a 17-year-old Hispanic with a baton even after the juvenile fell to the ground. Captured on videotape, the incident stirred the Hispanic community and resulted in a demonstration outside the City Hall in which some of the 40 protesters contended that the beating was racially motivated ("Vent Anger," 1994).

5. It should also be noted that African American officers had increasingly more negative attitudes toward whites as time progressed.

6. Her sample, although not representative of all public police departments, included city police departments, sheriffs' departments, and state patrols from Alabama, California, Connecticut, Florida, Iowa,

Minnesota, New Jersey, North Carolina, Oregon, Pennsylvania, Texas, and Virginia.

7. While not addressing racial differences among correctional officers, Kelsey Kauffman's (1988) description of the process through which correctional officers are socialized into a correctional officer subculture is particularly illuminating (see Chapter 8). The author, a former correctional officer, also shows how expulsion from the group helps to maintain adherence to the subcultural norms.

8. In 1991, 46 percent of all African American family households were headed by a female. The same statistic for white family households was 13 percent (U.S. Bureau of the Census, 1992, p. 47).

9. For example, the new job may require working a different shift which can result in child care difficulties for a single mother without an intact social support network.

10. Although not statistically significant, Walker and Barrow (1985, p. 606) found that African American judges were slightly more likely than their matched white counterparts to support criminal rights (50.0 percent versus 47.6 percent) and to take the black position on black policy issues (47.6 percent versus 42.1 percent).

11. It is possible that under certain conditions African American judges might hold black offenders more accountable for their illegal behavior than would white judges. As Cassia Spohn (1990b) notes, African American judges, rather than siding with black offenders, may envision themselves as advocates for the rights of black victims. Moreover, they may see themselves as potential victims of black-on-black crime. In either eventuality, the outcome could be harsher treatment of black offenders under African American judges than under white judges.

12. At the time of the decision, one-fifth of the state's population was African American (Colbert, 1990, p. 69).

13. This case involved a white criminal defendant who challenged the use of peremptory challenges to exclude potential black jurors.

14. However, Benokraitis (1982) found that excuses and exemptions did not substantially contribute to black underrepresentation on the southern jury panels in her sample.

15. The deletions also had the effect of substantially diminishing poverty-level white male representation on capital juries.

16. O'Reilly (1979) notes that jury terms vary by state ranging from 1 to 2 days to 3 months or longer.

CHAPTER 7
THE FUTURE OF RACE
AND CRIMINAL JUSTICE

To predict the future of race and criminal justice requires making assumptions about social conditions that are subject to change. Yet, despite these uncertainties, various indicators suggest that the high level of African American involvement in the criminal justice system, and the high rate of African American victimization will likely continue into the next century. To understand the foundations upon which these forecasts are based, let us now turn to a review of relevant factors.

AFRICAN AMERICANS
AS PERPETRATORS OF CRIME

At least three factors would seem to indicate that the high *official* rate of black offending will persist.[1] A perpetuation of the high level of poverty among African Americans, the continuation of America's war on drugs, and the presence of racial prejudice will likely preclude any amelioration of the racial imbalance in official crime statistics. While these factors could change in the future, the available evidence indicates a low probability of such an occurrence, at least in the immediate future.

Poverty and Crime

The relationship between social class and crime is an area that has been extensively examined in criminology. At issue is whether the typically high rates of official offending by the lower class is an artifact of criminal justice processing or a result of greater involvement in illegal activities.[2] Early self-report studies (Short & Nye, 1958; Nye, Short, & Olson, 1958) report no relationship between social class and delinquency, with the exception that lower-class youths are more likely to be officially processed. A 1972 survey by Charles Tittle and Wayne Villemez (1977) also found that social class is unrelated to self-reported crime. After reviewing the results of 35 studies of the social class-criminality relationship, Tittle, Villemez, and Smith (1978) conclude that the relationship between these two variables is largely a myth. However, Braithwaite's (1981) more comprehensive review of the evidence suggests that even self-report studies reveal more significant social class differences in criminality than would be anticipated based on chance alone. Moreover, Delbert Elliott and Suzanne Ageton's (1980) investigation of delinquency using more sensitive self-report measures indicates that lower-class youths are significantly (p ≤ .05) more likely to report involvement in predatory crimes against persons and total self-reported delinquency than middle-class youths. They surmise that earlier self-report measures finding no social class differences in delinquency were probably not sensitive enough to capture the differences in delinquency that exist. A later study by Tittle and Meier (1990) which reviewed recent empirical literature on this topic concludes that most of the recent research finds some condition under which social class is negatively related to delinquency, though the relationship is not general or pervasive.

As this selective review of the research discloses, the debate over the relationship between social class and self-reported delinquency and crime remains unresolved. Despite this lack of consensus, investigators generally acknowledge an inverse relationship between social class and *official* measures of offending (Braithwaite, 1981; Elliott & Ageton, 1980). Thus, African Americans and other groups that are overrepresented by members of the lower class typically exhibit high rates of official offending. If a disproportionate number of African Americans remain impoverished in the future, one would therefore anticipate a continuation of the high official offending rate. An analysis of three demographic trends (family income, unemployment, and single-parent families) suggests that indeed the high level of poverty among the African American population will persist, and thus the high official rate of offending among this group will likely continue into the future.

Family income. As revealed in Chapter 2, between 1970 and 1990 the median annual family income of African Americans fell $2,162 *below* that of white families. Also during the same period, the proportion of black families with incomes under $10,000 (using constant 1990 dollars) *increased* from 20.9 percent to 25.6 percent (U.S. Bureau of the Census, 1992, p. 449).

Given the limited educational background of many African Americans, there is little reason to believe that higher family incomes will prevail in the future. A recent study by the Economic Policy Institute, a non-partisan think tank, found that the workers least affected by falling wages were those who were best educated (Koch, 1994). Based on 1993 dollars the investigation compared the median hourly wages of several categories of workers for the years 1973 and 1993. The comparisons disclosed that during this period the median hourly wages of high school dropouts fell by 22.5 percent while the median hourly wages of high school graduates decreased at a somewhat slower pace (14.7 percent). The median hourly wages of college graduates, however, declined by only 7.5 percent. Several reasons were cited for this drop, including (1) the decreased value of the minimum wage, (2) the diminished clout of labor unions, (3) the expansion of low-wage jobs in the service sector, and (4) the movement toward a globalized economy. Since each of these trends is unlikely to change soon, it seems likely that many members of the African American population will continue to experience an erosion of their family incomes.

Unemployment. Another measure of economic well-being is the unemployment rate. In 1991 the black unemployment rate for civilians 16 years and over was more than twice the 1991 rate for whites (U.S. Bureau of the Census, 1992, p. 39). Perhaps of greater interest is the unemployment rate for African American youth, since younger people are disproportionately involved in crimes known to the police. In 1991 the unemployment rate for 16-to-19-year-old African Americans was 36.3 percent and 21.6 percent for those 20-to-24-years-old (U.S. Bureau of the Census, 1992, p. 399).

Projected civilian labor force participation rates for 2000 and 2005 offer little hope that a change is imminent. As depicted in Table 7.1, the civilian labor force participation rate for 16-to-24-year-old African American males is predicted to remain consistently low through 2005. And though the picture is brighter for African American males between the ages of 25 and 54 years, their participation rates still lag behind those of comparable white males. A slight increase (4 percent) in civilian labor force participation is forecast for African American females in the 16-to-24-year-old category, while older African American females can expect to improve their participation in the civilian labor force by almost 6 percentage points. More significant, however, is the fact that the younger African American females will remain substantially less likely to be employed than their white counterparts. Because researchers have detected a positive relationship between the unemployment rate for African American youths and the crime rate for that same group (Calvin, 1981; Duster, 1987), the inordinately high unemployment rates of African American youths seem to indicate little change in the offending patterns of this group.

Table 7.1
Actual and Projected Civilian Labor Force
Participation by Race and Gender

| | Civilian Labor Force Participation (in percents) | | |
| | Actual | Projected | |
	1992	2000	2005
White			
Males			
16 to 24 years	73.1%	74.9%	76.8%
25 to 54 years	94.1%	94.5%	95.3%
Females			
16 to 24 years	65.0%	66.0%	67.2%
25 to 54 years	75.0%	81.4%	84.7%
African American			
Males			
16 to 24 years	59.0%	58.3%	59.8%
25 to 54 years	86.1%	86.7%	86.5%
Females			
16 to 24 years	49.6%	51.8%	53.6%
25 to 54 years	74.2%	77.9%	80.0%

Source: U.S. Department of Labor. (1994). *The American Work Force: 1992-2005*. Washington, DC: U.S. Government Printing Office, Appendix A-1.

In *Sociology and the Race Problem: The Failure of a Perspective,* James McKee (1993) addresses the structural reasons behind the high unemployment rate of African Americans.

> Since the early 1970s, the American economy has been unable to continue the postwar expansion that made possible a period of racial progress in which blacks and other minorities found new economic opportunities. And even as expansion has faltered, a new global economy has emerged. To this point, the ideological claims of its proponents point to the significance of new levels of education and skill for any nation hoping to do well in the competitive struggles of a new world market. Beyond the issue of what this means for the American working class as a whole, it clearly diminishes even further the chances of ghetto-dwelling blacks to escape a life of poverty. Their economic future cannot remain unaffected by the movement toward a new high-tech economy, a new world market, and a reduction in the less skilled forms of employment that have been the mainstay of the working class. If there now is or there becomes a body of largely unneeded labor in a technologically advanced economy, blacks, and especially black males, will make up a substantial portion of it (p. 363).

Single-parent families. An increase in single-parent families (in particular, female-headed households) in the African American community further corroborates the forecast for a continuation of a high level of poverty among black families. It will be recalled from Chapter 2 that black female-headed households experienced a dramatic rise as a percentage of all African American households. Whereas in 1970, 28 percent of all African American households were headed by females, this figure had soared to 46 percent by 1991 (U.S. Bureau of the Census, 1992, p. 47). Although the reasons for this increase are not completely understood, part of the change may be attributable to the limited number of suitable marriage-age men. (It will be recalled from

Chapter 1 that 23 percent of African American males in their twenties were under the control of the criminal justice system in 1989.)

The rise in single-parent families is alarming given the increasing proportion of poor families headed by women. In 1960, for example, approximately 25 percent of all poor families were headed by women (Macionis, 1991, p. 273). By 1988, the percentage of all poor families that were headed by women had reached 53 percent (Macionis, 1991, p. 359). Further, the extent of economic disadvantage associated with the female-headed household is related to the race of the household head.   While 29.3 percent of all households headed by white women in 1988 were poor, 52.1 percent of comparable black households were poor (Macionis, 1991, p. 359).

The potentially negative impact of living in a female-headed household is evident when analyzing the effects of this type of family structure on school problems. Approximately one-fourth of all students who repeat a grade, are suspended or expelled, or have their parents contacted about their misbehavior in school come from mother-only families.   Additionally, over half (52 percent) of all students in the bottom half of their class live in mother-only families (Whitmire, 1994).   Given the documented inverse relationship between poor performance in school and delinquency (e.g., Brownfield, 1990; Hirschi, 1969; Wiatrowski, Griswold, & Roberts, 1981), and the greater likelihood of African Americans to live in mother-only families frequently associated with less successful academic careers, it seems reasonable to forecast the continued overrepresentation of young African Americans in the juvenile justice system.

The War on Drugs and Race

A glance at recent statistics on the most serious offense with which state prison inmates have been charged reveals important racial differences. Between 1986 and 1991, the proportion of white inmates imprisoned on drug-related charges rose modestly from 8 percent of all white inmates to 12 percent.   However, the proportion of African American inmates imprisoned for drug-related offenses spiraled from 7 percent in 1986 to 25 percent in 1991 (U.S. Department of Justice, 1993, figure 4). These trends parallel a dramatic expansion of federal funds for drug control programs. From fiscal year 1989 to 1993, the national drug control budget burgeoned from $6.6 billion to $12.7 billion, an increase of 93 percent (Office of National Drug Control

Policy, 1992, p. 139). Since law enforcement agencies typically target crack which is more commonly used by low-income African Americans and Hispanics than whites (Mauer, 1990), the "get tough" policies of drug control agencies are likely to result in the disproportionate processing of those minorities. Exemplary of this is Florida where blacks comprise 53.6 percent of prison admissions for offenses other than drugs, in contrast to 73.3 percent of prison admissions for drug-related offenses (Mauer, 1990, p. 5).

Indicative of this concern over drugs is a new initiative by the New York Police Department ("Around the Nation," 1994). The NYPD is preparing for a major offensive against purveyors of drugs. Over 12,500 locations have been identified by the police as major drug markets. Borough commanders will be permitted to select which of these areas in their borough to target. Then 56 undercover teams will engage in buy-and-bust tactics. Once an area has eliminated drug operators, each commander will be held responsible for maintaining a drug-free area.

Prejudice Toward Minorities

Three ways exist in which prejudice toward minorities can manifest itself in high rates of minority arrests. First, and perhaps most obvious, is the possibility that prejudice will translate into selective law enforcement. Although undoubtedly some of the disproportionality in arrest rates can be traced to selective law enforcement, precise figures elude us at the present time.

Prejudice toward minorities can also result in high arrest rates for minorities if the prejudice fosters discrimination, thereby reducing opportunities for upward mobility. The restricted mobility means that many African Americans will remain captives in the inner city where criminal influences are present. As fewer legitimate employment opportunities are available, one would expect the illegitimate employment opportunities (e.g., drug trafficking) to become increasingly attractive.

A third way in which prejudice toward minorities can manifest itself in high minority arrest rates is from the hostility engendered from minority prejudice against other minorities. As African Americans see other minorities surpass them in social status, resentment toward those minorities is likely to increase. The resentment may lead to greater antagonism between the groups. Statistics reveal that minorities are not only victims but also perpetrators of hate crimes.[3]

To reduce prejudice among groups, Americans have typically relied on educational institutions. For example, a short time ago the University of Wisconsin System began requiring more minorities courses to alleviate the problems it was experiencing with students who were intolerant of people from different backgrounds. While it is impossible to know what effect, if any, this exposure had on students' attitudes, this modification of the curriculum was based on the notion that education inhibits prejudice in individuals. Despite the commonly held belief that better-educated people tend to be less prejudiced than people with less education, some research indicates that there are limitations to what education can accomplish.

An investigation by Schuman, Steeh, and Bobo (1985), for instance, concludes that better-educated people are more likely than less-educated people to agree that African Americans have the right to live wherever they choose. Nonetheless, these differences decrease or disappear when the question refers to the implementation of this right. And, though better-educated individuals are more likely to accept racial integration involving a *few* African Americans, the differences by level of education fade when African Americans become a numerical *majority*.

Mary Jackman's (1978) analysis of national survey data collected during three presidential elections raises further questions about the relationship between education and racial tolerance. Controlling for southern upbringing and rural residence, she discovered that those with more education were somewhat more likely than those with less education to favor racial integration at the *abstract* level. But at the *applied* level (i.e., support for governmental intervention to achieve racial integration), the differences between the well- and poorly-educated respondents were trivial to nonexistent for each of the three time periods.

What does this research tell us about the possible reduction in prejudice over time as Americans increasingly attend institutions of higher learning? These studies allude to a possible improvement in racial attitudes, though they also caution against expecting education alone to eradicate the problems caused by racial prejudice. To the degree to which education is unable to eliminate racial mistrust, one can expect to see prejudice continue to manifest itself in a racial imbalance in official crime statistics.

AFRICAN AMERICANS AS VICTIMS OF CRIME

Because much crime is *intra*racial, a high rate of black offending should be associated with a high rate of black victimization. Victimization data generally support this assertion. In 1992, for instance, 84.1 percent of all black single-offender victimizations for crimes of violence involved black offenders (U.S. Department of Justice, 1994b, p. 61). Indicative of this high level of victimization are surveys showing that African Americans are more concerned with crime than whites. Surveys taken between 1985 and 1991 reveal that crime was more likely to be identified as a problem by black households than white households (U.S. Department of Justice, 1994a). Much of the concern over crime expressed by African Americans is probably a function of the location of many black households. Although 59 percent of all black households are in the central city where high crime rates are common, only 28 percent of white households are so situated (U.S. Department of Justice, 1994a, p. 1).

African Americans are also victimized by nonblacks. Recent research on hate crimes[4] alludes to their continued importance. Preliminary figures for 1993 reported by the Federal Bureau of Investigation (1994, p. 1) disclose that there were 7,684 incidents of hate crimes. Of the 46 states and District of Columbia that provided data, detailed information was available on 6,746 incidents (p. 4). A breakdown of the detailed information shows that 4,168 incidents (61.8 percent) were motivated by racial bias. A further disaggregation of the data reveals that 2,476 of the racial bias incidents (59.4 percent) were directed against African Americans. These preliminary figures also disclose that 3,117 of the 5,288 victims of racial bias (58.9 percent) were African American.[5]

In addition to the FBI data, other research has found that African Americans, in particular, are overrepresented as victims of hate crimes. Gerstenfeld's (1994, p. 6) data from various sources disclosed that the percentage of hate crimes involving African American victims ranged from 22.8 to 53.1 percent, depending upon the jurisdiction. Of the hate crimes known to the Boston police between 1983 and 1987, 31.6

percent of the victims were African American. And the offender was white in 91.5 percent of those cases (Levin & McDevitt, 1993, pp. 243-244).

Since 1981, when Oregon became the first state to enact hate crime legislation (Morsch, 1991), numerous states have adopted their own hate crime statutes. As of 1991, only Nebraska, Utah, and Wyoming had failed to pass hate crime legislation (Levin & McDevitt, 1993). Because the most frequent motivation for hate crimes is the race or ethnicity of the victim (Federal Bureau of Investigation, 1994; Gerstenfeld, 1994), and because our popular culture embraces hate and promotes stereotypical views of marginal groups (Levin & McDevitt, 1993), it would seem likely that hate crimes against African Americans will continue to flourish.[6]

THE NEED TO IMPROVE RESEARCH ON RACE AND CRIMINAL JUSTICE

Predicting the future of race and criminal justice involves speculation using incomplete and sometimes inaccurate information. Because of the state of our knowledge, much of what we know about the effect of race on the criminal justice system must be considered tentative. Improving the quality of research is absolutely essential if we are to progress in this area. Toward this end, this section offers some suggestions for ameliorating research focusing on race and criminal justice.

Longitudinal investigations of the criminal justice system are especially needed in this type of research. Particularly acute is the need to analyze decision making at several stages of the criminal justice system. As Zatz (1987) points out, even small, nonsignificant racial differences can, over various stages of arrest, prosecution, conviction, sentencing, and parole, result in a distinct cumulative disadvantage for minority defendants.

Also frequently overlooked is judicial decision making *prior* to sentencing. Because many states have adopted a policy of determinate sentencing, fewer racial differences should be apparent at the sentencing stage. Nonetheless, judicial discretion remains at earlier stages of processing. The offense with which an individual is charged is one example of judicial discretion. The bail decision represents another judicial decision that is typically neglected in the extant research.

We must additionally direct our attention to the differential impact of laws on minority populations. If the laws are discriminatory, there is no need for discriminatory processing to produce a racial imbalance in official crime statistics. Drug laws which equate one ounce of crack cocaine to 100 ounces of powdered cocaine aptly illustrate this issue. As stated earlier in this book, African Americans are much more likely to use the former and whites are much more likely to use the latter. Consequently, even without selective law enforcement, African Americans are more likely to receive stiffer sentences than whites for identical amounts of cocaine.

Future research should also redirect its analysis from aggregate data to disaggregated data in order to reveal possible racial differences by judge, jurisdiction, type of offense, and context. If, for instance, one is examining data on sentencing decisions in which the decisions of several jurisdictions are merged together, the racial disparities in one jurisdiction may be canceled out by the more lenient treatment of minorities in another jurisdiction. Only by disaggregating the data can we correctly ascertain the true extent of racial differences in sentencing.

Incomplete and inaccurate data further impede our understanding of the relationship between race and criminal justice. Nowhere is this more evident than in the case of hate crimes. When 1991 data on hate crimes were released by the FBI in 1993, the data contained a number of serious shortcomings. Less than 3,000 of the more than 16,000 law enforcement agencies in the United States provided information on these crimes. Additionally, 18 states failed to report any information at all. And in the populous state of California, only two police departments reported hate crime data to the FBI (Gerstenfeld, 1994). Although the preliminary 1993 statistics on hate crimes are based on data from 46 states and the District of Columbia, these jurisdictions still represent only 56 percent of the country's population (Federal Bureau of Investigation, 1994, p. 1). Further complicating matters is the absence of an agreed-upon definition of hate crime. Since definitions of hate-motivated crimes used by researchers typically lack conceptual clarity, it is difficult to know exactly what is being counted as hate crime in the literature (Byers & Venturelli, 1994).

Perhaps the most thorny issue involves criminological theory. Because criminologists frequently come from the academic discipline of sociology (Siegel, 1992), it seems logical to assume that they will rely heavily on sociological theories for an understanding of the relationship between race and criminal justice.   However, the sociological perspective of race relations that was popular when many criminological theories were being formulated was flawed.   McKee (1993) contends that from the 1920s through the 1970s the sociological image of African Americans was founded on two faulty assumptions. The first was an assumption of the cultural inferiority of African Americans.   This assumption was originally based on the rural black population in the South, although even after many African Americans migrated northward to large urban centers, black culture continued to be perceived as inferior to white culture.   According to McKee (1993, p. 343), northern black culture was seen as "a distorted, pathological version of American culture, marked only by the peculiarities of their reactions to pressures from the dominant whites."

Another failure of the sociological perspective on race in American society was its denial of a distinct African American culture.   From the 1930s to 1970 sociologists assumed that African Americans wanted to be assimilated into American society and wanted to lose their racial distinctiveness.   When dissenting views of race were voiced by African American sociologists, they were conveniently overlooked by white sociologists.

> Even such distinguished sociologists as Charles S. Johnson and E. Franklin Frazier were not exempt from this dilemma.   Though they were widely read and cited often and appreciatively by their white sociological colleagues, they nonetheless put forth some assessments of race relations that violated the assumptions of the perspective.   When that happened, their deviant views were effectively ignored by those same white colleagues (McKee, 1993, p. 4).

The inability of sociology to accurately portray race relations in the United States is reflected in its explanations of crime.   As alluded to in Chapter 3, mainstream sociological explanations of criminal behavior tend to be ahistorical.   The failure to incorporate elements of the black experience into explanations of black crime, as we will see in the next section, may preclude a comprehensive understanding of the etiology of minority crime.

IS THERE A NEED FOR
A "BLACK CRIMINOLOGY"?

Some prominent researchers have recently noted the paucity of African American scholars in the fields of criminology and criminal justice (Georges-Abeyie, 1984b; Heard & Bing, 1993; Russell, 1992; Young & Sulton, 1991).[7] Underrepresentation in criminology and criminal justice programs has been attributed to such factors as the lack of African American role models in college, racial prejudice on many predominantly white university campuses where the programs are offered, and the high cost of education (Heard & Bing, 1993). Further, the absence of aggressive minority recruitment programs in graduate education has contributed to a shortage of African Americans at the post-baccalaureate level (Russell, 1992). The dearth of African American scholars has meant that most explanations of crime have been promulgated by white criminologists.[8]

A pertinent question emerging from the recognition that African American input into criminological theory building has been limited is whether or not white criminologists can understand the black experience in America well enough to be able to discern the relevant factors associated with black crime. Young and Sulton (1991, p. 110) contend that white researchers are incapable of comprehending black behavior because "white criminologists generally lack familiarity with the history, gestures, values, and cultures of the African American community." A somewhat more moderate view is expressed by Mann (1993). She asserts that "Any research addressing the etiology of minority crime should be undertaken predominantly by minority researchers, *or by those who understand the nuances of the subject matter* (p. 112, italics mine)."

Regardless of the position one takes on this issue, it is important to recognize that whites and African Americans in the United States have had different experiences and those differences may necessitate the development of a criminological theory that takes into account the different experiences of the two groups. The significance of this is illustrated by LaFree, Drass, and O'Day (1992). Although commonly assumed in criminology that economic well-being is negatively related to criminal behavior (at least at the official level), the influence of economic well-being on behavior may be race specific. The authors posit that the erosion of social and legal barriers to black integration beginning in the late 1950s resulted in a division of African Americans into a stable middle class and a disorganized lower class. Consequently, aggregate measures showing an improvement in economic well-being may not necessarily be accompanied by a reduction in crime because aggregate measures conceal important class differences between whites and African Americans.

> The experiences of whites during this period are fundamentally different. Whites never faced the rigid segregation that forced even successful middle-class blacks to remain in black communities. Further, in comparison with blacks, the relative size of the white lower class . . . has always been much smaller and probably less influential (LaFree, Drass, & O'Day, 1992, p. 161).

Even the assumed inverse relationship between educational attainment and criminal behavior may vary along racial lines, according to LaFree, Drass, & O'Day (1992). The authors suggest that the expected effect of education on crime for African Americans at the aggregate level may not be realized under certain conditions. For instance, the anticipated decrease in criminal activity may not accompany an improvement in educational attainment if African Americans with less education perceive their position in society to be eroding, while the rising expectations of the better-educated African Americans are stifled by the inability of the labor force to provide them with appropriate employment opportunities.

Further evidence of a need for a black criminology comes from studies of the effect of skin tone (i.e., the darkness of the pigmentation of the skin of African Americans) on stratification within the black community. Referred to as the color complex by Russell, Wilson, and Hall (1992), the significance of skin tone was evident during slavery when lighter-skinned blacks were assigned more desirable jobs on the plantation. Although frequently overlooked in criminological theories of minority crime, many African American scholars have alluded to the relation between skin tone and social status among African Americans. E. Franklin Frazier, for instance, noted that in the Chicago African American community, mulattoes were disproportionately found in the zone with the largest concentration of blacks from higher level occupations (cited in Mann, 1993, p. 109).

More recently, Hughes and Hertel (1990) and Keith and Herring (1991), using the 1979-1980 National Survey of Black Americans, a national probability sample of 2,107 adult African Americans, observed that skin tone was significantly related to social status. After controlling for relevant variables, they determined that African Americans with lighter skin scored higher than their darker-skinned counterparts on all four measures of stratification (education, occupation, personal income, and family income). Further, Hughes and Hertel (1990) report that the effects of skin tone on the stratification variables were almost as strong as the effects of race (white versus African American) on those same variables. And when the researchers compared their data to earlier data, they detected *no* substantial change in the importance of skin tone on the socioeconomic status of African Americans.

Skin tone may theoretically affect criminality in at least three ways. First, the skin tone of African Americans may be important in that dark-skinned African American males, embodying the stereotypical features of the black criminal, may be viewed as more threatening by the larger society than African American males with fair skin (Georges-Abeyie, 1989; Russell, Wilson, & Hall, 1992). This perception of criminality, in turn, may lead to selective processing of African Americans based on skin tone.[9]

Another way in which skin tone may affect criminality is through its influence on the opportunity structure. Having more opportunities to advance as a result of their greater acceptance by the dominant group, fair-skinned African Americans may not experience the same frustrations as their darker-skinned counterparts. Consequently, lighter-skinned African Americans may feel less need to take advantage of illegitimate opportunities than African Americans with darker complexions.[10]

A third possibility is suggested by Alvin Poussaint (1983). Attempting to explain the high rate of black-on-black homicide, he posits that a history of institutional racism, in which the legal system places a premium on white lives at the same time that it devalues black lives, has produced racial self-hatred and low self-esteem among many African Americans. If racial self-hatred is a consequence of this history, then darker-skinned African Americans may have poorer self-

concepts than lighter-skinned African Americans because they more
nearly resemble the blackness that their society devalues. Their
impaired self-concepts, in turn, may facilitate their involvement in
violent crime.

TOWARD GREATER INVOLVEMENT
OF AFRICAN AMERICANS
IN CRIMINAL JUSTICE AND CRIMINOLOGY

The need for greater African American participation in criminal
justice and criminology is evident both in academe and in the various
criminal justice professions themselves. Each of these needs is now
addressed.

African Americans in Academe

To encourage the development of a criminological perspective that
takes into account the historical and life experiences of African
Americans, more African American faculty are needed in criminology
and criminal justice. The greater visibility of African American faculty
would also increase the probability that African American college
students would have exposure to black role models who could stimulate
potentially greater interest in careers in these fields. Increased visibility
would further serve to counteract the stereotype of the crime-prone
African American.

Accomplishing this task will require some restructuring of academe
itself. As evidenced by a recent investigation by Heard and Bing
(1993), African American faculty on predominantly white university
campuses face a number of obstacles based upon their race. The
authors report that a feeling of not being accepted by the academic
community is prevalent among African American criminal justice
faculty. Another problem that African American faculty members face
stems from their "protected class" status. This status may preclude the
development of collegial relationships with nonminority faculty if
African American faculty are viewed as having been hired solely
because of their race.

Two additional problems warrant discussion. The first is a
tendency for African American faculty to become absorbed in many
committee assignments as well as other service-related appointments

which are not highly evaluated for purposes of tenure, promotion, or merit. This is a consequence of the need for minority representation on committees at the same time that there are limited numbers of minority faculty available to fill those assignments. (African American women are particularly likely to be called upon to serve on committees as they represent two constituencies, African Americans and women.) A substantially greater minority presence among the faculty could alleviate this problem. Administrative and faculty recognition of the importance of committee assignments could also help to reduce the academic liability associated with service-related work.

Another problem is that relationships between African American and white faculty may be strained because starting salaries for African American faculty may exceed that of some recently hired white colleagues. This disparity results from increased faculty remuneration for all new faculty in conjunction with few, if any, merit increases for existing faculty. Since the problem is one of salary compression and marketing, the inequity can be remedied through equalization funds for white faculty members with low salaries.

The marginal status of African American scholars precedes their professorial careers. Many recently hired black faculty members report unpleasant experiences in graduate school. Heard and Bing's (1993, p. 10) survey of 16 African Americans who had recently received doctorates in criminal justice and related fields revealed that 46.7 percent agreed with the statement, "I was the victim of racism or discrimination by white college professors." Moreover, 60 percent of their sample believed that their professors were insensitive to black issues. Although the generalizability of the research is hampered by small sample size and nonrandom selection of subjects, the fact that they could document any perceptions of racism and discrimination is a call for concern.

The ambiguous status of African Americans in academe is reflected in many introductory criminal justice textbooks as well. Examining 19 illustrated introductory criminal justice textbooks listed in the 1989 edition of *Books in Print*, Dorworth and Henry (1992) found that, compared to their actual representation in these areas, African Americans were underrepresented in the areas of law enforcement and corrections. Pictures of African Americans as authorities approximated their actual representation in the legal field, however. More importantly, African Americans were *over*represented in photographs of offenders, thus reinforcing the negative image of African Americans.

African Americans as Practitioners

Notwithstanding the visible presence of African Americans in some high profile criminal justice positions,[11] African Americans remain underrepresented in the courts as attorneys, judges, and jurors, and in corrections as correctional officers. Even the relatively high percentage of African Americans in some municipal police departments may be misleading. As Walker (1985a) notes, the minority gains in police employment have come at the same time that minority representation in large American cities has been steadily increasing. Consequently, demographic changes have negated many of the gains made by minorities on the police force.

The shortage of African American personnel in the juvenile and criminal justice systems is especially conspicuous given the large numbers of African Americans processed through those systems annually. African Americans are particularly needed on the police force where they can provide positive role models for inner city youth while attenuating the stereotypical view of African Americans as criminals. A strong minority presence on the police force, moreover, legitimates the existence of the police in minority communities. Because police-minority relations are typically strained, the heightened visibility of minority officers could mitigate some of the minority hostility toward law enforcement officers. Further, to the extent that African Americans differ from their white colleagues, the notion of a police subculture based on white, prejudiced, authoritarian males from lower-middle and working-class backgrounds may no longer be valid.

Although the literature is inconclusive on the subject of attitudinal differences between African American and white correctional officers, other grounds exist for recommending the expansion of African American involvement in this profession. For one thing, the increased employment of African Americans in corrections, as with the police, will provide more positive role models that may serve to dispel the negative image of African Americans as criminals held by many nonblacks. The significance of this should not be overlooked given the disproportionately large number of black inmates in prison today. Secondly, minority recruitment expands legitimate employment opportunities in a field where nonwhites have traditionally been excluded.

The paucity of black jurists diminishes the legitimacy of the legal system, as does the exclusion of African Americans from jury service. To improve the perceived legitimacy of the legal system among African Americans, more African American attorneys, judges, and jurors are required. There is also evidence corroborating the notion that blacks and whites possess different views of the criminal justice system that could result in different sentencing patterns among prospective jurors. For instance, an analysis of responses from 239 adults in Cincinnati by Browning and Cao (1992) disclosed that African Americans subscribe to a different criminal justice ideology than whites. Compared to whites, African Americans appear to be more committed to combating crime through social reforms and offender rehabilitation. They also are more likely to be opposed to increased use of incapacitation to reduce crime. These racial differences suggest that the inclusion of African Americans on juries might indeed make a difference in sentencing outcomes. Moreover, indirect support for this view is provided by Tollett and Close (1991) who examined the juvenile justice system in Florida. The researchers found that minority members of that system were more likely than their white counterparts to make non-criminal justice policy recommendations to alleviate the overinvolvement of minority youth in the juvenile justice system.

Where punitive attitudes toward criminals do exist, moreover, there appear to be racial differences in their origins. Using data from the 1987 General Social Survey, Cohn, Barkan, and Halteman (1991) observed that African Americans and whites hold punitive attitudes toward criminals for somewhat different reasons. For African Americans, but not for whites, fear of crime was positively related to punitive attitudes toward criminals. In contrast, racial prejudice was positively related to punitive responses for whites only. Despite these racial differences, it should be noted that the predictor variables were only weakly related to these attitudes indicating that other unmeasured variables were responsible for much of the variance.

Research further reveals that African Americans are consistently more likely to oppose the death penalty than whites. Data from the 1990 General Social Survey show that 55.5 percent of the African Americans, compared to 82.8 percent of the whites, favor the death penalty for persons convicted of murder (Barkan & Cohn, 1994). A multivariate analysis of the white responses in the survey disclosed that only 4 of the 11 independent variables were significantly related to attitudes toward capital punishment. The two strongest predictors were gender (males were more likely to approve of capital punishment) and political conservatism (politically conservative individuals were more likely to approve of capital punishment). Antipathy to blacks, however, was almost as strongly related to approval of the death penalty as political conservatism.[12] Further, racial stereotyping was weakly ($B = .08$), but significantly ($p < .05$), associated with approval of the death penalty.

Increasing black representation in capital trials may be more difficult than in trials involving noncapital offenses given the opposition to the death penalty by many members of the African American population. In states using a bifurcated jury system for capital offenses (i.e., separate juries are used to ascertain guilt and, if guilty, the appropriate sentence), African Americans opposed to the death penalty could be seated on juries examining the first phase of the case. But, in states such as Texas, which has a non-bifurcated jury system (i.e., one jury decides both guilt and sentence), African Americans with strong beliefs against capital punishment would be excluded altogether. Although the impact of excluding from capital juries African Americans who disapprove of capital punishment is not known, a study containing a random sample of 1,131 adults in Texas disclosed that 54.1 percent of the African Americans were excluded when only those who would probably be eligible to sit on a death-penalty qualified jury were considered (McShane, Pelfrey, & Williams, 1986, table 4).

Even if African Americans are seated on a capital jury, it is unknown if the African Americans who favor capital punishment possess the same views on other issues as those who oppose capital punishment. Yet, it seems reasonable to assume that if African Americans approve of the death penalty, they may be different in other important ways from African Americans who oppose it. While not investigating racial differences, Williams and McShane's (1991) study of potential death-penalty qualified (DPQ) jurors and death-penalty excludable (DPE) jurors alludes to some possible differences. Compared to the DPE group, for instance, the DPQ group was *more* trusting of prosecutors, police officers, and prosecution witnesses and *less* trusting of defense witnesses, defense attorneys, and the defendant. Moreover, in the vignette contained in the survey, the DPQ individuals were more likely than the DPE individuals to convict the defendant.

Findings such as these, of course, do not conclusively demonstrate the existence of differences between African Americans. The extent to which these results are applicable to DPE and DPQ African American groups must be determined by future research.

CONCLUSION

Poverty, a continuation of the war on drugs, and prejudice toward minorities will help to perpetuate the high official rate of black offending in the United States. The high rate of black crime will, in turn, disproportionately involve black victims as much crime is intraracial. In addition, research on hate crimes suggests that popular culture will continue to provide the justifications needed for hate-motivated offenses. African Americans, therefore, will continue to be a favorite target for many of the perpetrators of this type of crime.

A thorough comprehension of the race-crime relationship must await improvements in research. While time-consuming and expensive, longitudinal studies are required to more effectively understand racial differences in criminal justice processing at various stages of the criminal justice system. Further, as more states move toward determinate sentencing, the focus of future research must change from a concentration on the sentencing phase to presentencing decision making stages. In addition to an analysis of the presentencing stage, we need to investigate more fully the differential impact of laws on minority populations. Future research should also focus more on disaggregated data since some investigators have shown that racial differences become apparent only after the data are disaggregated. Furthermore, the use of incomplete data and imprecise definitions of key concepts have made many studies incomparable.

Our comprehension of race and crime has also been impeded by inadequate theory. Criminological theory has typically neglected historical forces that may shape criminal behavior (or the *perception* of criminality by nonminority social control agents). Moreover, criminological theory, being frequently based on sociological interpretations of race, has tended to inaccurately depict African American culture. This inaccurate portrayal of black culture has led some researchers to conclude that only African Americans should research black crime.

There is a pressing need for more African American faculty and practitioners in the fields of criminology and criminal justice. Enhanced legitimacy of the criminal justice system and increased visibility of positive role models for minority youth are two of the benefits that would accrue from the increased hiring of African Americans. Some recent research additionally suggests that the expanded use of African Americans as jurors may result in a change in sentencing patterns, at least in noncapital trials.

NOTES

1. This list is not meant to be exhaustive, however, as other factors could have an equal or greater impact on the official black offending rate. Unknown, for example, is the effect of the crime bill (HR3355) passed by the Senate on August 25, 1994. This bill authorizes $30.2 billion for crime control and prevention. Of that amount, $13.45 billion has been set aside for state, local, and federal law enforcement, including matching funds for up to 100,000 new police officers for communities. It further authorizes $9.85 billion for prisons and contains a "three strikes and you're out" provision that will probably inflate the prison population since it mandates a life sentence for offenders convicted for a third time in federal court of any of 60 offenses. This provision may have a pronounced effect on African Americans since third-time violent felons and drug convicts would be imprisoned for life. Moreover, the bill creates over 50 new federal death penalty crimes for such offenses as carjacking slayings, drive-by shooting fatalities, and major drug-trafficking. Also authorized is $6.9 billion for various crime prevention programs. Deleted from the final bill was the Racial Justice Act which would have permitted minority defendants to use racial disparity statistics to challenge death sentences as discriminatory ("Death Penalty Offenses," 1994; "Evolution of," 1994; Jackson & Ostrow, 1994; "Senate Sends," 1994).

2. Explanations for this relationship are many and varied. Some researchers argue that the differential rate of official offending is due in part to the fact that the lower class is concentrated in heavily patrolled areas of the city. Others contend that the typical lower-class street crime is more visible than the typical upper-class crime (e.g., embezzlement, tax evasion, etc.) and is therefore more likely to be detected. Another view states that the relationship is the result of actual differences in patterns of offending along social class lines. Whatever the reason(s), people with limited resources are more likely than their wealthier counterparts to appear in official statistics on crime.

3. Hate crimes, sometimes referred to as "ethnoviolence," "bias crimes," or "ethnic intimidation" (Byers & Venturelli, 1994), disproportionately involve black offenders. Using data from the FBI,

several major metropolitan police departments, and published sources, Phyllis Gerstenfeld (1994, p. 6) found that the percentage of hate crimes committed by black offenders varied from 14.9 to 33.8 percent. Although undoubtedly some of these hate crimes involved white victims (consider the highly publicized case of Reginald Denny who was dragged from his truck by five African American men and severely beaten after the acquittal of Los Angeles police officers charged with beating Rodney King), Levin and McDevitt (1993) acknowledge the existence of minority-on-minority hate crimes. They contend that the largest number of minority-on-minority hate crimes involves African Americans and Jews, Asians, or Hispanics (p. 147).

4. According to Levin and McDevitt (1993) hate crimes reported to the police differ from other kinds of crime in several important ways. For one thing, hate crimes often entail excessive brutality. Moreover, many hate crimes are random in occurrence, are directed at total strangers, and appear to be irrational or senseless. Hate crimes also typically involve multiple offenders. And, contrary to popular opinion, most hate crimes are not the result of the activities of organized hate groups, such as the Ku Klux Klan, the Aryan Nations, or the Silent Brotherhood.

5. Regional differences do exist, nonetheless. In Los Angeles County in 1993, for example, for the first time since the county began keeping records of hate crimes in 1980, gay men were more likely than African Americans to be targets of hate crimes. Of the 783 hate crimes in that county, 27 percent of the crimes involved gay men whereas 22.9 percent of the crimes involved African Americans (Hamilton, 1994, p. B1). Part of the greater victimization of gay men in Los Angeles County may be a reflection of the greater visibility of the gay community in that area.

6. Although the Hate Crime Statistics Act of 1990 promises to keep public attention focused on these types of offenses, relative to other crimes, hate crimes occur infrequently. For instance, in Boston in 1990 hate crimes comprised only 2 percent of the violent crimes known by the police (Levin & McDevitt, 1993, p. 196).

7. A recent estimate of the total number of African Americans in the United States who have been awarded doctorates in either criminology or criminal justice stands at under 50 (Russell, 1992, p. 675). This situation may be changing somewhat, however, as Russell (1992, p. 677) also reports that in 1990 there were 59 African Americans enrolled in criminology and criminal justice doctoral programs in the United States.

8. The limited number of African American scholars in these fields is not the only reason that minority views have been largely silent. According to Young and Sulton (1991), the views of African American scholars have been typically overlooked due to the exclusion of many African Americans from the editorial boards of criminology and criminal justice journals. They are also frequently omitted from committees of professional organizations and from interviews by the news media about the causes of crime. In addition to being overlooked as consultants for criminal justice agencies and policymakers, African Americans are commonly passed over for large research grants. And when white criminologists receive large grants, African Americans are seldom used as project consultants or data collectors.

9. In fact, darker-skinned African Americans are overrepresented in the black population in prison (Poussaint, 1983; Russell, Wilson, & Hall, 1992).

10. The effect of skin tone on behavior may actually vary by age. While black males with fair complexions may benefit from their lighter skin later in life (through greater acceptance by whites and more opportunities for social advancement), light-skinned black males may be at a disadvantage during adolescence. Russell, Wilson, and Hall (1992) argue that lighter-skinned black males may need to act tough and streetwise (two traits which increase their risk of arrest as juveniles) to prove to their darker-skinned peers that they really are African American.

11. Two notable examples of African Americans in the upper echelon of criminal justice administration are Robert Matthews and Harry Singletary, Jr. In 1981, at the age of 33, Matthews became the youngest warden in the history of the Federal Bureau of Prisons. Six years later, he was named warden at the Leavenworth facility, thereby

becoming the first African American to serve in that capacity at that prison (Earley, 1992, p. 45). Then, in 1990 Matthews took over the warden's position at the federal penitentiary in Atlanta, Georgia, thus breaking the racial barrier at that institution as well ("New Warden," 1990).

Singletary provides another illustration of an African American who has risen to the top. When he was appointed Secretary of the Florida Department of Corrections in 1991, he became the first African American to head that agency which is composed of 145 facilities, over 22,000 employees, and 44,000 inmates ("New Prisons Chief," 1991).

12. Antipathy to blacks was based on responses to two questions that asked respondents to indicate to what extent they favor or oppose the following: (1) "living in a neighborhood where half your neighbors were Blacks" and (2) "having a close relative or family member marry a Black person."

EPILOGUE

> Research has established that the socioeconomic
> conditions associated with crime are more prevalent
> among blacks than among whites, and demographic trends
> appear to be reinforcing the difference. As long as these
> conditions and trends continue, the prison population is
> likely to contain even higher percentages of black
> inmates--with or without sentencing reform (Petersilia &
> Turner, 1988, p. 94).

As the above quote suggests, any attempt to address the racial
disparity in criminal justice processing must begin with
recommendations for ameliorating the socioeconomic circumstances of
African Americans.[1] While implementation of these suggestions will
not be easy or inexpensive, failure to recognize the significance of these
conditions in crime and delinquency causation will surely lead to a
furtherance of the current racial imbalance. Improving the economic
situation of African Americans must therefore be a priority in crime
and delinquency prevention.

Reducing poverty will necessitate a commitment to providing
meaningful work to everyone capable of working. To accomplish this
task, better education and job training programs will be required. Two
feasible proposals include the search for innovative ways to finance
public education (so that schools in poorer school districts will not be
less adequately financed than schools in wealthier districts) and the
development of more alternatives to traditional schools (e.g., magnet
schools). Moreover, once African Americans possess the requisite job
skills, government incentives may be needed to encourage employers
to hire minority applicants.

As the impoverished female-headed family has become increasingly
common in the African American community, an attempt must be made
to buttress this type of family. Especially problematic in many single-

parent families is the supervision of children. Adequate supervision may become difficult if one's work does not coincide with school hours or if child care is either unavailable or prohibitively expensive. To strengthen the single-parent family, public schools in inner cities could offer at no cost (or at a substantially subsidized rate) child care both immediately before as well as immediately after school hours. By certifying some of the inhabitants in the housing projects as child care providers, accessibility of child care could be enhanced. This would also have the desirable effect of expanding employment opportunities for other tenants in the projects. State or federal funds could be designated for upgrading the apartments to ensure safety of the children.

A sense of personal worth is essential if illegal behavior is to be discouraged. Providing African Americans with greater control over those institutions and agencies that serve their communities could convey a message of self-worth to the individuals living there. The recruitment of successful middle-class black professionals to interact with inner-city youth might strengthen racial identity. This could be supplemented with classes aimed at fortifying racial identity and self-esteem.

Better and safer public housing is another prerequisite for the nurturing of self-worth. Teaching conflict resolution skills to the at-risk African American population (primarily young males) might reduce the intraracial homicide rate in black communities, particularly if these skills are taught in conjunction with social programs whose objective is the socioeconomic betterment of the target population. The homicide rate might also be favorably affected by legislation directed at the reduction of handgun sales.

Besides preventive measures, changes in the criminal justice system itself must be forthcoming. Increased African American representation in municipal police departments would enhance the perceived legitimacy of the police in African American communities, provide more positive role models for African American youth, and increase the number of legitimate employment opportunities for African Americans. To substantially improve the position of African Americans on the police force would probably require some modifications of present hiring and promotion criteria (e.g., some aptitude tests used in hiring and promotion decisions have been found to discriminate against black applicants). Further, administrative leave and tuition assistance to obtain advanced education should be available to police officers to increase the likelihood that African Americans and other minorities will receive satisfactory consideration for promotions. To facilitate the movement of larger numbers of minorities into the police profession and to enhance their retention, all police officers should be required to undergo periodic cultural/minority sensitivity training.

The decriminalization of some offenses (e.g., drug offenses) could have a two-fold effect on African Americans. First, it could reduce the number of African Americans who are disqualified from holding criminal justice positions because of their prior criminal records. Second, it could have a profound effect on the overrepresentation of African Americans in prison. And for very minor crimes, Mobley (1982) suggests the establishment of Community Dispute and Mediation Centers to prevent minor offenders from becoming enmeshed in the criminal justice system.

For nonviolent offenders, a greater reliance on alternatives to incarceration could further alleviate the racial disparity in prison. Some frequently mentioned possibilities include the greater use of restitution or community service, fines (based on a proportion of one's income to equalize its impact on people of varying financial means), probation, and suspended sentences.

The pre-sentence investigation report (PSR) may also inadvertently discriminate against African Americans (Petersilia, 1983). Typically prepared by probation officers, the PSR contains extensive information on the defendant's personal background. Used in sentencing and parole decisions, such "objective" indicators of recidivism as family instability and unemployment are more prevalent in the African American population than in the white population. Yet, as Petersilia (1983) points out, the recidivism rates for both groups are comparable. Consequently, modifications of the PSR are necessary if greater racial parity is to be achieved.

Other suggestions for enhancing racial parity in the criminal justice system focus on the judiciary. Even a cursory glance at the court system reveals a crucial need for more African American lawyers and judges. To increase racial sensitivity, special training programs should be developed for judges and other judicial personnel. States should also have strict, specific guidelines and criteria for transferring juveniles to adult court to minimize the possibility of racial bias. Because many African American defendants are drawn from the lower social classes, to ensure sufficient legal representation, states should expand their funding for public defenders. The present system of jury selection needs alteration too, so that racially balanced juries will be the norm and not the exception. In practice, this means selecting potential jurors from lists that include a good cross section of African Americans. Moreover, a reappraisal of the value of the *voir dire* examination in juror selection should be conducted, given its proclivity to exclude potential African American jurors. And since relative to the white population, minority group members are more financially disadvantaged by participation on juries, a more equitable method of juror compensation must be developed to ensure adequate representation among these segments of society.

Changes are also needed in prison. To reduce recidivism, there should be a renewed interest in rehabilitation. If African Americans are to be dissuaded from resuming their previous illegal activities, they should be taught appropriate job-related skills and offered remedial education while still in prison. Further, since many African Americans are incarcerated on drug-related charges, drug abuse programs should be readily available as part of the rehabilitation experience. Follow-up programs should also be implemented.

Although these recommendations are not meant to be exhaustive of all possibilities, they include the most frequently mentioned suggestions. While none of these can guarantee an appreciable improvement in the racial disparity between African Americans and whites, to ignore these potential solutions is to assure a perpetuation of existing racial inequity.

NOTES

1. Although the recommendations contained in this epilogue were drawn from many diverse sources encountered while researching this topic, I am particularly indebted to the scholarly works of Flowers (1990), Mauer (1990), Mobley (1982), Petersilia (1983), Pope and Ross (1992), Tollett and Close (1991), and Young and Sulton (1991).

BIBLIOGRAPHY

Adams, R. (1973). Differential association and learning principles revisited. *Social Problems*, *20*, 447-458.

Adamson, C.R. (1983). Punishment after slavery: Southern state penal systems, 1865-1890. *Social Problems*, *30*, 555-569.

Adler, F., Mueller, G., & Laufer, W. (1991). *Criminology*. New York: McGraw-Hill.

Agnew, R. (1985). A revised strain theory of delinquency. *Social Forces*, *64*, 151-166.

Akers, R.L. (1968). Problems in the sociology of deviance: Social definitions and behavior. *Social Forces*, *46*, 455-465.

Akers, R.L., Krohn, M.D., Lanza-Kaduce, L., & Radosevich, M. (1978). Social learning and deviant behavior: A specific test of a general theory. *American Sociological Review*, *44*, 636-655.

Alex, N. (1969). *Black in blue: A study of the negro policeman*. New York: Appleton-Century-Crofts.

Alpert, G.P. (1993). The role of psychological testing in law enforcement. In R.G. Dunham & G.P. Alpert (Eds.), *Critical issues in policing: Contemporary readings* (2nd ed., pp. 96-105). Prospect Heights, IL: Waveland Press.

Alpert, G.P., & Dunham, R.G. (1988). *Policing urban America*. Prospect Heights, IL: Waveland Press.

Anson, R.H., & Cole, J.N. (1984). Inmate suicide: Ethnic adaptations to the prisonization experience. *Justice Quarterly*, *1*, 563-567.

Around the nation: New York. (1994, April 15). *Law Enforcement News*, p. 2.

Arthur, J.A. (1994). Correctional ideology of black correctional officers. *Federal Probation*, *58*, 57-66.

Backstrand, J.A., Gibbons, D.C., & Jones, J.F. (1992). Who is in jail? An examination of the rabble hypothesis. *Crime & Delinquency*, *38*, 219-229.

Baldus, D.C., Pulaski, C., & Woodworth, G. (1983). Comparative review of death sentences: An empirical study of the Georgia experience. *Journal of Criminal Law & Criminology, 74*, 661-753.

Baldus, D.C., Woodworth, G., & Pulaski, C.A. (1985). Monitoring and evaluating contemporary death sentencing systems: Lessons from Georgia. *U.C. Davis Law Review, 18*, 1375-1407.

Balkwell, J.W. (1990). Ethnic inequality and the rate of homicide. *Social Forces, 69*, 53-70.

Bannon, J.D., & Wilt, G.M. (1973). Black policemen: A study of self images. *Journal of Police Science & Administration, 1*, 21-30.

Barkan, S.E., & Cohn, S.F. (1994). Racial prejudice and support for the death penalty by whites. *Journal of Research in Crime & Delinquency, 31*, 202-209.

Barnett, A. (1985). Some distribution patterns for the Georgia death sentence. *U.C. Davis Law Review, 18*, 1327-1374.

Bartollas, C., & Sieverdes, C.M. (1981). The victimized white in a juvenile correctional system. *Crime & Delinquency, 27*, 534-543.

Bayley, D.H., & Mendelsohn, H. (1969). *Minorities and the police: Confrontation in America.* New York: Free Press.

Beck, E.M., & Tolnay, S.E. (1990). The killing fields of the Deep South: The market for cotton and the lynching of blacks, 1882-1930. *American Sociological Review, 55*, 526-539.

Becker, H.S. (1963). *Outsiders: Studies in the sociology of deviance.* New York: Free Press.

Bell, D., Jr., & Lang, K. (1985). The intake dispositions of juvenile offenders. *Journal of Research in Crime & Delinquency, 22*, 309-328.

Benokraitis, N. (1982). Racial exclusion in juries. *Journal of Applied Behavioral Science, 18*, 29-47.

Benokraitis, N., & Griffin-Keene, J.A. (1982). Prejudice and jury selection. *Journal of Black Studies, 12*, 427-449.

Berry, M.F., & Blassingame, J. (1992). American archipelago: Blacks and criminal justice. In M.L. Andersen & P.H. Collins (Eds.), *Race, class, and gender: An anthology* (pp. 429-442). Belmont, CA: Wadsworth.

Bishop, D.M., & Frazier, C.E. (1988). The influence of race in juvenile justice processing. *Journal of Research in Crime & Delinquency, 25*, 242-263.

Black, D.J., & Reiss, A.J. (1970). Police control of juveniles. *American Sociological Review, 35*, 63-77.

Black males line up for fingerprinting to help frustrated police solve rape spree. (1987, September 29). *Law Enforcement News, 13*, p. 7.

Blalock, H.M., Jr. (1972). *Social statistics* (2nd ed.). New York: McGraw-Hill.

Blau, J.R., & Blau, P.M. (1982). The cost of inequality: Metropolitan structure and violent crime. *American Sociological Review, 47*, 114-129.

Blau, P.M., & Golden, R.M. (1986). Metropolitan structure and criminal violence. *Sociological Quarterly, 27*, 15-26.

Bloom, L. (1971). *The social psychology of race relations*. Cambridge, MA: Schenkman.

Blumstein, A. (1982). On the racial disproportionality of United States' prison populations. *Journal of Criminal Law & Criminology, 73*, 1259-1281.

Blumstein, A., & Graddy, E. (1981/1982). Prevalence and recidivism in index arrests: A feedback model. *Law & Society Review, 16*, 265-290.

Bobbitt, D.M. (1993, March). Racial discrimination in the jury selection process: The future of the peremptory challenge. Paper presented at the meeting of the Academy of Criminal Justice Sciences, Kansas City, MO.

Bohm, R. (1991). Race and the death penalty in the United States. In M.J. Lynch & E.B. Patterson (Eds.), *Race and criminal justice* (pp. 71-85). Albany, NY: Harrow & Heston.

Boocock, S.S. (1972). *An introduction to the sociology of learning*. Boston: Houghton Mifflin.

Bortner, M.A., Sunderland, M.L., & Winn, R. (1985). Race and the impact of juvenile deinstitutionalization. *Crime & Delinquency, 31*, 35-46.

Bowers, W.J., & Pierce, G.L. (1980). Arbitrariness and discrimination under post-*Furman* capital statutes. *Crime & Delinquency, 26*, 563-635.

Braithwaite, J. (1981). The myth of social class and criminality reconsidered. *American Sociological Review, 46*, 36-57.

Branson, R. (1988, September 11). Parchman officials face rising gang participation by inmates. *(Jackson, Mississippi) Clarion-Ledger*, p. 1.

Bresler, L., & Lewis, D.K. (1983). Black and white women prisoners: Differences in family ties and their programmatic implications. *The Prison Journal, 63*, 116-123.

Bridges, G.S., & Crutchfield, R.D. (1988). Law, social standing and racial disparities in imprisonment. *Social Forces, 66*, 699-724.

Bridges, G.S., Crutchfield, R.D., & Simpson, E.E. (1987). Crime, social structure and criminal punishment: White and nonwhite rates of imprisonment. *Social Problems, 34*, 345-361.

Brown, S.E., Esbensen, F., & Geis, G. (1991). *Criminology: Explaining crime and its context.* Cincinnati, OH: Anderson.

Brown, S.V. (1979). Race and parole hearing outcomes. In R. Alvarez, K.G. Lutterman, & Associates (Eds.), *Discrimination in organizations: Using social indicators to manage social change* (pp. 355-374). San Francisco: Jossey-Bass.

Brownfield, D. (1990). Adolescent male status and delinquent behavior. *Sociological Spectrum, 10*, 227-248.

Browning, S.L., & Cao, L. (1992). The impact of race on criminal justice ideology. *Justice Quarterly, 9*, 685-701.

Buentello, S. (1992, July). Combatting gangs in Texas. *Corrections Today*, pp. 58-60.

Burgess, R.L., & Akers, R.L. (1966). A differential association-reinforcement theory of criminal behavior. *Social Problems, 14*, 128-147.

Byers, B., & Venturelli, P.J. (1994, March). Researching hate crimes and hate crime offenders: Methods, issues and opportunities. Paper presented at the meeting of the Academy of Criminal Justice Sciences, Chicago, IL.

Calvin, A.D. (1981). Unemployment among black youths, demographics, and crime. *Crime & Delinquency, 27*, 234-244.

Campbell, V. (1980). Double marginality of black policemen. *Criminology, 17*, 477-484.

Carroll, L. (1974). *Hacks, blacks, and cons: Race relations in a maximum security prison.* Lexington, MA: Lexington.

Carroll, L. (1990). Race, ethnicity, and the social order of the prison. In D.H. Kelly (Ed.), *Criminal behavior: Text and readings in criminology* (2nd ed., pp. 510-527). New York: St. Martin's.

Carroll, L., & Mondrick, M.E. (1976). Racial bias in the decision to grant parole. *Law & Society Review, 11*, 93-107.

Chilton, R. (1993). Twenty-five years after the crime commission report: Is the field still data starved? *The Criminologist, 18* (5), pp. 1, 6-8.

Christianson, S. (1980). Legal implications of racially disproportionate incarceration rates. *Criminal Law Bulletin, 16*, 59-63.

Christianson, S. (1981). Our black prisons. *Crime & Delinquency, 27*, 364-375.

Cicourel, A.V. (1968). *The social organization of juvenile justice.* New York: John Wiley & Sons.

Clarke, F.I. (1991). Hate violence in the United States. *FBI Law Enforcement Bulletin, 60*, 14-17.

Clarke, S.H., & Koch, G.G. (1976). The influence of income and other factors on whether criminal defendants go to prison. *Law & Society Review, 11*, 57-92.

Clines, F.X. (1993, February 7). When black soldiers were hanged: A war's footnote. *The New York Times*, p. 20.

Cloward, R.A., & Ohlin, L.E. (1960). *Delinquency and opportunity: A theory of delinquent gangs.* New York: Free Press.

Cohen, A.K. (1955). *Delinquent boys: The culture of the gang.* New York: Free Press.

Cohn, S.F., Barkan, S.E., & Halteman, W.A. (1991). Punitive attitudes toward criminals: Racial consensus or racial conflict? *Social Problems, 38*, 287-296.

Colbert, D.L. (1990). Challenging the challenge: Thirteenth Amendment as a prohibition against the racial use of peremptory challenges. *Cornell Law Review, 76*, 1-128.

Corzine, J., Creech, J., & Corzine, L. (1983). Black concentration and lynchings in the South: Testing Blalock's power-threat hypothesis. *Social Forces, 61*, 774-796.

Corzine, J., & Huff-Corzine, L. (1992). Racial inequality and black homicide: An analysis of felony, nonfelony and total rates. *Journal of Contemporary Criminal Justice, 8*, 150-165.

Crew, B.K. (1991). Race differences in felony charging and sentencing: Toward an integration of decision-making and negotiation models. *Journal of Crime & Justice, 14*, 99-122.

Crouch, B.A. (1984). A spirit of lawlessness: White violence; Texas blacks, 1865-1868. *Journal of Social History, 18*, 217-232.

Crouch, B.M., & Alpert, G.P. (1982). Sex and occupational socialization among prison guards: A longitudinal study. *Criminal Justice & Behavior, 9,* 159-176.

Cullen, F., Link, B., Wolfe, N., & Frank, J. (1985). The social dimension of correctional officer stress. *Justice Quarterly, 2,* 505-533.

Curriden, M. (1992). Selective prosecution: Are black officials investigative targets? *ABA Journal, 78,* 54-57.

Dannefer, D., & Schutt, R.K. (1982). Race and juvenile justice processing in court and police agencies. *American Journal of Sociology, 87,* 1113-1132.

Dantzler, W.G., Jr. (1991). *Why black males are conditioned to fail.* East Saint Louis, IL: Essai Seay Publications.

Death penalty offenses. (1994, August 27). *Waco Tribune-Herald,* p. 11A.

"Disturbing increase" reported in young black male homicides. (1990, December 17). *Crime Control Digest, 24,* pp. 1 & 4.

Dorworth, V.E., & Henry, M. (1992). Optical illusions: The visual representation of blacks and women in introductory criminal justice textbooks. *Journal of Criminal Justice Education, 3,* 251-260.

Duster, T. (1987). Crime, youth unemployment, and the black urban underclass. *Crime & Delinquency, 33,* 300-316.

Dye, T.R. (1994). *Politics in America.* Englewood Cliffs, NJ: Prentice-Hall.

Earley, P. (1992). *The hot house: Life inside Leavenworth prison.* New York: Bantam Books.

Ekland-Olson, S. (1988). Structured discretion, racial bias, and the death penalty: The first decade after *Furman* in Texas. *Social Science Quarterly, 69,* 853-873.

Elliott, D.S., & Ageton, S.S. (1980). Reconciling race and class differences in self-reported and official estimates of delinquency. *American Sociological Review, 45,* 95-110.

Ellison, C.G. (1991). An eye for an eye? A note on the southern subculture of violence thesis. *Social Forces, 69,* 1223-1239.

Eterno, J.A. (1993, March). Ethnicity and sentencing: A study of the effect of ethnicity on sentencing of female prostitutes in New York City. Paper presented at the meeting of the Academy of Criminal Justice Sciences, Kansas City, MO.

Evolution of a crime bill. (1994, September 5). *Time,* p. 23.

Fagan, J., & Deschenes, E.P. (1990). Determinants of judicial waiver decisions for violent juvenile offenders. *Journal of Criminal Law & Criminology, 81*, 314-347.

Fagan, J., Forst, M., & Vivona, T.S. (1987). Racial determinants of the judicial transfer decision: Prosecuting violent youth in criminal court. *Crime & Delinquency, 33*, 259-286.

Fagan, J., Slaughter, E., & Hartstone, E. (1987). Blind justice? The impact of race on the juvenile justice process. *Crime & Delinquency, 33*, 224-258.

Farnworth, M., & Horan, P.M. (1980). Separate justice: An analysis of race differences in court processes. *Social Science Research, 9*, 381-399.

Federal Bureau of Investigation. (1993). *Crime in the United States, 1992*. Washington, DC: U.S. Government Printing Office.

Federal Bureau of Investigation. (1994). *Hate crime--1993* (Press release from the Criminal Justice Information Services Division). Washington, DC: U.S. Department of Justice.

Felkenes, G.T. (nd). *Executive summary: The impact of* Fanchon Blake v. the city of Los Angeles *on the selection, recruitment, training, appointment, and performance of women and minorities for the Los Angeles police department and the city of Los Angeles*. Claremont Graduate School, Center for Politics and Policy.

Ferdinand, T.N., & Luchterhand, E.G. (1970). Inner-city youth, the police, the juvenile court, and justice. *Social Problems, 17*, 510-527.

Flanagan, T.J., & Maguire, K. (Eds.) (1992). *Sourcebook of criminal justice statistics 1991* (U.S. Department of Justice, Bureau of Justice Statistics). Washington, DC: U.S. Government Printing Office.

Flowers, R.B. (1990). *Minorities and criminality*. New York: Praeger.

Fong, R.S. (1990). The organizational structure of prison gangs: A Texas case study. *Federal Probation, 54*, 36-43.

Fong, R.S., & Buentello, S. (1991). The detection of prison gang development: An empirical assessment. *Federal Probation, 55*, 66-69.

Fox, J.G. (1982). *Organizational and racial conflict in maximum-security prisons*. Lexington, MA: Lexington Books.

Franklin, J.H. (1968). Jim Crow goes to school: The genesis of legal segregation in the South. In C.E. Wynes (Ed.), *The negro in the*

South since 1865: Selected essays in American negro history (pp. 135-148). New York: Harper Colophon Books.

Frazier, C.E., Bishop, D.M., & Henretta, J.C. (1992). The social context of race differentials in juvenile justice dispositions. *Sociological Quarterly, 33,* 447-458.

Free, M.D., Jr. (1991). Clarifying the relationship between the broken home and juvenile delinquency: A critique of the current literature. *Deviant Behavior, 12,* 109-167.

French, H.W. (1987, November 1). New York's police feel the chill of racial tension. *The New York Times,* p. 6E.

French, L. (1983). A profile of the incarcerated black female offender. *The Prison Journal, 63,* 80-87.

Fukurai, H., Butler, E.W., & Krooth, R. (1993). *Race and the jury: Racial disenfranchisement and the search for justice.* New York: Plenum.

Fyfe, J. (1981). Who shoots? A look at officer race and police shooting. *Journal of Police Science & Administration, 9,* 367-382.

Fyfe, J. (1986). *Police personnel practices, baseline data reports* (Vol. 18, No. 6). Washington, D.C.: International City Management Association.

Garfinkel, H. (1956). Conditions of successful degradation ceremonies. *American Journal of Sociology, 61,* 420-424.

Geller, W.A. (1982). Deadly force: What we know. *Journal of Police Science & Administration, 10,* 151-177.

Genovese, E.D. (1974). *Roll, Jordan, roll: The world the slaves made.* New York: Pantheon Books.

Georges-Abeyie, D. (interviewer). (1984a). Black police officers: An interview with Alfred W. Dean, Director of Public Safety, city of Harrisburg, Pennsylvania. In D. Georges-Abeyie (Ed.), *The criminal justice system and blacks* (pp. 161-165). New York: Clark Boardman.

Georges-Abeyie, D. (1984b). The criminal justice system and minorities--A review of the literature. In D. Georges-Abeyie (Ed.), *The criminal justice system and blacks* (pp. 125-156). New York: Clark Boardman.

Georges-Abeyie, D. (1989). Race, ethnicity, and the spatial dynamic: Toward a realistic study of black crime, crime victimization, and criminal justice processing of blacks. *Social Justice, 16,* 35-54.

Gerstenfeld, P.B. (1994, March). Race and allegations of hate crime offenses: What the statistics can tell us. Paper presented at the meeting of the Academy of Criminal Justice Sciences, Chicago, IL.

Gibbons, D.C., & Krohn, M.D. (1991). *Delinquent behavior* (5th ed.). Englewood Cliffs, NJ: Prentice-Hall.

Gibson, J.L. (1978). Race as a determinant of criminal sentences: A methodological critique and a case study. *Law & Society Review, 12*, 455-478.

Goetting, A. (1985). Racism, sexism, and ageism in the prison community. *Federal Probation, 49*, 10-22.

Goetting, A., & Howsen, R.M. (1983). Blacks and prison: A profile. *Criminal Justice Review, 8*, 21-31.

Goldberg, H. (1993, August 27). Poll: Equal justice dream for minority. *Waco Tribune-Herald*, pp. 1A, 11A.

Golden, R.M., & Messner, S.F. (1987). Dimensions of racial inequality and rates of violent crime. *Criminology, 25*, 525-541.

Goldman, N. (1963). *The differential selection of offenders for court appearance*. Washington, DC: National Research & Information Center on Crime & Delinquency.

Goodstein, L., & MacKenzie, D.L. (1984). Racial differences in adjustment patterns of prison inmates--Prisonization, conflict, stress, and control. In D. Georges-Abeyie (Ed.), *The criminal justice system and blacks* (pp. 271-306). New York: Clark Boardman.

Goring, C.B. (1913). *The English convict: A statistical study*. London: His Majesty's Stationery Office.

Gottschall, J. (1983). Carter's judicial appointments: The influence of affirmative action and merit selection on voting on the U.S. Courts of Appeals. *Judicature, 67*, 165-173.

Gould, L.C. (1969). Who defines delinquency: A comparison of self-reported and officially reported indices of delinquency for three racial groups. *Social Problems, 16*, 325-336.

Gould, S.J. (1994, November 28). Curveball. *The New Yorker*, pp. 139-149.

Green, E. (1970). Race, social status, and criminal arrest. *American Sociological Review, 35*, 476-490.

Hagan, F.E. (1990). *Introduction to criminology: Theories, methods, and criminal behavior*. Chicago, IL: Nelson-Hall.

Hagan, J. (1974). Extra-legal attributes and criminal sentencing: An assessment of a sociological viewpoint. *Law & Society Review, 8,* 357-383.

Hagan, J., & Albonetti, C. (1982). Race, class, and the perception of criminal injustice in America. *American Journal of Sociology, 88,* 329-355.

Hagan, J., Gillis, A.R., & Simpson, J. (1985). The class structure of gender and delinquency: Toward a power-control theory of common delinquent behavior. *American Journal of Sociology, 90,* 1151-1178.

Hamilton, D. (1994, May 10). Gay men become number one hate-crime targets. *The Los Angeles Times,* pp. B1, B4.

Harer, M.D., & Steffensmeier, D. (1992). The differing effects of economic inequality on black and white rates of violence. *Social Forces, 70,* 1035-1054.

Hawkins, D.F. (1983). Black and white homicide differentials: Alternatives to inadequate theory. *Criminal Justice and Behavior, 10,* 407-440.

Hawkins, D.F. (1986). Race, crime type and imprisonment. *Justice Quarterly, 3,* 251-269.

Hawkins, D.F., & Hardy, K.A. (1989). Black-white imprisonment rates: A state-by-state analysis. *Social Justice, 16,* 75-94.

Heard, C.A., & Bing, R.L., III. (1993). African American faculty and students on predominantly white university campuses. *Journal of Criminal Justice Education, 4,* 1-13.

Heilbrun, A.B., Jr., Foster, A., & Golden, J. (1989). The death sentence in Georgia, 1974-1987: Criminal justice or racial injustice? *Criminal Justice & Behavior, 16,* 139-154.

Herrnstein, R.J., & Murray, C. (1994). *The bell curve: Intelligence and class structure in American life.* New York: Free Press.

Hickey, E.W. (1991). *Serial murderers and their victims.* Pacific Grove, CA: Brooks/Cole.

Hindelang, M.J. (1978). Race and involvement in common law personal crimes. *American Sociological Review, 43,* 93-109.

Hirschi, T. (1969). *Causes of delinquency.* Berkeley, CA: University of California Press.

Hirschi, T., & Hindelang, M. (1977). Intelligence and delinquency: A revisionist review. *American Sociological Review, 42,* 471-486.

Hochstedler, E. (1984). Impediments to hiring minorities in public police agencies. *Journal of Police Science & Administration, 12*, 227-240.

Holmes, M.D., & Daudistel, H.C. (1984). Ethnicity and justice in the southwest: The sentencing of anglo, black, and Mexican origin defendants. *Social Science Quarterly, 65*, 265-277.

Holmes, M.D., Daudistel, H.C., & Farrell, R.A. (1987). Determinants of charge reductions and final dispositions in cases of burglary and robbery. *Journal of Research in Crime & Delinquency, 24*, 233-254.

Huff-Corzine, L., Corzine, J., & Moore, D.C. (1991). Deadly connections: Culture, poverty, and the direction of lethal violence. *Social Forces, 69*, 715-732.

Hughes, M., & Hertel, B.R. (1990). The significance of color remains: A study of life chances, mate selection, and ethnic consciousness among black Americans. *Social Forces, 68*, 1105-1120.

Huizinga, D., & Elliott, D.S. (1987). Juvenile offenders: Prevalence, offender incidence, and arrest rates by race. *Crime & Delinquency, 33*, 206-223.

Humphrey, J.A., & Fogarty, T.J. (1987). Race and plea bargained outcomes: A research note. *Social Forces, 66*, 176-182.

Inciardi, J.A. (1990). *Criminal justice* (3rd ed.). New York: Harcourt Brace Jovanovich.

Independent Commission on the Los Angeles Police Department. (1991). *Report of the independent commission on the Los Angeles police department.* Los Angeles, CA: Author.

Jackman, M.R. (1978). General and applied tolerance: Does education increase commitment to racial integration? *American Journal of Political Science, 22*, 302-324.

Jackson, P.I. (1986). Black visibility, city size, and social control. *Sociological Quarterly, 27*, 185-203.

Jackson, P.I., & Carroll, L. (1981). Race and the war on crime: The sociopolitical determinants of municipal police expenditures in 90 non-southern U.S. cities. *American Sociological Review, 46*, 290-305.

Jackson, R.L., & Ostrow, R.J. (1994, August 27). Justice to distribute anti-crime funds. *Waco Tribune-Herald*, p. 10A.

Jacobs, J.B., & Grear, M.P. (1977). Dropouts and rejects: An analysis of the prison guard's revolving door. *Criminal Justice Review, 2*, 57-70.

Jacobs, J.B., & Kraft, L.J. (1978). Integrating the keepers: A comparison of black and white prison guards in Illinois. *Social Problems, 25,* 304-318.

Jendrek, M.P. (1984). Sentence length: Interactions with race and court. *Journal of Criminal Justice, 12,* 567-578.

Johnson, L.B. (1989). The employed black: The dynamics of work-family tension. *The Review of Black Political Economy, 17,* 69-85.

Jones, J. (1981). *Bad blood: The Tuskegee syphilis experiment--A tragedy of race and medicine.* New York: Free Press.

Jurik, N.C. (1985). Individual and organizational determinants of correctional officer attitudes toward inmates. *Criminology, 23,* 523-539.

Jurik, N.C., & Winn, R. (1987). Describing correctional-security dropouts and rejects: An individual or organizational profile? *Criminal Justice & Behavior, 14,* 5-25.

Kamin, L.J. (1995, February). Behind the curve. *Scientific American,* pp. 99-103.

Kauffman, K. (1988). *Prison officers and their world.* Cambridge, MA: Harvard University Press.

Keil, T.J., & Vito, G.F. (1989). Race, homicide severity, and application of the death penalty: A consideration of the Barnett scale. *Criminology, 27,* 511-535.

Keil, T.J., & Vito, G.F. (1990). Race and the death penalty in Kentucky murder trials: An analysis of post-*Gregg* outcomes. *Justice Quarterly, 7,* 189-207.

Keil, T.J., & Vito, G.F. (1992). The effects of the *Furman* and *Gregg* decisions on black-white execution ratios in the South. *Journal of Criminal Justice, 20,* 217-226.

Keith, V.M., & Herring, C. (1991). Skin tone and stratification in the black community. *American Journal of Sociology, 97,* 760-778.

Kempf, K.L., & Austin, R.L. (1986). Older and more recent evidence on racial discrimination in sentencing. *Journal of Quantitative Criminology, 2,* 29-48.

Kennedy, L.W., & Baron, S.W. (1993). Routine activities and a subculture of violence: A study of violence on the street. *Journal of Research in Crime & Delinquency, 30,* 88-112.

Kirkegaard-Sorensen, L., & Mednick, S.A. (1977). A prospective study of predictors of criminality: Intelligence. In S.A. Mednick &

K.O. Christiansen (Eds.), *Biosocial bases of criminal behavior* (pp. 267-273). New York: Gardner Press.

Kitsuse, J., & Dietrick, D. (1959). Delinquent boys: A critique. *American Sociological Review*, *24*, 208-215.

Kleck, G. (1981). Racial discrimination in criminal sentencing: A critical evaluation of the evidence with additional evidence on the death penalty. *American Sociological Review*, *46*, 783-805.

Klein, H.S. (1967). *Slavery in the Americas: A comparative study of Virginia and Cuba*. Chicago: University of Chicago Press.

Klein, S., Petersilia, J., & Turner, S. (1990). Race and imprisonment decisions in California. *Science*, *247*, 812-816.

Klofas, J.M. (1986). Discretion among correctional officers: The influence of urbanization, age and race. *International Journal of Offender Therapy & Comparative Criminology*, *30*, 111-124.

Koch, W. (1994, September 5). Study: Wages continue to fall, minorities hit hardest. *Wausau Daily Herald*, p. 10A.

Kowalski, G.S., & Rickicki, J.P. (1982). Determinants of juvenile postadjudication dispositions. *Journal of Research in Crime & Delinquency*, *19*, 66-83.

Kposowa, A.J., & Breault, K.D. (1993). Reassessing the structural covariates of U.S. homicide rates: A county level study. *Sociological Focus*, *26*, 27-46.

Kramer, J., & Steffensmeir, D. (1993). Race and imprisonment decisions. *Sociological Quarterly*, *34*, 357-376.

Krisberg, B., Schwartz, I., Fishman, G., Eisikovits, Z., Guttman, E., & Joe, K. (1987). The incarceration of minority youth. *Crime & Delinquency*, *33*, 173-205.

Kruttschnitt, C. (1983). Race relations and the female inmate. *Crime & Delinquency*, *29*, 577-592.

Kruttschnitt, C., & Krmpotich, S. (1990). Aggressive behavior among female inmates: An exploratory study. *Justice Quarterly*, *7*, 371-389.

Kvaraceus, W., & Miller, W.B. (1967). Norm-violating behavior in middle-class culture. In E.W. Vaz (Ed.), *Middle-class delinquency* (pp. 233-241). New York: Harper & Row.

LaFree, G. (1980). The effect of sexual stratification by race on official reactions to rape. *American Sociological Review*, *45*, 842-854.

LaFree, G., Drass, K.A., & O'Day, P. (1992). Race and crime in postwar America: Determinants of African American and white rates, 1957-1988. *Criminology, 30,* 157-188.

Lane, C. (1994, December 1). The tainted sources of "The bell curve." *The New York Review of Books,* pp. 14-19.

Langan, P.A. (1985). Racism on trial: New evidence to explain the racial composition of prisons in the United States. *Journal of Criminal Law & Criminology, 76,* 666-683.

Larsen, P. (1991, July 10). Racism "widespread" in LAPD: Panel cites comments on patrol-car computers. *The San Bernardino Sun,* p. 1A.

Leinen, S. (1984). *Black police, white society.* New York: New York University Press.

Less racial disparity in death sentences? (1983, November 7). *Criminal Justice Newsletter, 14,* pp. 7-8.

Letman, S.T., & Scott, H., Jr. (1981, November 9). For blacks and social justice, it's still "the dream deferred." *Law Enforcement News, 7,* pp. 6 & 13.

Levin, J., & McDevitt, J. (1993). *Hate crimes: The rising tide of bigotry and bloodshed.* New York: Plenum.

Lewis, D.O., Shanok, S.S., Cohen, R.J., Kligfeld, M., & Frisone, G. (1980). Race bias in the diagnosis and disposition of violent adolescents. *American Journal of Psychiatry, 137,* 1211-1216.

Lewis, W.G. (1989). Toward representative bureaucracy: Blacks in city police organizations, 1975-1985. *Public Administration Review, 49,* 257-268.

Liska, A.E., & Chamlin, M.B. (1984). Social structure and crime control among macrosocial units. *American Journal of Sociology, 90,* 383-395.

Lizotte, A.J. (1978). Extra-legal factors in Chicago's criminal courts: Testing the conflict model of criminal justice. *Social Problems, 25,* 564-580.

Locke, H.G. (1979). *The impact of affirmative action and civil service on American police personnel systems.* Chicago: Public Administration Service.

Luckenbill, D.F., & Doyle, D.P. (1989). Structural position and violence: Developing a cultural explanation. *Criminology, 27,* 419-436.

Lundman, R., Sykes, R.E., & Clark, J.P. (1978). Police control of juveniles: A replication. *Journal of Research in Crime & Delinquency, 15*, 74-91.

Lynch, M.J., & Patterson, E.B. (1991). *Race and criminal justice.* Albany, NY: Harrow & Heston.

Macionis, J.J. (1991). *Sociology* (3rd ed.). Englewood Cliffs, NJ: Prentice-Hall.

Maghan, J. (1993). The changing face of the police officer: Occupational socialization of minority police recruits. In R.C. Dunham & G.P. Alpert (Eds.), *Critical issues in policing: Contemporary readings* (2nd ed., pp. 348-360). Prospect Heights, IL: Waveland Press.

Maghan, J., & McLeish-Blackwell, L. (1991). Black women in correctional employment. In J.B. Morton (Ed.), *Change, challenge and choices: Women's role in modern corrections* (pp. 82-99). Laurel, MD: American Correctional Association.

Malcolm, A.H. (1990, April 23). New police chiefs put new ideas on the force. *The New York Times*, p. 12A.

Mann, C.R. (1984). Race and sentencing of female felons: A field study. *International Journal of Women's Studies, 7*, 160-172.

Mann, C.R. (1993). *Unequal justice: A question of color.* Bloomington, IN: Indiana University Press.

Marquart, J.W. (1986). Prison guards and the use of physical coercion as a mechanism of prisoner control. *Criminology, 24*, 347-366.

Marquart, J.W., & Crouch, B.M. (1985). Judicial reform and prisoner control: The impact of *Ruiz v. Estelle* on a Texas penitentiary. *Law & Society Review, 19*, 557-586.

Martin, R., Mutchnick, R.J., & Austin, W.T. (1990). *Criminological thought: Pioneers past and present.* New York: Macmillan.

Martin, S.E. (1993). Female officers on the move? A status report on women in policing. In R.G. Dunham & G.P. Alpert (Eds.), *Critical issues in policing: Contemporary readings* (2nd ed., pp. 327-347). Prospect Heights, IL: Waveland Press.

Martin, S.E. (1994). "Outsider within" the station house: The impact of race and gender on black women police. *Social Problems, 41*, 383-400.

Martino, M. (1989). Georgia study reveals racial bias in sentencing. *National Prison Project, 20*, p. 8.

Matza, D. (1964). *Delinquency and drift.* New York: John Wiley.

Mauer, M. (1990). *Young black men and the criminal justice system: A growing national problem.* Washington, DC: The Sentencing Project.

McCarthy, B.R., & Smith, B.L. (1986). The conceptualization of discrimination in the juvenile justice process: The impact of administrative factors and screening decisions on juvenile court dispositions. *Criminology, 24,* 41-64.

McCormick, D. (1994, June 8). Rangers swear in first black woman. *Waco Tribune-Herald,* pp. 1A, 6A.

McGarrell, E.F. (1993). Trends in racial disproportionality in juvenile court processing: 1985-1989. *Crime & Delinquency, 39,* 29-48.

McKee, J.B. (1993). *Sociology and the race problem: The failure of a perspective.* Champaign, IL: University of Illinois Press.

McNeely, R.L., & Pope, C.E. (1980). Racial issues in the measurement of criminal involvement. *Journal of African-Afro-American Affairs, 4,* 9-26.

McShane, M.D., Pelfrey, W.V., & Williams, F.P., III. (1986). *Eligibility for jury service in capital trials: A question of potential exclusion and bias.* Huntsville, TX: Sam Houston State University, Research Program of the Criminal Justice Center.

Merton, R.K. (1938). Social structure and anomie. *American Sociological Review, 3,* 672-682.

Messner, S.F., & Golden, R.M. (1992). Racial inequality and racially disaggregated homicide rates: An assessment of alternative theoretical explanations. *Criminology, 30,* 421-447.

Meyer, C.L., Larson, P., & Markway, L.D. (1994, March). Hate crimes and the criminal justice system. Paper presented at the meeting of the Academy of Criminal Justice Sciences, Chicago, IL.

Meyer, M.W. (1980). Police shootings at minorities: The case of Los Angeles. *Annals of the American Academy of Political & Social Science, 452,* 98-110.

Michalowski, R.J. (1985). *Order, law and crime.* New York: Random House.

Miethe, T.D., & Moore, C.A. (1986). Racial differences in criminal processing: The consequences of model selection on conclusions about differential treatment. *Sociological Quarterly, 27,* 217-237.

Miller, W. (1958). Lower-class culture as a generating milieu of gang delinquency. *Journal of Social Issues, 14* (3), 5-19.

Mitford, J. (1974). *Kind and usual punishment: The prison business.* New York: Vintage.

Mobley, L. (1982). Construction of new prisons: Increased oppression of minorities. *The Crisis, 89* (3), 13-14.

Moore, R. (1983). Strategies for increasing the number of black police executives (conclusion). *FBI Law Enforcement Bulletin, 52,* 14-20.

Morsch, J. (1991). The problem of motive in hate crimes: The argument against presumptions of racial motivation. *Journal of Criminal Law & Criminology, 82,* 659-689.

Morstain, B.R. (1984). Minority-white differences on a police aptitude exam: EEO implications for police selection. *Psychological Reports, 55,* 515-525.

Mydans, S. (1991, March 29). Los Angeles force accused from within. *The New York Times,* p. 10A.

Myers, M.A., & Massey, J.L. (1991). Race, labor, and punishment in postbellum Georgia. *Social Problems, 38,* 267-286.

Myers, M.A., & Talarico, S.M. (1986). The social contexts of racial discrimination in sentencing. *Social Problems, 33,* 236-251.

Myers, S.L., Jr. (1985). Statistical tests of discrimination in punishment. *Journal of Quantitative Criminology, 1,* 191-218.

Myrdal, G. (1987). Inequality of justice. *Review of Black Political Economy, 16,* 81-98.

Nelson, J.F. (1992). Hidden disparities in case processing: New York State, 1985-1986. *Journal of Criminal Justice, 20,* 181-200.

Nettler, G. (1974). *Explaining crime.* New York: McGraw-Hill.

New prisons chief targets toughest criminals. (1991, May 20). *Tampa Tribune,* pp. 1, 4.

New warden faces task of transforming post-riot Atlanta pen. (1990, January 15). *Atlanta Journal,* pp. D1, D3.

Newman, D.J., & Anderson, P.R. (1989). *Introduction to criminal justice* (4th ed.). New York: Random House.

Nye, F.I., Short, J.F., Jr., & Olson, V.J. (1958). Socioeconomic status and delinquent behavior. *American Journal of Sociology, 63,* 381-389.

Office of National Drug Control Policy. (1992). *National drug control strategy: A nation responds to drug use.* Washington, DC: U.S. Government Printing Office.

O'Reilly, J.M. (1979). Jury representation by neighborhood. In R. Alvarez, K.G. Lutterman, & Associates (Eds.), *Discrimination in organizations: Using social indicators to manage social change* (pp. 300-328). San Francisco: Jossey-Bass.

Owen, B.A. (1985). Race and gender relations among prison workers. *Crime & Delinquency, 31,* 147-159.

Paternoster, R. (1983). Race of victim and location of crime: The decision to seek the death penalty in South Carolina. *Journal of Criminal Law & Criminology, 74,* 754-785.

Paternoster, R. (1984). Prosecutorial discretion in requesting the death penalty: A case of victim-based racial discrimination. *Law & Society Review, 18,* 437-478.

Patterson, E.B., & Lynch, M.J. (1991). Bias in formalized bail procedures. In M.J. Lynch & E.B. Patterson (Eds.), *Race and criminal justice* (pp. 36-53). Albany, NY: Harrow & Heston.

Peek, C.W., Lowe, G.D., & Alston, J.P. (1981). Race and attitudes toward local police: Another look. *Journal of Black Studies, 11,* 361-374.

Petersilia, J. (1979). Which inmates participate in prison treatment programs? *Journal of Offender Counseling, Services & Rehabilitation, 4,* 121-135.

Petersilia, J. (1983). *Racial disparities in the criminal justice system.* Santa Monica, CA: Rand.

Petersilia, J., & Turner, S. (1988, June). Minorities in prison: Discrimination or disparity? *Corrections Today, 50,* pp. 92-94.

Peterson, R.D. (1988). Youthful offender designations and sentencing in the New York criminal courts. *Social Problems, 35,* 111-130.

Piliavin, I., & Briar, S. (1964). Police encounters with juveniles. *American Journal of Sociology, 69,* 206-214.

Pinkney, A. (1987). *Black Americans* (3rd ed.). Englewood Cliffs, NJ: Prentice-Hall.

Pisciotta, A.W. (1983). Race, sex, and rehabilitation: A study of differential treatment in the juvenile reformatory, 1825-1900. *Crime & Delinquency, 29,* 254-269.

Police car tipped in protest. (1993, October 11). *Wausau Daily Herald,* p. 4A.

Poll: Young more anti-black. (1993, June 13). *Wausau Daily Herald,* p. 7A.

Pollock-Byrne, J.M. (1990). *Women, prison, and crime.* Pacific Grove, CA: Brooks/Cole.

Poole, E.D., & Regoli, R. (1980). Race, institutional rule breaking, and disciplinary response: A study of discretionary decision making in prison. *Law & Society Review, 14,* 931-946.

Poole, E.D., & Regoli, R. (1983, March). Self-reported and observed rule-breaking: A look at disciplinary response. Paper presented at the meeting of the Academy of Criminal Justice Sciences, San Antonio, TX.

Pope, C.E. (1979). Race and crime revisited. *Crime & Delinquency, 25,* 347-357.

Pope, C.E., & Feyerherm, W.H. (1981). Race and juvenile court dispositions: An examination of initial screening decisions. *Criminal Justice & Behavior, 8,* 287-301.

Pope, C.E., & Ross, L.E. (1992). Race, crime and justice: The aftermath of Rodney King. *The Criminologist, 17* (6), pp. 1, 7-10.

Pope, L. (1991, May 26). Department lags in hiring practices despite 10-year-old court agreement. *The San Bernardino Sun,* p. 12A.

Potter, J. (1980). Should women guards work in prisons for men? *Corrections Magazine, 6* (5), 30-38.

Poussaint, A.F. (1983). Black-on-black homicide: A psychological-political perspective. *Victimology, 8,* 161-169.

Promotion--19-year-old affirmative action plan no longer serves compelling state interest--Plan terminated by court order. (1993, October). *Police Officer Grievances Bulletin,* pp. 3-4.

Promotion--Police department affirmative action promotion quota constitutional. (1993, August). *Police Officer Grievances Bulletin,* pp. 3-4.

Pruitt, C.R., & Wilson, J.Q. (1983). A longitudinal study of the effect of race on sentencing. *Law & Society Review, 17,* 613-635.

Quinn, J.F., & Downs, W. (1993). Police perceptions of the severity of local gang problems: An analysis of noncriminal predictors. *Sociological Spectrum, 13,* 209-226.

Rabinowitz, H.N. (1976). From exclusion to segregation: Southern race relations, 1865-1890. *Journal of American History, 63,* 325-350.

Radelet, M.L. (1981). Racial characteristics and the imposition of the death penalty. *American Sociological Review, 46,* 918-927.

Radelet, M.L. (1989). Executions of whites for crimes against blacks: Exceptions to the rule? *Sociological Quarterly, 30,* 529-544.

Radelet, M.L., & Pierce, G.L. (1985). Race and prosecutorial discretion in homicide cases. *Law & Society Review, 19,* 587-621.

Ralph, P.H., Sorensen, J.R., & Marquart, J.W. (1992). A comparison of death-sentenced and incarcerated murderers in pre-*Furman* Texas. *Justice Quarterly, 9,* 185-209.

Ramirez, J. (1983). Race and the apprehension of inmate misconduct. *Journal of Criminal Justice, 11,* 413-427.

Reynolds, L.H., & Flynn, M.S. (1981). Retention rates of minority police officers. *Urban League Review, 6,* 62-70.

Roberts, J.V., & Gabor, T. (1990). Lombrosian wine in a new bottle: Research on crime and race. *Canadian Journal of Criminology, 32,* 291-313.

Rogers, R. (1991). The effects of educational level on correctional officer job satisfaction. *Journal of Criminal Justice, 19,* 123-137.

Rose, H.M. (1987). Homicide and minorities. *Public Health Reports, 102,* 613-615.

Ross, L.E. (1992). Blacks, self-esteem, and delinquency: It's time for a new approach. *Justice Quarterly, 9,* 609-624.

Russell, K., Wilson, M., & Hall, R. (1992). *The color complex: The politics of skin color among African Americans.* New York: Harcourt Brace Jovanovich.

Russell, K.K. (1992). Development of a black criminology and the role of the black criminologist. *Justice Quarterly, 9,* 667-683.

Sabol, W.J. (1989). Racially disproportionate prison populations in the United States. *Contemporary Crises, 13,* 405-432.

Sampson, R.J. (1986). Effects of socioeconomic context on official reaction to juvenile delinquency. *American Sociological Review, 51,* 876-885.

Savitz, L. (1982). Official statistics. In L. Savitz & N. Johnston (Eds.), *Contemporary criminology* (pp. 3-15). New York: John Wiley.

Scaglion, R., & Condon, R.G. (1980). The structure of black and white attitudes toward police. *Human Organization, 39,* 280-283.

Schaefer, R.T. (1984). *Racial and ethnic groups* (2nd ed.). Boston: Little, Brown and Company.

Schrag, C. (1971). *Crime and justice: American style.* Washington, DC: U.S. Government Printing Office.

Schuman, H., Steeh, C., & Bobo, L. (1985). *Racial attitudes in America: Trends and interpretations*. Cambridge, MA: Harvard University Press.

Senate sends anti-crime bill to Clinton. (1994, August 26). *Wausau Daily Herald*, pp. 1A, 2A.

Serr, B.J., & Maney, M. (1988). Racism, peremptory challenges, and the democratic jury: The jurisprudence of a delicate balance. *Journal of Criminal Law & Criminology, 79*, 1-65.

Shapiro, S.R. (1985). Juries under judgment. *Human Rights, 13*, 32-37.

Sheldon, W. (1949). *Varieties of delinquent youth*. New York: Harper Brothers.

Shoemaker, D.J. (1990). *Theories of delinquency: An examination of explanations of delinquent behavior* (2nd ed.). New York: Oxford University Press.

Shoemaker, D.J., & Williams, J.S. (1987). The subculture of violence and ethnicity. *Journal of Criminal Justice, 15*, 461-472.

Short, J.F., Jr., & Nye, F.I. (1958). Extent of unrecorded delinquency: Tentative conclusions. *Journal of Criminal Law, Criminology and Police Science, 49*, 296-302.

Siegel, L.J. (1992). *Criminology* (4th ed.). St. Paul, MN: West.

Siegel, L.J., & Senna, J.J. (1991). *Juvenile delinquency: Theory, practice and law* (4th ed.). St. Paul, MN: West.

Sieverdes, C.M., & Bartollas, C. (1982). Race, sex, and juvenile inmate roles. *Deviant Behavior, 3*, 203-218.

Simons, R.L., & Gray, P.A. (1989). Perceived blocked opportunity as an explanation of delinquency among lower-class black males: A research note. *Journal of Research in Crime & Delinquency, 26*, 90-101.

Simpson, S., & White, M.F. (1985). The female guard in the all-male prison. In I.L. Moyer (Ed.), *The changing roles of women in the criminal justice system: Offenders, victims, and professionals* (pp. 276-300). Prospect Heights, IL: Waveland Press.

Single-day study finds all blacks in state youth prisons. (1990, July 4). *Juvenile Justice Digest, 18*, pp. 5-6.

Slotnick, E. (1984). The paths to the federal bench: Gender, race and judicial recruitment variation. *Judicature, 67*, 371-388.

Smith, D.A., Graham, N., & Adams, B. (1991). Minorities and the police: Attudinal and behavioral questions. In M.J. Lynch & E.B.

Patterson (Eds.), *Race and criminal justice* (pp. 22-35). Albany, NY: Harrow & Heston.

Smith, D.A., & Visher, C.A. (1981). Street-level justice: Situational determinants of police arrest decisions. *Social Problems, 29,* 167-177.

Smith, D.A., Visher, C.A., & Davidson, L.A. (1984). Equity and discretionary justice: The influence of race on police arrest decisions. *Journal of Criminal Law & Criminology, 75,* 234-249.

Smith, M.D. (1983). *Race versus robe: The dilemma of black judges.* Port Washington, NY: National University Publications.

Smith, M.D. (1987). Patterns of discrimination in assessments of the death penalty: The case of Louisiana. *Journal of Criminal Justice, 15,* 279-286.

Sorensen, J.R., Marquart, J.W., & Brock, D.E. (1993). Factors related to killings of felons by police officers: A test of the community violence and conflict hypotheses. *Justice Quarterly, 10,* 417-440.

South, J. (1993, September 4). Minorities more likely to do time. *Waco Tribune-Herald,* pp. 1A, 12A.

Spohn, C. (1990a). Decision making in sexual assault cases: Do black and female judges make a difference? *Women & Criminal Justice, 2,* 83-105.

Spohn, C. (1990b). The sentencing decisions of black and white judges: Expected and unexpected similarities. *Law & Society Review, 24,* 1197-1216.

Spohn, C., & Cederblom, J. (1991). Race and disparities in sentencing: A test of the liberation hypothesis. *Justice Quarterly, 8,* 305-327.

Spohn, C., Gruhl, J., & Welch, S. (1981-1982). The effect of race on sentencing: A re-examination of an unsettled question. *Law & Society Review, 16,* 71-88.

Spohn, C., Gruhl, J., & Welch, S. (1987). The impact of the ethnicity and gender of defendants on the decision to reject or dismiss felony charges. *Criminology, 25,* 175-191.

Stewart, S.A. (1993, August 5). Judge "favorable" to defendants: Pins much of blame on King. *USA Today,* p. 3A.

Stewart, S.A., & Fields, G. (1993, August 5). Judge says King was "threat" to officers. *USA Today,* p. 1A.

Stolberg, S. (1992, July 21). Christopher panel drew map that showed Kolts the way. *The Los Angeles Times,* p. 19A.

Sullivan, P.S., Dunham, R.G., & Alpert, G.P. (1987). Attitude structures of different ethnic and age groups concerning police. *Journal of Criminal Law & Criminology, 78,* 177-196.

Takagi, P. (1981). Race, crime, and social policy: A minority perspective. *Crime & Delinquency, 27,* 48-63.

Tatum, B. (1994). The colonial model as a theoretical explanation of crime and delinquency. In A.T. Sulton (Ed.), *African American perspectives on: Crime causation, criminal justice administration and crime prevention* (pp. 33-52). Englewood, CO: Sulton Books.

Taylor Greene, H. (1994a). Black perspectives on police brutality. In A.T. Sulton (Ed.), *African American perspectives on: Crime causation, criminal justice administration and crime prevention* (pp. 139-148). Englewood, CO: Sulton Books.

Taylor Greene, H. (1994b, February). Black police in Virginia. Paper presented at the meeting of the National Association of African American Studies, Petersburg, VA.

Teahan, J.E. (1975). A longitudinal study of attitude shifts among black and white police officers. *Journal of Social Issues, 31,* 47-56.

Terry, R. (1967). The screening of juvenile offenders. *Journal of Criminal Law, Criminology & Police Science, 58,* 173-181.

Thomas, J. (1991). Racial codes in prison culture: Snapshots in black and white. In M.J. Lynch & E.B. Patterson (Eds.), *Race and criminal justice* (pp. 126-144). Albany, NY: Harrow & Heston.

Thomas, S.B., & Quinn, S.C. (1991). The Tuskegee syphilis study 1932 to 1972: Implications for HIV education and AIDS risk education programs in the black community. *American Journal of Public Health, 81,* 1498-1505.

Thomson, R.J., & Zingraff, M.T. (1981). Detecting sentencing disparity: Some problems and evidence. *American Journal of Sociology, 86,* 869-880.

Thornberry, T.P. (1973). Race, socioeconomic status and sentencing in the juvenile justice system. *Journal of Criminal Law & Criminology, 64,* 90-98.

Tittle, C., & Curran, D. (1988). Contingencies for dispositional disparities in juvenile justice. *Social Forces, 67,* 23-58.

Tittle, C., & Meier, R. (1990). Specifying the ses/delinquency relationship. *Criminology, 28,* 271-299.

Tittle, C., & Villemez, W. (1977). Social class and criminality. *Social Forces, 56,* 474-502.

Tittle, C., Villemez, W., & Smith, D. (1978). The myth of social class and criminality: An empirical assessment of the empirical evidence. *American Sociological Review, 43,* 643-656.

Toch, H. (1976). *Living in prison: The ecology of survival.* New York: John Wiley.

Toch, H., & Klofas, J. (1982). Alienation and desire for job enrichment among correction officers. *Federal Probation, 46,* 35-44.

Tollett, T., & Close, B.R. (1991). The overrepresentation of blacks in Florida's juvenile justice system. In M.J. Lynch & E.B. Patterson (Eds.), *Race and criminal justice* (pp. 86-99). Albany, NY: Harrow & Heston.

Trout, C.H. (1992, July). Taking a new look at an old problem. *Corrections Today,* pp. 62, 64, 66.

Turner, J.H., Singleton, R., Jr., & Musick, D. (1984). *Oppression: A socio-history of black-white relations in America.* Chicago: Nelson-Hall.

Twelve blind jurors. (1992, May 2). *The Economist, 323,* p. 27.

Uhlman, T.M. (1978). Black elite decision making: The case of trial judges. *American Journal of Political Science, 22,* 884-895.

Unnever, J.D. (1982). Direct and organizational discrimination in the sentencing of drug offenders. *Social Problems, 30,* 212-225.

Unnever, J.D., Frazier, C.E., & Henretta, J.C. (1980). Race differences in criminal sentencing. *Sociological Quarterly, 21,* 197-205.

Unnever, J.D., & Hembroff, L.A. (1988). The prediction of racial/ethnic sentencing disparities: An expectation states approach. *Journal of Research in Crime & Delinquency, 25,* 53-82.

U.S. Bureau of the Census. (1992). *Statistical abstract of the United States: 1992* (112th ed.). Washington, DC: U.S. Government Printing Office.

U.S. Department of Justice. (1988). *Report to the nation on crime and justice* (2nd ed.). Washington, DC: Bureau of Justice Statistics.

U.S. Department of Justice. (1990). *BJS data report, 1989* (Office of Justice Programs). Washington, DC: Bureau of Justice Statistics.

U.S. Department of Justice. (1992a). *Criminal victimization in the United States: 1973-1990 trends* (Office of Justice Programs). Washington, DC: Bureau of Justice Statistics.

U.S. Department of Justice. (1992b). *Criminal victimization in the United States, 1991* (Office of Justice Programs). Washington, DC: Bureau of Justice Statistics.

U.S. Department of Justice. (1993). *Survey of state prison inmates, 1991* (Office of Justice Programs). Washington, DC: Bureau of Justice Statistics.

U.S. Department of Justice. (1994a). *Crime and neighborhoods* (Office of Justice Programs). Washington, DC: Bureau of Justice Statistics.

U.S. Department of Justice. (1994b). *Criminal victimization in the United States, 1992* (Office of Justice Programs). Washington, DC: Bureau of Justice Statistics.

U.S. Department of Justice. (1994c). *Women in prison: Survey of state prison inmates, 1991* (Office of Justice Programs). Washington, DC: Bureau of Justice Statistics.

U.S. Department of Labor. (1994). *The American work force: 1992-2005* (Bulletin 2452). Washington, DC: U.S. Government Printing Office.

Van Voorhis, P., Cullen, F.T., Link, B.G., & Wolfe, N.T. (1991). The impact of race and gender on correctional officers' orientation to the integrated environment. *Journal of Research in Crime & Delinquency, 28,* 472-500.

Vandal, G. (1991). "Bloody Caddo": White violence against blacks in a Louisiana parish, 1865-1876. *Journal of Social History, 25,* 373-388.

Vent anger. (1994, August 6). *Wausau Daily Herald,* p. 12A.

Vetter, H.J., & Silverman, I.J. (1986). *Criminology and crime: An introduction.* New York: Harper & Row.

Virginia blacks get tougher sentences, new survey finds. (1983, October 24). *Crime Control Digest, 17,* pp. 8-9.

Vito, G.F., & Keil, T.J. (1988). Capital sentencing in Kentucky: An analysis of the factors influencing decision making in the post-*Gregg* period. *Journal of Criminal Law & Criminology, 79,* 483-503.

Vold, G.B., & Bernard, T.J. (1986). *Theoretical criminology* (3rd ed.). New York: Oxford University Press.

Walker, S. (1985a). Racial minority and female employment in policing: The implications of "glacial" change. *Crime & Delinquency, 34,* 555-572.

Walker, S. (1985b). The limits of segregation in prisons: A reply to Jacobs. *Criminal Law Bulletin, 21,* 485-494.

Walker, S. (1989). *Employment of black and hispanic police officers, 1983-1988: A follow-up study.* Omaha, NE: University of Nebraska, Center for Applied Urban Research.

Walker, T.G., & Barrow, D.J. (1985). The diversification of the federal bench: Policy and process ramifications. *Journal of Politics, 47*, 596-617.

Watts, J.G. (1983). "It just ain't righteous": On witnessing black crooks and white cops. *Dissent, 30*, 347-353.

Weiner, N.L., & Willie, C.V. (1971). Decisions by juvenile officers. *American Journal of Sociology, 77*, 199-210.

Welch, S., Combs, M., & Gruhl, J. (1988). Do black judges make a difference? *American Journal of Political Science, 32*, 126-136.

Wellford, C. (1975). Labeling theory and criminology: An assessment. *Social Problems, 22*, 332-345.

Werthman, C., & Piliavin, I. (1967). Gang members and the police. In D.J. Bordua (Ed.), *The police: Six sociological essays* (pp. 56-98). New York: John Wiley & Sons.

West, D.J., & Farrington, D.P. (1973). *Who becomes delinquent?* London: Heinemann.

Whitehead, J.T., & Lab, S.P. (1990). *Juvenile justice: An introduction.* Cincinnati, OH: Anderson.

Whitehead, J.T., & Lindquist, C.A. (1989). Determinants of correctional officers' professional orientation. *Justice Quarterly, 6*, 69-87.

Whitmire, R. (1994, September 4). Stepfamilies: "Brady Bunch" they're not. *Wausau Daily Herald*, pp. 1A, 9A.

Wiatrowski, M., Griswold, D., & Roberts, M. (1981). Social control theory and delinquency. *American Sociological Review, 46*, 525-541.

Wilbanks, W. (1987). *The myth of a racist criminal justice system.* Monterey, CA: Brooks/Cole.

Williams, F.P., III, & McShane, M.D. (1988). *Criminological theory.* Englewood Cliffs, NJ: Prentice-Hall.

Williams, F.P., III, & McShane, M.D. (1991). Psychological testimony and the decisions of prospective death-qualified jurors. In R. Bohm (Ed.), *The death penalty in America: Current research* (pp. 71-87). Cincinnati, OH: Anderson.

Williams, L. (1988, February 14). Police officers tell of strains of living as a "black in blue." *The New York Times*, pp. 1 & 26.

Wilson, J.Q., & Herrnstein, R.J. (1985). *Crime and human nature.* New York: Simon & Schuster.

Wiltz, C.J. (1982). Fear of crime, criminal victimization, and elderly blacks. *Phylon, 43,* 283-294.

Wolfgang, M., & Ferracuti, F. (1967). *The subculture of violence: Towards an integrated theory in criminology.* London: Tavistock Publications.

Wolfgang, M., & Riedel, M. (1973). Race, judicial discretion, and the death penalty. *Annals of the American Academy of Political & Social Science, 407,* 119-133.

Wood, N.P., Jr. (1990). Black homicide--A public health crisis: Introduction and overview. *Journal of Interpersonal Violence, 5,* 147-150.

Wright, B.S., Doerner, W.G., & Speir, J.C. (1990). Pre-employment psychological testing as a predictor of police performance during an FTO program. *American Journal of Police, 9,* 65-84.

Wright, K.N. (1989). Race and economic marginality in explaining prison adjustment. *Journal of Research in Crime & Delinquency, 26,* 67-89.

Wright, K.N., & Saylor, W.G. (1992). A comparison of perceptions of the work environment between minority and non-minority employees of the federal prison system. *Journal of Criminal Justice, 20,* 63-71.

Wubnig, M. (1975). Black police attitudes in the New York City police department: An exploratory study (Doctoral dissertation, City University of New York, 1975). *Dissertation Abstracts International, 36,* 4803-4804A.

Wycliff, D. (1988). Black and blue encounters. *Criminal Justice Ethics, 7,* pp. 2, 84.

Young, V., & Sulton, A.T. (1991). Excluded: The current status of African American scholars in the field of criminology and criminal justice. *Journal of Research in Crime & Delinquency, 28,* 101-116.

Zalman, M., Ostrom, C.W., Jr., Guilliams, P., & Peaslee, G. (1979). *Sentencing in Michigan: Report of the Michigan felony sentencing project.* Lansing, MI: Michigan Felony Sentencing Project.

Zatz, M.S. (1987). The changing forms of racial/ethnic biases in sentencing. *Journal of Research in Crime & Delinquency, 24,* 69-92.

Zimbardo, P.G. (1972). Pathology of imprisonment. *Society, 9,* 4-8.

NAME INDEX

SUBJECT INDEX

Act of 1875, 167, 168
African Americans
    age composition of, 3, 25n
    criminal justice control rate
      of, 14, 15
    as depicted in introductory
      criminal justice
      textbooks, 195, 196
    educational attainment of,
      37
    empowerment of, 206
    family income of, 36, 180,
      181
    and female-headed
      households, 35, 36,
      183, 184
      improving supervision
        of children in, 206
    in jail and prison, 12-15
    and the juvenile justice
      system, 11, 12
    and migration to the North,
      33
    number of, 3
    as percentage of U.S.
      population, 3
    and perception of criminal
      injustice, 27, 28
    poverty reduction of, 205
    prejudice of, 185, 186,
      201n, 202n
    prejudice toward, 37, 185,
      195
    regional distribution of, 3
    and unemployment, 36, 37,
      181-183
    urbanization of, 3, 25n
Akins v. Texas, 169
Arrests of African Americans,
    6-8, 25n, 76-78
Attica Prison Riot, 122
Batson v. Kentucky, 23, 169,
    170
Bell Curve, The, 65, 66
Bias, Overt, 95
Bias, Subtle, 95
Blacks, *see* African Americans
Brown v. Topeka Board of
    Education, 35
California Personality
    Inventory, 145
Capital Punishment, *see* Judicial
    System
Cassell v. Texas, 169
Civil Rights Program, 39
Coker v. Georgia, 105, 110
Color Complex
    and criminality, 193, 194,
      203n
    and stratification, 192, 193
Convict Lease System, 30, 31